Contents

Principle Woods, Inc.
One San Jose Place, Suite 11
Jacksonville, Florida 32257
www.pwimpact.com

Writers: Tiffany Clark, Tori Friedrich, Deborah Hansen,
Jon Kern, Rebecca Minardi
Editor: Laura Jacqmein
Project Manager: Susan Anderson
Graphic Design: Rebecca Russo, Principle Creative, Inc.

Printed in the United States of America
ISBN 978-0-9827353-2-9

Syllable Guide

The Syllable Guide is an instructional tool designed to help students learn to break unfamiliar words into manageable parts.

Guide to Breaking Words into Syllables	Detailed Guide to Breaking Words into Syllables	Quick Reference Guide
1. Count the vowel sounds in the word. 2. Subtract any silent vowels (like *e*). 3. The final number should be the number of syllables. 4. Break the word into that many chunks. 5. The chunks should be small parts you can say.	1. Count the vowel sounds in the word. 2. Subtract any silent vowels (like *e*). 3. The final number should be the number of syllables. 4. Slash between parts of compound words. 5. Slash after beginning parts. 6. Slash before end parts. 7. Slash between two middle consonants (except for two different consonants that make one sound, like *ph, th, ch, wh*). 8. Sometimes slash before a single middle consonant (except for short vowel sounds, like *cabin: cab-in*). 9. Slash before a consonant-*le* (like - *ble, -cle, -tle*). 10. Try to say the words using these small "chunks."	1. Circle vowel sounds (don't count silent vowels). 2. / compound parts (*cup/cake*) 3. prefixes/ & /suffixes (*con/fine/ment*) 4. C/C (*inves/tigative*) (not *ph, th, ch*, etc.) 5. Sometimes /C (*trau/ma*) 6. /Cle (like *-ble, -cle, -tle*, etc.) 7. Say the word using these "chunks."

Basic Vowel Sounds

ai (raid) *au* (taught) *ay* (may) *ea* (bread, seat) *ee* (sleep) *oa* (road) *oi* (coin) *oo* (soon, look) *ou* (proud)	*ow* (cow, flow) *oy* (toy) *ar* (harm) *er* (perm) *ir* (sir) *or* (horn) *ur* (burn) *a*(c)*e* (date) *e*(c)*e* (eve)	*i*(c)*e* (slide) *o*(c)*e* (note) *u*(c)*e* (accuse) *a* (hat, carry, father) *e* (let, merry) *i* (tin) *o* (go, to, mop) *u* (up) *y* (sky)

Basic Beginning Parts (Prefixes) and Their Meanings

ab-: from *ad-*: to, at, toward *an-*: not *be-*: to make, about, by *co-, col-, con-, com-*: together/ with *de-*: from, down, away, off *dis-*: apart, not, opposite	*en-*: in, into, make *ex-*: out *fore-*: in front, before *in-, im-, il-, ir-*: in, into, without, not *mis-*: wrongly, incorrect *post-*: after *pre-*: before	*pro-*: moving forward, in front of, defending *re-*: back, again *sub-*: under *trans-*: across, through, beyond *un-*: not *uni-*: one

Basic End Parts (Suffixes) and Their Meanings

-al: relating to, process (adj.) *-ance*: action, state of (n.) *-ar, -er, -or*: one who/that/which (n.) *-ate*: make, cause (v.) *-cide*: kill (n.) *-dom*: quality (n.) *-en*: make (v.), made of (adj.) *-ful*: full of (adj.)	*-fy*: make (v.) *-ice*: condition (n.) *-ion, -sion, -tion*: state of (n.) *-ish*: a characteristic of (adj.) *-ism*: system, condition (n.) *-ive*: related to, tending (adj.) *-ize*: to cause or make (v.) *-less*: without (adj.) *-like*: resembling (adj.) *-ly*: manner of (adv.)	*-ment*: process, result of, act of (n.) *-ness*: state of (n.) *-ous*: having (adj.) *-ology, -alogy*: study of (n.) *-tude*: condition of (n.) *-ward*: in a particular direction (adj.) (adv.) *-y*: having (adj.)

Reading Assessment Answer Document

Student Name: _____   Grade: _____

Directions: Using capital letters, write the answer to each multiple-choice question in the boxes below. Note that each question has a benchmark or concept that is being reviewed.

	HIGH-INTEREST ARTICLES					
	Truth in Satire?	Batting Against Social Anxiety	The Dangers and Benefits of Social Networking	Beating the Odds	The Sound of Success	
	Date:	Date:	Date:	Date:	Date:	
	Score:	Score:	Score:	Score:	Score:	Concepts/Benchmarks
WORDS AND PHRASES						
1.						Analyze Words/Text
2.						Analyze Words/Text
3.						Conclusions/Inferences
MAIN IDEA/AUTHOR'S PURPOSE						
4.						Details/Facts
5.						Author's Point of View
6.						Patterns of Organization
7.						Author's Purpose
8.						Main Idea/Essential Message
COMPARE & CONTRAST/CAUSE & EFFECT						
9.						Cause and Effect
10.						Cause and Effect
11.						Comparison
REFERENCE & RESEARCH						
12.						Validity/Accuracy of Information
13.						Locate, Organize, Interpret Information
14.						Synthesize Information

Reading Assessment Answer Document

Student Name: _____ Grade: _____

Directions: Using capital letters, write the answer to each multiple-choice question in the boxes below. Note that each question has a benchmark or concept that is being reviewed.

	The Home Front	How Do You Fix a Broken Brain?	Taylor Swift: Road to the Top	Second Chances	Blanco: Mexican Soccer Legend	
	Date:	Date:	Date:	Date:	Date:	
	Score:	Score:	Score:	Score:	Score:	Concepts/Benchmarks
WORDS AND PHRASES						
1.						Analyze Words/Text
2.						Analyze Words/Text
3.						Conclusions/Inferences
MAIN IDEA/AUTHOR'S PURPOSE						
4.						Details/Facts
5.						Author's Point of View
6.						Patterns of Organization
7.						Author's Purpose
8.						Main Idea/Essential Message
COMPARE & CONTRAST/CAUSE & EFFECT						
9.						Cause and Effect
10.						Cause and Effect
11.						Comparison
REFERENCE & RESEARCH						
12.						Validity/Accuracy of Information
13.						Locate, Organize, Interpret Information
14.						Synthesize Information

Reading Assessment Answer Document

Student Name: _____ Grade: _____

Directions: Using capital letters, write the answer to each multiple-choice question in the boxes below. Note that each question has a benchmark or concept that is being reviewed.

	Anime	Teen Depression	Show Me the Money!	Homeless Children in America	Leadership 101	
TECHNICAL ARTICLES						
	Date:	Date:	Date:	Date:	Date:	
	Score:	Score:	Score:	Score:	Score:	Concepts/Benchmarks
WORDS AND PHRASES						
1.						Analyze Words/Text
2.						Analyze Words/Text
3.						Conclusions/Inferences
MAIN IDEA/DETAILS						
4.						Details/Facts
5.						Patterns of Organization
6.						Main Idea/Essential Message
COMPARE & CONTRAST/CAUSE & EFFECT						
7.						Cause and Effect
8.						Comparison
REFERENCE & RESEARCH						
9.						Validity/Accuracy of Information
10.						Locate, Organize, Interpret Information
11.						Synthesize Information

Reading Assessment Answer Document

Student Name: _____ Grade: _____

Directions: Using capital letters, write the answer to each multiple-choice question in the boxes below. Note that each question has a benchmark or concept that is being reviewed.

	Can Equality Exist ...?	Who Wins? Who Loses?	Can My Music Make Me Smarter?	The Success Mechanism	Soccer: Ballet of the Masses	
	TECHNICAL ARTICLES					
	Date:	Date:	Date:	Date:	Date:	
	Score:	Score:	Score:	Score:	Score:	Concepts/Benchmarks
WORDS AND PHRASES						
1.						Analyze Words/Text
2.						Analyze Words/Text
3.						Conclusions/Inferences
MAIN IDEA/DETAILS						
4.						Details/Facts
5.						Patterns of Organization
6.						Main Idea/Essential Message
COMPARE & CONTRAST/CAUSE & EFFECT						
7.						Cause and Effect
8.						Comparison
REFERENCE & RESEARCH						
9.						Validity/Accuracy of Information
10.						Locate, Organize, Interpret Information
11.						Synthesize Information

— Unit 1 —
AnimationDomination

READING INSTRUCTIONAL GUIDE FOR HIGH-INTEREST ARTICLE

BEFORE READING

Looking at the Words

Determining How the Word Sounds (Phonics)

Using the Syllable Guide found in the beginning of the book, read the steps to learn how to break a word into manageable parts. Follow these steps to sound out the words below.

Determining What the Word Means (Vocabulary)

Look at the words below before beginning to read the article. Before reading the definitions, use prefixes and suffixes from the Syllable Guide to predict meaning.

Words to Study	Breaking into Syllables	Short Definition
foible	foi-ble	(n.) a minor character flaw or weakness
industrious	in-dus-tri-ous	(adj.) hardworking
influential	in-flu-en-tial	(adj.) having strong influence; powerful
insatiable	in-sa-tia-ble	(adj.) unable to be content or satisfied
manipulative	ma-nip-u-la-tive	(adj.) skillfully controlling, especially to one's advantage
oblivious	ob-liv-i-ous	(adj.) unmindful; unaware
resilient	re-sil-ient	(adj.) able to recover easily; rebounding

Activating Background Knowledge

Anticipation Guide

Mark each of the following statements True or False:

1. _____ *The Simpsons* is the name of a popular musical group.

2. _____ *SpongeBob SquarePants* is an animated series.

3. _____ Homer Simpson is the name of a paternal character.

4. _____ SpongeBob is a snail.

5. _____ Bart Simpson demonstrates strong moral character.

Starter Questions

After completing the Anticipation Guide, participate in a group or class discussion using the following questions:

1. What is the primary setting for *SpongeBob SquarePants*?

2. Who is the most mischievous character in *The Simpsons*?

3. What are the names of SpongeBob's friends?

4. Where does *The Simpsons* take place?

5. What grade is Bart Simpson perpetually in?

Make a prediction about what you think the article will be about.

DURING READING

- Skim the article for 45–60 seconds. Circle any words you don't know.
- When you are finished, decode and determine the meaning of unknown words.
- Skim the questions for 30–45 seconds.
- Predict what the article is about.
- Read the article.
- Reread to clarify as needed.
- Answer the questions.

AFTER READING

Discussion Starter Questions

1. Which character is most similar to your personality? Why?

2. If you were Bart Simpson's teacher, how would you motivate him to stay out of trouble?

3. Do you think Homer Simpson could work for Mr. Krabs? Why or why not?

4. Would you rather have a friendship with SpongeBob or Bart Simpson? Why?

5. If you were given the opportunity to be a writer for either *The Simpsons* or *SpongeBob SquarePants*, how would you change the show?

Truth in Satire?
The Simpsons and SpongeBob SquarePants

The Simpsons

Duh-dum-dum-da-da-dum-da-da-da-da-da-dum. Doh! Their theme song is familiar to an entire generation. Their family first introduced itself to the American living room in December of 1989 on the Fox network. *The Simpsons* is the longest-running comedy in the history of television. It targets preteen through adult viewers. One would have never expected a show about an underachieving boy and his clueless father from a generic town known as Springfield to have such an impact on American culture. But with a movie, postage stamps, toys, lunchboxes, and countless t-shirts related to the show, it certainly has.

SpongeBob SquarePants

Beginning 10 years after *The Simpsons*, another animated comedy found its way into the hearts of a generation of after-school cartoon viewers. A sea sponge named SpongeBob SquarePants and his friends have entertained younger and older viewers alike. *SpongeBob SquarePants* is arguably one of the most popular animated comedies on television. Since 1999 it has been attracting viewers to the Nickelodeon cable television network. The show takes place in the fictitious underwater setting of Bikini Bottom in the Pacific Ocean.

The Characters

Bart Simpson

For a 4th-grade **underachiever**, Bart sure is **clever**. He can be **disrespectful** at times but uses his quick wit to get himself out of trouble by the show's end. His **mischievous** nature causes him to spend most of his time annoying people. You might find him making prank phone calls to Moe, the local tavern owner. And even though he gives his sister Lisa a hard time, deep down inside he truly cares for all the members of his family. Even though he can be bad, his best friends tend to be the types of "uncool" kids that the popular crowd wouldn't want to hang out with.

Homer Simpson

Homer is Bart's donut-loving father. Despite all of his flaws, he's **committed** to his family and friends. He is the "longest-term entry-level employee" at the Springfield Nuclear Power Plant. His **clueless** and **sluggish** behavior tends to get him into trouble, but he often manages to work his way out of it by the end of an episode.

SpongeBob

This **fun-loving** sea sponge from Bikini Bottom is **kindhearted** and **hardworking**. His **curious** and **enthusiastic** mindset takes him on many adventures. He has a **selfless** attitude and **optimistic** nature. He is a happy sea creature, a **go-getter**, and a **dependable** friend.

Patrick Star

Patrick, a pink starfish, is SpongeBob's **loyal** buddy. He is truly **naïve**, but that doesn't stop him from offering advice and support to SpongeBob. The two get themselves into silly situations throughout the show. Patrick's **kindhearted** intentions provide SpongeBob with the kind of friend he needs to keep him happy.

Marge Simpson

Marge is Bart's blue-haired, **unselfish** mother. Her **patient** and **nurturing** manner offers stability to the family. She keeps the household running smoothly, even with the problems that Bart and Homer get themselves into. Despite their antics, she is **proud** of Bart and remains a **faithful** spouse to Homer. She is also a **tidy** homemaker and enjoys raising her other two children, Lisa and Maggie.

Santa's Little Helper

The Simpson family dog has managed to survive in the Simpson house. He can be **unruly**—doing things like tearing up the furniture and eating from the table. This strains his relationship with Homer, who got the dog while trying to win money at a greyhound racetrack. Yet Santa's Little Helper has been **resilient** enough to overcome several painful experiences. He stays **steadfast** to his sometimes ungrateful owners.

Mr. Burns

C. Montgomery Burns is Homer's boss and Springfield's richest man. As the owner of the Springfield Nuclear Power Plant, he is also one of the town's most **influential** men. This isn't always good. Even though he's rich, he is still **greedy** and **power-hungry**. He even built a device that blocked out the sun in order to blanket the town in complete darkness.

Lisa and Maggie Simpson

Lisa and Maggie are Bart's younger sisters. Lisa, an **intellectual** 8-year-old girl, is incredibly smart and loves to show it. She always tries to make things right in Springfield but can come across as **judgmental**. Maggie is only 1 year old, but in her short life she's managed to spell her name and shoot Mr. Burns when he tried to steal her lollipop. She's best known for smacking on her pacifier and crawling around **carefree**, **oblivious** to potential danger.

Sandy Cheeks

Sandy Cheeks is the **intelligent** friend of SpongeBob. She's a squirrel from the state of Texas and doesn't belong in the water. She lives in a large glassed-in, underwater dome. She is **industrious**, performing fun experiments and inventing cool things. She is also **athletic** and enjoys karate, especially with SpongeBob. One of her flaws is that she can come across as **haughty** at times. She tends to have an inflated opinion of herself and her ideas.

Gary

Gary is SpongeBob's **loyal** pet snail. He is **slow** and doesn't accomplish much, leaving a trail of slime wherever he goes. He says only one word: "Meow." However, SpongeBob can understand exactly what he means. Gary is not a human-like creature.

Mr. Krabs

Mr. Krabs is the owner of the Krusty Krab, Bikini Bottom's home of the Krabby Patty. He is **obsessive** about counting and protecting his money. His insatiable desire for wealth leads him to practice questionable business. He can be **manipulative**. He takes advantage of SpongeBob, his favorite employee, who works long, hard hours for little pay. Mr. Krabs spends much of his time keeping his Krabby Patty's secret formula safe from his enemy, Plankton, the owner of the Chum Bucket. Despite his **greedy** personality, Mr. Krabs has strong **paternal** instincts when it comes to his daughter, Pearl—a whale.

Squidward

Squidward is SpongeBob's **pessismistic** co-worker at the Krusty Krab. One word could describe Squidward: **annoyed**. Nearly everything annoys him. He is **narcissistic** and thinks of himself as better than others, when he is really pretty average. SpongeBob believes that Squidward has a good heart on the inside of his **grumpy** exterior.

A Mirror of Our Lives?

Both shows use satire. The writers use their wit to poke fun at the characteristics of everyday people. Though we laugh at the characters, we may also see a bit of ourselves in each of them. And while we hope we can say, "We aren't *that* bad," maybe recognizing these human weaknesses and foibles can help us think about becoming better people.

READING COMPREHENSION

After reading "Truth in Satire? *The Simpsons* and *SpongeBob SquarePants*," choose the options that best answer questions 1–14.

1. Read this sentence.
   He stays steadfast to his sometimes ungrateful owners.

   What is the meaning of the word *steadfast*?
   A. unruly
   B. friendly
   C. disloyal
   D. dependable

2. Read these sentences.
   Both shows use satire. The writers use their wit to poke fun at the characteristics of everyday people.

   Based on these lines, which of the following is an element of satire?
   F. ridicule
   G. tragic hero
   H. dark humor
   I. dramatic irony

3. From this article, the reader can tell that
   A. Bart Simpson is a strong student.
   B. Mr. Krabs's employees respect him.
   C. Maggie Simpson has gotten herself into dangerous situations.
   D. *SpongeBob SquarePants* has higher viewer ratings than *The Simpsons*.

4. Based on the article, which of these is likely to occur?
   F. *SpongeBob* will be canceled soon.
   G. The creator of *The Simpsons* will allow Bart to age.
   H. *The Simpsons* and *SpongeBob SquarePants* will combine to make one show.
   I. *The Simpsons* and *SpongeBob SquarePants* will continue to influence television.

5. What is the author's purpose for the concluding paragraph of the article?
   A. to make the reader feel better
   B. to magnify the characteristics of the characters
   C. to show how the shows' characters mirror each other
   D. to explain that the shows can be a basis for improving our own character

6. The author organizes the article by
   F. summarizing the characteristics of the main characters.
   G. providing and analyzing scripts from two popular animated series.
   H. comparing and contrasting *The Simpsons* and *SpongeBob SquarePants*.
   I. proving why *The Simpsons* and *SpongeBob SquarePants* should receive more praise.

7. Why does the author place the character traits in bold print?
    A. to draw the reader's attention
    B. to check the reader's understanding
    C. to add rhythm to the reading of the article
    D. to make it easier for the reader to clearly see the font

8. What is the main idea of the first paragraph?
    F. *SpongeBob* is a better show.
    G. Animated comedies are only for adults.
    H. Our society needs to spend less time watching television.
    I. *The Simpsons* has proven to be quite a successful animated program.

9. Why does Mr. Burns cover Springfield in darkness?
    A. to protect the town from the sun's rays
    B. because he is greedy and wants more money
    C. to hide the pollution created by his power plant
    D. so that Springfield citizens won't have to see his nuclear power plant

10. What is it about Bart Simpson that often enables him to get out of trouble?
    F. his humor
    G. his respect
    H. his honesty
    I. his sharp wit

11. How are Gary and Patrick Star similar?
    A. They are both slow.
    B. They both work for Mr. Burns.
    C. They are both faithful companions to SpongeBob.
    D. They are both friends who lead SpongeBob into trouble.

12. Which of the following BEST supports the idea that *The Simpsons* may have influenced *SpongeBob*?
    F. SpongeBob is a human.
    G. *The Simpsons* was created before *SpongeBob*.
    H. *SpongeBob SquarePants* is one of the most popular comedies on television.
    I. Younger and older viewers have enjoyed *SpongeBob SquarePants* and *The Simpsons*.

13. Which of SpongeBob's friends would Mr. Burns most likely hire?
    A. Gary
    B. Patrick
    C. Mr. Krabs
    D. Sandy Cheeks

14. Which of the following phrases BEST applies to both Homer and Gary?
    F. slow and steady wins the race
    G. between a rock and a hard place
    H. what goes around, comes around
    I. don't throw stones in glass houses

READING STRATEGY

Directions: The characters of *SpongeBob SquarePants* and *The Simpsons* are characterized by descriptive words throughout the high-interest article. In the space provided for each character, write three words to describe him or her. Use different descriptive words than those highlighted in the article.

Patrick

Gary

Squidward

Homer

Santa's Little Helper

Lisa

SpongeBob

Sandy

Mr. Krabs

Bart

1. Intelligent

2. Naughty

3. Amusing

Marge

Mr. Burns

INTERPRETING THE DATA

PART I

Would it be better to live with The Simpsons in Springfield or SpongeBob in Bikini Bottom?

The creator of *The Simpsons* has said that the town of Springfield is modeled after his hometown of Portland, Oregon. *SpongeBob*'s creator has said that Bikini Bottom is most like Seattle, Washington. Table 1 includes various data on Portland and Seattle. Study the data and then answer questions 15 and 16.

Table 1. Comparisons between Portland and Seattle

	Portland (Springfield, *The Simpsons*)	Seattle (Bikini Bottom, *SpongeBob SquarePants*)
Population in July 2008	557,706	598,541
Estimated median household income in 2008	$50,979	$61,786
Estimated median household income in 2000	$40,146	$45,736
Estimated median house or condo value in 2008	$310,900	$491,600
Estimated median house or condo value in 2000	$154,700	$252,100
Mean price of all housing units in 2008	$350,431	$584,836
Median gross rent (housing) in 2008	$779	$940
Percentage of residents living in poverty in 2008	14.4%	11.6%
Land area	134.3 square miles	83.9 square miles
Population density	4,152 people per square mile	7,136 people per square mile

For population 25 years and over:	High school or higher	85.7%	89.5%
	Bachelor's degree or higher	32.6%	47.2%
	Graduate or professional degree	11.4%	17.3%

Unemployed in October 2009	10.7%	7.8%
Median real estate property taxes paid for housing units with mortgages in 2008	$2,784	$3,638
Median real estate property taxes paid for housing units with no mortgage in 2008	$2,942	$3,668

	Year	1999	2003	2008	1999	2003	2008
Crime per 100,000 people	Murders	6.9	5.0	4.7	8.3	5.9	4.8
	Auto thefts	921.4	1,076.2	603.8	1,591.3	1,570.7	614.5
	Burglaries	1,199.8	1,189.1	778.8	1,191.4	1,481.2	1,087.3

15. Which city would be better to live in: Portland (Springfield) or Seattle (Bikini Bottom)? Use data from Table 1 to support your answer.

**ANALYZE
EVALUATE
EXPLAIN**

PART II

Which production method provides the best investment opportunity: digital animation (*The Simpsons*) or hand animation (*SpongeBob*)?

The tags in Figure 1 include data on 10 of the top hand-animated and digitally animated films of the last two decades. Use Table 3 to organize the data to help you determine which production method provides a better investment opportunity. The gross and the production budgets for each method are rounded to the nearest whole million dollars.

Table 2. Definitions of two production methods used in making films

Definitions	
Hand animation	"Cartoons" in which each picture is drawn by hand and then flashed rapidly in order to show movement of characters. *The SpongeBob SquarePants Movie* was released November 19, 2004. It was a hand-animated film. Its total gross earnings were $85 million. Its production budget was $30 million.
Digital animation	Using a computer to draw and create a "cartoon" in which pictures are flashed rapidly in order to show movement of characters. *The Simpsons Movie* was released July 27, 2007. It was digitally animated. Its total gross earnings were $183 million. Its production budget was $73 million.

Figure 1. Gross production budgets and total gross earnings of top 10 hand-animated and digitally animated films of the last two decades

The Little Mermaid 11/15/1989 Total Gross: $112M Production Budget: N/A	Beauty and the Beast 11/31/1991 Total Gross: $171M Production Budget: $20M	Aladdin 11/11/1992 Total Gross: $217M Production Budget: $28M	The Lion King 6/15/1994 Total Gross: $329M Production Budget: $79M
Pocahontas 6/10/1995 Total Gross: $142M Production Budget: $55M	Toy Story 11/22/1995 Total Gross: $192M Production Budget: $30M	The Hunchback of Notre Dame 6/21/1996 Total Gross: $100M Production Budget: $100M	Hercules 6/15/1997 Total Gross: $99M Production Budget: $70M
Mulan 6/19/1998 Total Gross: $121M Production Budget: $90M	Tarzan 6/16/1999 Total Gross: $171M Production Budget: $145M	Toy Story 2 11/19/1999 Total Gross: $246M Production Budget: $90M	Shrek 5/18/2001 Total Gross: $268M Production Budget: $50M
Monsters, Inc. 11/2/2001 Total Gross: $256M Production Budget: $115M	Lilo & Stich 6/21/2002 Total Gross: $146M Production Budget: $80M	Finding Nemo 5/30/2003 Total Gross: $340M Production Budget: $94M	Shrek 2 5/19/2004 Total Gross: $441M Production Budget: $70M
The Incredibles 11/5/2004 Total Gross: $261M Production Budget: $92M	Cars 6/9/2006 Total Gross: $244M Production Budget: $70M	Shrek the Third 5/18/2007 Total Gross: $323M Production Budget: $160M	Up 5/29/2009 Total Gross: $293M Production Budget: $175M

16. Use the data in Figure 1 to Complete Table 3.

Table 3. Total gross earnings and production budgets of top hand-animated and digitally animated movies of the last decade, rounded to the nearest million

Hand animation			Digital animation		
Movie	Total gross earnings	Production budget	Movie	Total gross earnings	Production budget
The Little Mermaid	112	N/A	Toy Story		
Beauty and the Beast			Toy Story 2		
Aladdin			Shrek		
The Lion King			Monsters, Inc.		
Pocahontas			Finding Nemo		
Hunchback of Notre Dame			Shrek 2		
Hercules			The Incredibles		
Mulan			Cars		
Tarzan			Shrek the Third		
Lilo & Stich			Up		

17. Complete the double bar graph in Figure 2 for the hand-animated movies.

Figure 2. Total gross earnings and production budgets of top hand-animated movies of the last decade, rounded to the nearest million

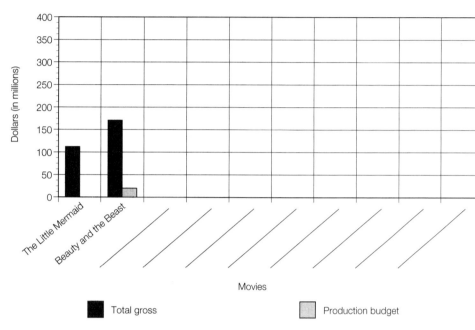

18. In Figure 3 create your own bar graph for the digitally animated movies.

Figure 3. Total gross earnings and production budgets of top digitally animated movies of the last decade, rounded to the nearest million

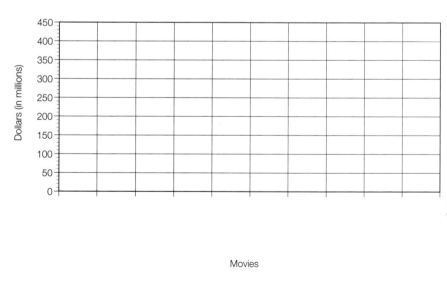

19. According to your bar graphs, which production method (hand animation or digital animation) provides the best return to filmmakers? Use data to support your answer.

ANALYZE
EVALUATE
EXPLAIN

REFLECT AND RESPOND

20. The cartoon characters in this unit possess unique personality traits that have been made obvious. Look at the article again for the various characteristics that are showcased in these two cartoons. Then think about your own personality characteristics that would be highlighted if you were the subject of a popular cartoon. Write to explain what those characteristics are and whether you are proud of those qualities or would like to change them.

Reflect
&
Respond

READING INSTRUCTIONAL GUIDE FOR TECHNICAL EXTENSION

BEFORE READING

Looking at the Words

Determining What the Word Means (Vocabulary)

Words to Study	Breaking into Syllables	Short Definition
composition	com-po-si-tion	(n.) general makeup
genre	gen-re	(n.) the kind or type of a work of art
hybrid	hy-brid	(adj.) composed of mixed elements or characteristics
inspire	in-spire	(v.) to influence
progressive	pro-gres-sive	(adj.) advanced; cutting-edge
sophisticated	so-phis-ti-cat-ed	(adj.) complex
straightforward	straight-for-ward	(adj.) direct

Activating Background Knowledge

Graphic Organizer

Either individually or in groups, brainstorm about animation, recalling anything previously learned and any prior experience with the subject. Next, complete the Venn diagram to compare and contrast historical animation with present-day animation.

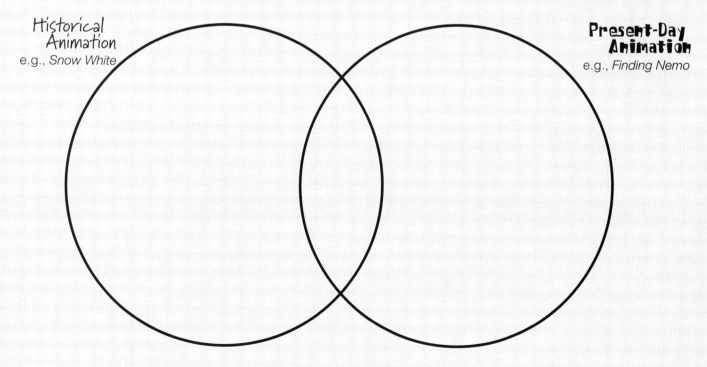

Historical
Animation
e.g., *Snow White*

Present-Day
Animation
e.g., *Finding Nemo*

Starter Questions

After completing the Graphic Organizer, participate in a group or class discussion to come up with questions about the subject, a prediction about the article, and at least one learning goal. The first question has been provided for you.

Question: Besides America, what is another country with a strong fan base for animation?

Question: _____

Prediction: _____

Goal: _____

DURING READING

- Skim the article for 45–60 seconds. Circle any words you don't know.

- When you are finished, decode and determine the meaning of unknown words.

- Skim the questions for 30–45 seconds.

- Predict what the article is about.

- Read the article.

- Reread to clarify as needed.

- Answer the questions.

AFTER READING

After reading, you may do the following:

- Review, paraphrase, and summarize

- Participate in main-idea discussions by describing the information in their own words

- Reflect on concept maps and generate additional discussion starter questions based on the mappings

- Participate in small-group discussions using discussion starter questions

Discussion Starter Questions

The first question has been provided for you.

1. How has animation changed over the years?

2. _____

3. _____

TECHNICAL EXTENSION

Anime

The Simpsons, SpongeBob, Mickey Mouse, and Beavis are all well-known cartoon characters to most of us. But what about Goku, Astro Boy, Speed Racer, and Spike Spiegel? Do you know who they are?

These are the most popular characters in the world of Japanese anime. Anime is a form of animation that has a huge following both in Japan and in the United States. Fans are known as "anime otaku," which means those who are obsessed, sometimes to the point of insanity, with this subculture.

Artists have been trying to add movement to their illustrations since people started drawing on cave walls. Early animation devices were strange contraptions like the thaumotrope invented by Paul Roget in France in the 1800s. This was a disc that had the picture of a bird on one side and the bird's cage on the other. When it was spun using string attached to both ends, the bird appeared to be in the cage.

Thomas Edison's motion camera and projector led to the sophisticated animation we have today. An artist that also contributed to this evolution was Winsor McCray. McCray was an American who added personality to a dinosaur in his movie, *Gertie the Dinosaur*. Prior to this time, most cartoons concentrated on the action instead of the characters. Of course, Walt Disney took animation to a higher level when he added sound to movie cartoons in *Steamboat Willie* in 1928. Then in 1937, Disney Studios released the first full length animation feature film, *Snow White and the Seven Dwarfs*.

But let's get back to anime. In the early 1900s, graphic artists in Japan were influenced by the Western inventions of the newspaper comic strip and motion pictures. Soon, the Japanese comic book, or "magna," was born through the work of artists like Rakiten Kitazawa and Ippei Okamoto. Next, these artists experimented with moving pictures of their cartoons.

Followers of anime think that Osamu Tezuka is the man who made both anime and manga successful in Japan. He earned the title "God of Manga" in the mid-1900s with his novel-length *Shintakarajima (New Treasure Island)*. Tezuka's illustrations were filled with action and exaggerated emotion. Before this, stories were told in a lifeless, straightforward way.

Another influence of Tezuka that is still seen in anime is how the characters are drawn. They are often given large eyes and exaggerated facial expressions. Tezuku was inspired by the earliest Disney cartoon characters, like Mickey Mouse and Donald Duck, who also had round heads and expressive eyes. Anime artists use specific lines to show certain emotions, such as bulging lines across a forehead to show that a character is upset. Over-sized sweat drops are drawn to show embarrassment. Anime also includes non-human and hybrid characters, like robots, animals, spirits, and demons.

The plot lines in anime are a mixture of fantasy and fact and generally fall into five basic genres, or categories: action/adventure, drama, horror, science fiction, and progressive. One characteristic of anime is the lack of a specific end or *resolution* to an episode. Something in the story is usually left unfinished, which makes the viewer want to come back for more.

Much like action figures and cartoons in the United States, an anime character or story line often becomes so popular that it crosses media categories. It might start out as a comic book and then become a television series as well as a movie. Each format might be a little different, but all feature the same central characters. A similar example in America might be the GI Joe character. It started out as a cartoon, but now you can buy GI Joe lunchboxes and toys.

So who are the anime otaku, those obsessed fans who have embraced this art form in America? An anime blogger did a survey using the Internet and a large fan club in California to find out who these people are. What she found is interesting. Most are male between the ages of 18 and 25. The racial composition is mixed, with slightly more Asians and Caucasians.

Those surveyed said the biggest attraction to this style of animation lies in the characters. Typical characters that are popular in anime are the young male who is shy around girls and a "magical" girl with superhuman powers. Some popular anime in this romantic genre are *Video Girl Ai Urusei Yatsura, Tenchi Muyo*, and *Ah! My Goddess!* There have been examples of similar characters in American television with programs like *Bewitched*, *I Dream of Jeannie*, and *Wizards of Waverly Place*.

Animation added life to still-life comic book characters. Japanese artists were inspired by this marriage of American comic strips and motion pictures, and anime was born. Today, it is ironic that American anime otaku are fascinated with this art form that was born in our country, developed in Japan, and is now one of the most popular Japanese imports back into America!

READING COMPREHENSION

After reading "Anime," answer questions 1–12.

1. Read the following sentence.
    Early animation devices were strange contraptions like the thaumotrope invented by Paul Roget in France in the 1800s.

    Which of the following words or phrases could be used as a synonym for the word *contraption* as it is used in the sentence?
    A. a trap
    B. a circular disc
    C. a thermometer
    D. a mechanical tool of some kind

2. Read the following sentence.
    They are often given large eyes and exaggerated facial expressions.

    What is the meaning of the word *exaggerated* as used in this sentence?
    F. smaller
    G. summarized
    H. emphasized
    I. decreased to be barely noticed

3. According to this article, what is one of the main reasons that fans of anime are attracted to this art form?
    A. the artists
    B. the history of the art form
    C. personalities of the characters
    D. the crossover into various media

4. What was the biggest contribution of Osamu Tezuka to anime?
    F. action and emotion
    G. animation of all characters
    H. adding sound to animated illustrations
    I. creating a blog for followers of anime

5. What is the purpose of paragraphs 3 and 4?
    A. to introduce anime
    B. a brief history of animation
    C. to compare Edison and Disney
    D. a discussion of the creation of the first full-length animated film

6. Which of the following would be the BEST subtitle of this article?
    F. Osamu Tezuka
    G. Disney Animation
    H. A Japanese Art Form
    I. Magical Girl and Tenchi Muyo

7. Why might Winsor McCray be called a contributor to the popularity of today's animated movies?
    A. He worked for Walt Disney.
    B. He concentrated on the story.
    C. He created a full-length animated cartoon.
    D. He added personality to a cartoon character.

8. What do American action figure GI Joe and many anime characters have in common?
    F. They are available in several media.
    G. GI Joe started out as a video game character.
    H. Anime characters are drawn with exaggerated expressions.
    I. GI Joe is no longer available as an action figure since the character became so popular as a cartoon.

9. Which fact from the article BEST supports the idea that anime otaku will continue to follow their favorite characters?
    A. There are many genres.
    B. Most stories are unfinished.
    C. Most anime otaku are young males.
    D. Tezuka is still very popular in Japan.

10. Which of the following was NOT a step in the evolution toward today's sophisticated animation?
    F. downplaying personalities
    G. adding sound to movie cartoons
    H. developing the motion camera and projector
    I. concentrating on the characters instead of just the action

11. One article about anime states that **"some of what may be satisfying for American otaku about their fan culture is that it allows them to 'steal' Japanese culture. In part, this could be conceived as a form of revenge."**

    According to the article, what is the "revenge" being carried out by American anime otaku?
    A. The obsessive interest of the otaku.
    B. Anime stories are often a combination of two or more categories.
    C. The culture of Japan as a whole holds no interest to anime otaku.
    D. Americans are embracing a Japanese art form that was initially created using American concepts.

12. What were some of the ideas and inventions that led to the current art form known as Japanese anime?

    _____

    _____

    _____

    _____

    _____

    _____

    _____

    _____

TECHNICAL WRITING PROMPT

13. You have been asked to give a presentation on anime for the Japan-America Society in your city, and you would like to include a timeline in your PowerPoint presentation. Create a general timeline (you do not need to include dates) of the history of anime in Japan and the United States. Be sure to illustrate how cartoons and animation from the two countries have impacted one another. Your timeline should recap events in a succinct, easy-to-read manner and include specific details from the article.

VOCATIONAL EXTENSION

HELP WANTED:

Experienced sous chef to work alongside world-renowned executive chef Hubert Keller in upscale French restaurant Fleur de Lys. Must be energetic, creative, and calm under pressure. Salary negotiable depending on experience. E-mail resume and list of references to lyscuisine@kellercorp.com.

Do you dream of a job in the service industry? Do you love food? Have you always wondered what secret ingredient makes a Krabby Patty so appealing? Then the food service industry may be for you!

The food industry has over 12.7 million employees and $1.6 billion per day in food sales. It gets 49% of the average food dollar. It's one of the largest industries and employers in the United States. Even in a down economy, it continues to grow.

At the top of this profitable field are professionals such as managers, CEOs, and CFOs. However, the restaurant industry is so big that there are job opportunities for almost any background. Below are just some of the available restaurant positions:

- General manager
- Assistant manager
- Executive chef
- Sous chef
- Cook
- Line cook
- Front-of-house manager
- Waiter/Waitress

Most everyone loves to eat out. In fact, 78% of Americans say they would rather eat out than cook and clean up. Not only that, but most Americans believe that eating out or grabbing food "on the go" makes them more productive in their everyday routines. Given these facts, the food industry is likely to survive, even when the economy is doing poorly.

Salaries for food service employees range anywhere from $17,000 to $60,000, depending on the position and experience. A waiter starting out may make only $15,000 a year. Another with over 10 years of experience may earn around $45,000.

Education can make a difference as well. An uneducated chef will probably start out as a busboy making around $10,000. He can work his way up the ranks through promotions. A chef graduating from a culinary school (such as the Culinary Institute of America) can go straight into a career as either a sous chef or executive chef—and will probably start with a substantial salary. A four- or even two-year college degree can decide whether someone works as a fry cook, like SpongeBob, or as a chef in a five-star French bistro. With or without a college degree, though, the restaurant industry has opportunities for everyone. In fact, nearly 71% of all food service employees have only a high school diploma.

Does the restaurant industry sounds like a match for you? If so, you better get cooking!

LOOKING FORWARD

14. When you apply for a job in a restaurant, the owner tells you that she actually has several positions available in four different restaurants ranging from upscale to burgers. She wants to determine which job is the best fit for you. She asks you to write a paragraph explaining what kind of position and restaurant environment best suit your personality, and skills. Think this over, using personal knowledge and information from the article, and write your answer here.

Looking Forward

ETHICAL DILEMMA

15. You own a business with one partner who isn't involved in the business on a daily basis. After returning some office supplies to your local office supply store, you realize that the cashier refunded the money in cash instead of crediting the business debit card. You would like to use the cash to pay off some personal bills. What do you do?

Ethical Dilemma

UNIT VOCABULARY ASSESSMENT

Matching
Match each word in Column I to its definition in Column II.

Column I

_____ 1. resilient
_____ 2. insatiable
_____ 3. influential
_____ 4. manipulative

Column II

A.   unable to be content or satisfied
B.   skillfully controlling
C.   powerful
D.   rebounding

Multiple Choice
Choose the word that MOST NEARLY replaces the underlined word in each sentence.

5. The more <u>industrious</u> you are, the more likely you are to get a promotion.
   A. idle   C. indifferent
   B. animated   D. hardworking

6. I like to read books that <u>inspire</u> me to be a better person.
   A. seek   C. influence
   B. support   D. discourage

7. Karli is often <u>oblivious</u> to what is happening around her.
   A. aware   C. instinctive
   B. obvious   D. unmindful

8. Some people have trouble with change and dislike <u>progressive</u> ideas.
   A. modern   C. cutting-edge
   B. professional D. old-fashioned

9. Though at times difficult to hear, I appreciated her <u>straightforward</u> advice.
   A. direct   C. dishonest
   B. serious   D. complicated

Word Bank

composition
foibles
genre
hybrid
sophisticated

Fill in the Blank
Choose a word from the word bank to fill in the blank in the sentence below.

10. My favorite _____ of literature is historical fiction.

11. The coaches will determine the _____ of the relay team.

12. Despite his _____, he was remembered as a great president.

13. A tangelo is a _____ fruit resulting from a cross between a mandarin orange and a tangerine.

14. The equations in biochemical engineering are _____ and difficult to understand.

AUTHENTIC ASSESSMENT

Students will complete a comic book strip based on the unit "Animation Domination."

Instructions for Comic Strip

1. **Prompt.** Students will create a satirical cartoon based on something in their own lives. In order to do this, students should understand that satire often takes human shortcomings, mishaps, or vices and pokes fun at them, hoping to bring improvement. Following are some literary elements that may be used in satire:

    a) Sarcasm- sometimes harsh or ironic comment, intended to ridicule its subject

    b) Irony- using words to express a meaning that is the opposite of what is true

    c) Parody- a funny or sarcastic imitation of something or someone

    d) Analogy- a similarity between two things, used to compare

2. **Story plan.** Students may work individually to create an idea for a satirical situation involving themselves or something directly impacting their lives. Students will then brainstorm to create a storyline that is interesting but simple enough to take up only six panels. Students may use information from the unit as well as prior knowledge and experience. At least one of the four elements of satire should be used. Each student should write a draft of the story and submit it to the teacher for approval. The following are questions that may be addressed in the story:

    a) What real-life situation does the comic strip satirize?

    b) Who are the major characters?

    c) What is the major conflict?

    d) What elements of satire are used?

3. **Comic strip planner.** Once the story is approved, students may begin planning the comic strip. Each student must completely fill in the comic strip planner provided. The following are items to consider when planning a comic:

    a) What should the caption express?

    b) What action is occurring, and who is involved?

    c) What is the best transition from one panel to another?

    d) Is there a good conclusion?

4. **Comic strip.** Once the comic strip planner is completed and approved, the comic strip itself may be completed. Text and illustrations included should effectively tell the story written in the story plan. The comic strip may be hand drawn or created on the computer.

5. **Assessment.** Work will be assessed using the rubric that follows.

COMIC STRIP PLANNER

Scene	Actions Occurring	Characters Present	Background	Caption
1				
2				
3				
4				
5				
6				

RUBRIC

Requirement	8-10 Points	4-7 Points	0-3 Points	Points Earned
Story Plan	The student creates an interesting and informative story plan that is well written.	The student creates a story plan that lacks some interest or information.	The student does not create a story plan, or the plan is incomplete.	
Comic Strip Planner	The student fully completes each element of the comic strip planner.	The student completes most elements of the comic strip planner.	The student does not complete the comic strip planner or completes only a small portion.	
Comic Strip	The comic strip is neatly drawn/written, with no errors in spelling, punctuation, or grammar.	The comic strip is neatly drawn/written, with a few errors in spelling, punctuation, or grammar.	The comic strip is not completed, is difficult to read, or has many errors in spelling, punctuation, or grammar.	
Content	The comic strip tells a complete story and uses at least one element of satire.	The comic strip tells a story that is mostly complete and uses at least one element of satire.	The comic strip does not tell a complete story and/or uses no elements of satire.	

READING INSTRUCTIONAL GUIDE FOR HIGH-INTEREST ARTICLE

BEFORE READING

Looking at the Words

Determining How the Word Sounds (Phonics)

Using the Syllable Guide found in the beginning of the book, read the steps to learn how to break a word into manageable parts. Follow these steps to sound out the words below.

Determining What the Word Means (Vocabulary)

Look at the words below before beginning to read the article. Before reading the definitions, use prefixes and suffixes from the Syllable Guide to predict meaning.

Words to Study	Breaking into Syllables	Short Definition
candid	can-did	(adj.) open and sincere
contemplate	con-tem-plate	(v.) to consider thoroughly
debilitating	de-bil-i-tat-ing	(adj.) causing a loss of strength or energy
franchise	fran-chise	(n.) a professional sports team
psychiatric	psy-chi-at-ric	(adj.) relating to the science and treatment of mental disorders
overwhelm	o-ver-whelm	(v.) to overcome completely in mind and feeling
psychological	psy-cho-log-i-cal	(adj.) relating to the mind or emotions

Activating Background Knowledge

Anticipation Guide

Mark each of the following statements True or False:

1. _____ Zack Greinke is a famous NFL athlete.

2. _____ Anxiety affects only women.

3. _____ Anxiety can be an obstacle for athletes.

4. _____ Zack Greinke's sports career is over.

5. _____ Anxiety disorders can be overcome with proper treatment from trained physicians.

Starter Questions

After completing the Anticipation Guide, participate in a group or class discussion using the following questions:

1. What professional team does Greinke play for?

2. What position does Greinke play?

3. Who is Ricky Williams?

4. What is social anxiety disorder?

5. What are symptoms of social anxiety disorder? If you don't know, what would you *guess* that some symptoms might be?

Make a prediction about what you think the article will be about.

DURING READING

- Skim the article for 45–60 seconds. Circle any words you don't know.
- When you are finished, decode and determine the meaning of unknown words.
- Skim the questions for 30–45 seconds.
- Predict what the article is about.
- Read the article.
- Reread to clarify as needed.
- Answer the questions.

AFTER READING

Discussion Starter Questions

1. What similarities do Zack Greinke and Ricky Williams share?

2. What can the reader learn from both Greinke and Williams?

3. How did Greinke overcome his difficulties?

4. What honors and awards has Greinke won?

5. Do you think more celebrities should come forward and open up about their anxiety difficulties in order to increase awareness? Why or why not?

BATTING AGAINST Social Anxiety

Pounding heart, fuzzy thoughts.

Shallow breathing, blank mind.

Panic.

It should have been the prime time of his career and possibly of his life. He should have been enjoying life as one of the most successful young baseball players ever. Instead, as Zack Greinke struggled through his third major league training camp, his mind raced. He couldn't concentrate long enough to throw a decent pitch, much less a strike. He felt like he was losing his mind.

Zack Greinke was a star on his Florida high school baseball team. At his 2002 graduation, he was a first-round draft pick as well as the Gatorade National Player of the Year. Passing up a college scholarship, Greinke spent a winter in the Puerto Rican League and then a season in the minor leagues. After being named the Royals' minor league pitcher of the year, he suited up as a 20-year-old major league rookie for the Kansas City Royals.

His first year with the Royals was a successful one, and he was named the Royals' pitcher of the year. Greinke was expected to be a major part of the franchise's future. Life and work were turning out like the American dream, at least on the outside.

Behind the scenes, Greinke suffered from social anxiety disorder and depression. Social anxiety disorder is a psychiatric disorder that involves panic and stress when relating to others. It can include a constant fear of being embarrassed or judged. These debilitating conditions had overwhelmed Greinke for most of his life, although he was able to hide it. Even during his successful stretch in the minor leagues, he contemplated quitting baseball. The constant social pressures had led him to hate the game.

During the 2005 season, Zack Greinke lost 17 games and won only 5. For any player, that kind of breakdown could lead to a mental strain. But for already struggling Greinke, it only deepened his depression and made him pull even further away from his teammates. Every little part of the game had become difficult. He argued with his pitching coach, who thought his game might improve if he moved just five inches to the left. Greinke refused. He was unfriendly to his teammates. He dreaded even going to the ballpark.

In February of 2006, at the end of a training session, he broke down and had a talk with managers Buddy Bell and Allard Baird. In the often harsh world of baseball, they did something unusual—they told Greinke to take a break. They told him to concentrate on himself and return to baseball when he was ready. He left the Royals' spring training camp and took a break from baseball to seek psychological help. It was then that he was officially diagnosed with social anxiety disorder and began receiving therapy and anti-anxiety medication. Feeling better, he found a renewed enthusiasm for baseball.

After two months off, Greinke returned to the minor leagues and began rebuilding his career. His entry back into the major leagues wasn't nearly as easy the second time. He had to prove himself physically and prove to the

staff and to himself that he could handle the mental pressures of the game. He spent the 2007 training season as a relief pitcher and fighting for a spot on the team. At the end of the season, he signed a one-year contract for the 2008 season. He pitched well enough that year to land a four-year, $38 million contract with the Royals. The first season of his contract, he pitched 24 consecutive innings without giving up a run. He went on to win the prestigious American League Cy Young award.

Part of how Greinke is learning to deal with his disorder is to take some of the "extras" out of his career. He no longer focuses on awards and numbers. Instead, he just concentrates on winning games with his team. After his recent high-profile *Sports Illustrated* cover article he said, "Really, all that matters is winning games. Winning is what always mattered (most), but I would still like the other stuff. But now, I don't care one bit about it—any of it, any award stuff, All-Star or anything. All this is about is winning games. That's all it's about."

Zack Greinke proved that early success followed by overwhelming failure doesn't have to be the end of the game. He's still young, and at the moment, he's better than ever. He knows that social anxiety will always be a struggle. Just as an athlete has to train his body, Greinke will have to constantly monitor his state of mind, seeking help when he needs it. But for now, his mind and body are working together, and he's back to being called the future of baseball.

Zack Greinke is not the only well-known person to suffer from social anxiety disorder. Although not many celebrities have publicly announced their struggles with social anxiety, a few like Barbara Streisand, Donny Osmond, and Ricky Williams have discussed it.

Greinke rarely talks about his diagnosis. But former NFL player Ricky Williams often talks about how social anxiety disorder affects his life and career. He was a shy Heisman Trophy winner, drafted and then thrown into the spotlight as a star player. He had everything he ever wanted but was afraid to do simple tasks like go to the grocery store. He explained, "I hit rock bottom after my second year in the NFL. I was 22 years old, I had all the money I could ever imagine, I had the opportunity literally to go anywhere in the whole world and do anything I wanted. But for some reason, I couldn't leave the house. I hated being at airports, where everyone recognized me and was going to try to come up to me and say 'Hi.' I was just deathly afraid of it."

After Williams realized that he needed treatment if he was going to function as a player, he participated in cognitive therapy and began a medication regimen that allowed him some normalcy in his life. He is serious about being a role model, especially to other men. It's why he is so honest about his struggles. "If my story can help even one person to seek help, it will feel as though I've scored the game-winning touchdown."

READING COMPREHENSION

After reading "Batting Against Social Anxiety," choose the options that best answer questions 1–14.

1. Read this sentence.
    It should have been the prime time of his career and possibly his life.

    As it is used in this sentence, what does the author mean by the phrase "prime time"?
    A. future
    B. evening
    C. best phase
    D. time for change

2. Read this sentence.
    After Williams realized that he needed treatment if he was going to function as a player, he participated in cognitive therapy and began a medication regimen that allowed him some normalcy in his life.

    What is the meaning of the word *regimen* as it is used in this sentence?
    F. plan
    G. change
    H. withdrawal
    I. experiment

3. From this article, the reader can tell that
    A. social anxiety is an easy disorder to overcome.
    B. athletes have an easier life than non-celebrities.
    C. celebrities have to battle some of the same issues that the rest of us face.
    D. athletes should attend college before beginning a career in professional sports.

4. What change did Greinke's managers make to help him with his career?
    F. They offered him more money.
    G. They provided additional training to improve his performance.
    H. He was traded to another team that could give him more playing time.
    I. They suggested that he take a break from baseball to deal with the difficulties he was having.

5. What character trait in Greinke does the author seem to admire the most?
    A. fairness
    B. athleticism
    C. perseverance
    D. outgoing personality

6. The author organizes the article by
    F. explaining the ups and downs of Greinke's career.
    G. comparing Greinke with other famous baseball players.
    H. presenting a series of questions and answers from Greinke.
    I. presenting an argument about why Greinke should be selected MVP.

7. Why does the author choose to begin the article with the symptoms of a panic attack?
   A. to introduce Greinke to the reader
   B. to encourage the reader to support Greinke's professional career
   C. to prove how panic attacks are more common than people realize
   D. to illustrate how a person feels when suffering from a panic attack

8. What is the main idea of the first full paragraph?
   F. Greinke is a famous pitcher.
   G. Greinke's anxiety affected his career.
   H. Panic attacks are common among athletes.
   I. The symptoms of a panic attack are often overlooked.

9. Which experience seemed to have the most direct influence on Greinke's decision to seek help for his disorder?
   A. losing a game
   B. a conversation with his managers
   C. the request for a television interview
   D. the comments fans were making about his performance

10. What finally helped Greinke develop a renewed enthusiasm for baseball?
    F. a new coach
    G. proper treatment for his disorder
    H. playing for another baseball team
    I. receiving an award for his pitching ability

11. Greinke and Williams are alike in that they both
    A. pitch in the MLB.
    B. play for the Royals.
    C. suffer from social anxiety disorder.
    D. graduated from Clemson University.

12. Which fact from the article provides the BEST evidence that one can have social anxiety and still perform successfully?
    F. Greinke pitched 24 innings without giving up a run.
    G. Greinke had a serious conversation with his managers.
    H. Greinke knows that winning games is all that really matters.
    I. Greinke is not the only well-known person to suffer from social anxiety disorder.

13. Those who read this article will learn
    A. how to play baseball under pressure.
    B. how to throw a fast pitch despite distractions.
    C. that social anxiety is more common among celebrities than one might think.
    D. the pros and cons of beginning a career as a professional athlete in today's society.

14. Based on the information about BOTH Greinke and Williams, which of these conclusions is accurate?
    F. Both men have overcome difficulties to become successful athletes.
    G. Social anxiety has forced both Greinke and Williams to give up their careers.
    H. Williams and Greinke are opposed to others receiving treatment for social anxiety.
    I. Social anxiety is an uncommon disorder that does not affect the performance of athletes.

READING STRATEGY

Directions: A chain-of-events organizer is used to describe the stages of a series of events or the actions of a subject. Using the article, fill in at least two facts about each stage of Zack Greinke's career. When you reach home plate, write a summary of how the events have impacted his career.

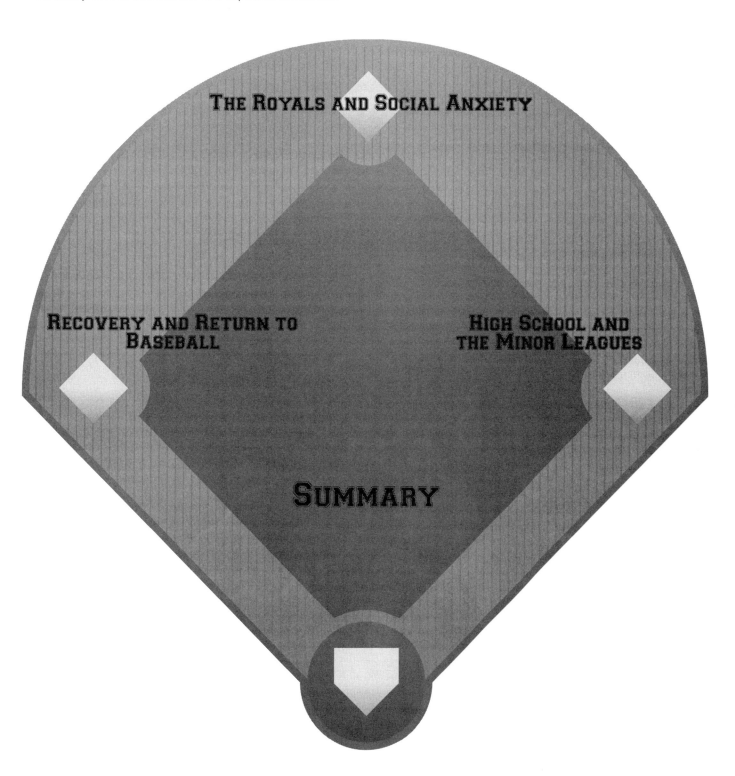

INTERPRETING THE DATA

PART I

Who suffers from anxiety disorders?

In any given year, millions of adults in the United States suffer from some type of anxiety disorder. Women are twice as likely as men to suffer from many of these conditions, and many of the forms of anxiety disorders occur during the teen years. Compute the totals in Table 1 to answer questions 15 and 16.

Table 1. Prevalence of anxiety disorders among American adults (ages 18-54)

Type of anxiety disorder	Number of American adults suffering from disorder	Percentage of American adults suffering from disorder
Panic disorder	2.4 million	1.7%
Obsessive-compulsive disorder	3.3 million	2.3%
Post-traumatic stress disorder	5.2 million	3.6%
Generalized anxiety disorder	4 million	2.8%
Social anxiety disorder	5.3 million	3.7%
All anxiety disorders	15.	16.

17. Which two types of anxiety disorders are the most prevalent among American adults?

_____

18. Is the percentage of adults that suffer from panic disorder more or less than the percentage that suffer from generalized anxiety disorder?

_____

_____

19. Another study indicates that the percentage of Americans of all ages suffering from anxiety disorders is 28.8%. This separate study also reveals that the median age of onset (when the disorder appears) is 11 years old. What is a possible explanation for why the percentage in this study is so much different than the total found in #16?

ANALYZE
EVALUATE
EXPLAIN

_____

_____

_____

_____

_____

_____

PART II

How does social anxiety disorder affect a sufferer's life?

Read the following quotations of those suffering from social anxiety disorder:

"In any social situation, I felt fear. I would be anxious before I even left the house, and it would escalate as I got closer to a college class, a party, or whatever. I would feel sick to my stomach — it almost felt like I had the flu. My heart would pound, my palms would get sweaty, and I would get this feeling of being removed from myself and from everybody else."

"When I would walk into a room full of people, I'd turn red and it would feel like everybody's eyes were on me. I was embarrassed to stand off in a corner by myself, but I couldn't think of anything to say to anybody. It was humiliating. I felt so clumsy; I couldn't wait to get out."

"I couldn't go on dates, and for a while I couldn't even go to class. My sophomore year of college I had to come home for a semester. I felt like such a failure."

Social anxiety disorder (SAD) is a specific type of anxiety disorder where a person feels overwhelmingly nervous and/or self-conscious in everyday social situations such as going to the grocery store, attending school, or hanging out with friends. SAD is one of the most common psychiatric disorders and can affect not only the social aspects of a person's life, but also his or her career.

Table 2. Effect of SAD on employment and income

	People diagnosed with SAD	People labeled psychiatrically well
Have full-time employment	31%	54%
Hold professional positions	1.7%	7.1%
Have a lower-level household income	14.9%	7.2%

20. In general, how do people diagnosed with SAD fare in employment and income versus those labeled psychiatrically well? Use data from Table 2 to support your answer.

ANALYZE EVALUATE EXPLAIN

21. Study the information in Table 2 and the paragraphs before it. Then determine some possible reasons for the data in Table 2. Using details in your answer, explain what it might feel like to have a job or to go to work while suffering from the social anxiety described.

ANALYZE EVALUATE EXPLAIN

REFLECT AND RESPOND

22. If you had a friend who was showing signs of social anxiety disorder, what could you do to encourage that person to get help? Using examples from the article and facts learned through Interpreting the Data, discuss why it is important not to ignore the issue, but instead to pursue treatment for social anxiety.

Reflect & Respond

READING INSTRUCTIONAL GUIDE FOR TECHNICAL EXTENSION

BEFORE READING

Looking at the Words

Determining What the Word Means (Vocabulary)

Words to Study	Breaking into Syllables	Short Definition
acupuncture	ac-u-punc-ture	(n.) a practice that pierces the body with needles to treat illness or relieve pain
agitation	ag-i-ta-tion	(n.) the state of being disturbed or troubled
biofeedback	bi-o-feed-back	(n.) a technique that teaches control of body functions such as blood pressure
chiropractic	chi-ro-prac-tic	(n.) a system of therapy that focuses on the spine and nervous system
complementary	com-ple-men-ta-ry	(adj.) serving as a needed addition; completing
episode	ep-i-sode	(n.) an event in a person's life
isolate	i-so-late	(v.) to set apart

Activating Background Knowledge

Graphic Organizer

Either individually or in groups, brainstorm about depression, recalling anything previously learned and any prior experience with the subject. Next, complete the concept map to demonstrate what you already know about the varying causes of depression.

Starter Questions

After completing the Graphic Organizer, participate in a group or class discussion to come up with questions about the subject, a prediction about the article, and at least one learning goal. The first question has been provided for you.

Question: What is depression?

Question: _____

Prediction: _____

Goal: _____

DURING READING

- Skim the article for 45–60 seconds. Circle any words you don't know.

- When you are finished, decode and determine the meaning of unknown words.

- Skim the questions for 30–45 seconds.

- Predict what the article is about.

- Read the article.

- Reread to clarify as needed.

- Answer the questions.

AFTER READING

After reading, you may do the following:

- Review, paraphrase, and summarize

- Participate in main-idea discussions by describing the information in their own words

- Reflect on concept maps and generate additional discussion starter questions based on the mappings

- Participate in small-group discussions using discussion starter questions

Discussion Starter Questions

The first question has been provided for you.

1. What are the similarities and differences between the different types of depression?

2. _____

3. _____

©2010 PRINCIPLE WOODS, INC. Removal of copyright notice and copying are violations of Federal Law.

TECHNICAL EXTENSION

Teen Depression
A Common Mental Health Disorder

Maybe you have known someone like Zack Greinke. Or maybe you recognize yourself in his story. To the outside world, he had everything a young man could want as a major league baseball player right out of high school. However, Zack lost his concentration while he was pitching, fought with those trying to help him succeed, and was rude to his teammates. He often disappeared when he was scheduled to pitch. He was overwhelmed with his life in general and told his family that every day was just "another gray day."

Zack suffers from depression, a common disorder among adults as well as teens. Look around your classroom at five people sitting near you. The odds are that 1 teen in that group will suffer with depression before he or she reaches adulthood. In addition, about 1 in 10 teens will struggle with depression. The average episode lasts about 8 months. If this sounds familiar, you can be assured that it is common within your age group. It is also very treatable if help is sought.

More young women than young men report being depressed. However, this might be because girls are more comfortable talking about their feelings. Teens in both groups, though, often believe their feelings or behaviors are "strange" or "weird," which only makes the problem worse. Rather than seek help, they isolate themselves or behave in upsetting ways.

Not all depression is the same, either:

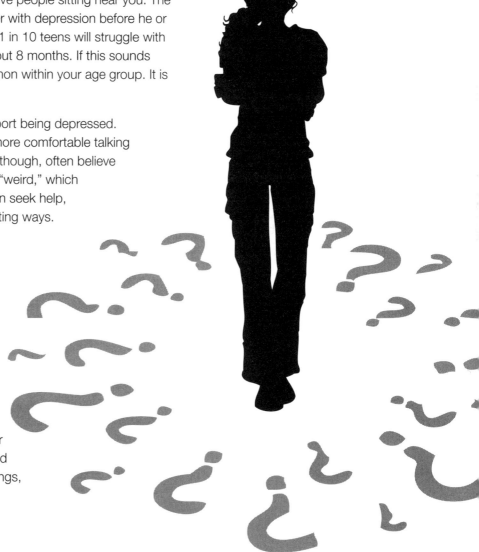

Major depression is also called "clinical depression." Prolonged sadness or other symptoms (see text box) lasting longer than 2 weeks may indicate major depression.

Dysthymia is similar to major depression, but the symptoms are not as severe. It can last longer than major depression, though, and is marked by sad or hopeless feelings, irritability, and mood swings.

Adjustment disorder is a reaction to a difficult event within the last 3 months.

Bipolar disorder refers to extreme swings between high and low moods.

Seasonal affective disorder (SAD) has the same characteristics as depression but happens each year during a specific season. The change in available sunlight during the winter months in many parts of the country has been identified as a cause of SAD.

It is hard to identify the causes of depression during the teen years because of the normal changes that go on at this time of life. Being a teen is stressful in itself, marked by many hormonal changes. It is also the time when teens struggle to become independent from parents or other important adults. However, some instances of depression are the result of an event in the teen's life. These events could be the death of a friend or family member, a break-up, failure at school, or even world events such as the terrorist attacks in recent years.

Following are some other risk factors that mean teens might be *more likely* to experience depression:

- a traumatic incident

- some form of abuse

- long-term illness or disability

- a family history of depression or other mental disorders

- other untreated problems, like drug or alcohol abuse or antisocial behaviors

It is important for teens to be aware of these risk factors. Hopefully, then they will be more comfortable asking for help, especially if there is a history of depression in their families.

Zack Greinke knew that something was wrong, but he did not know what to do about it. He started to hate pitching, something that he had always loved. However, it wasn't until he talked to two of his coaches about his depression that he began to get the help he needed.

Symptoms of Teen Depression

Sadness that overwhelms

Feelings of hopelessness

Rage or irritability over small things

Withdrawal from friends and family

Loss of interest in activities

Changes in sleeping or eating habits

Restlessness or agitation

Feelings of guilt

Feelings of worthlessness

Excessive fatigue or lack of energy

Difficulty with concentration

Thoughts or dreams of suicide or death

Treatment for depression can range from meeting with a counselor or therapist to taking medication. Many professionals recommend talk therapy first in the cases of mild to moderate depression. These sessions alone often resolve the problem. Complementary therapies such as massage and yoga are also often included in the treatment plan. Other therapies in this category might be proper diet and exercise, biofeedback, chiropractic care, and acupuncture. Experts do not recommend any plan that relies only on medication, especially for teenagers.

Teen depression is common and treatable, as long as it is identified. Zack got the help he needed and successfully returned to pitching. More importantly, his "gray days" seem to be over.

READING COMPREHENSION

After reading "Teen Depression," answer questions 1–12.

1. Read this sentence.
   If this sounds familiar, you can be assured that it is prevalent within your age group and is very treatable if help is sought.

   What does the word *prevalent* mean as used in the sentence?
   - A. odd
   - B. rare
   - C. unusual
   - D. common

2. What does the phrase "complementary therapies" mean in the following sentence?
   Complementary therapies such as massage and yoga are also often included in the treatment plan.
   - F. methods that rotate
   - G. treatments that stand alone
   - H. treatments that assist in curing
   - I. methods that attack a non-curable disease

3. According to the article, seasonal affective disorder (SAD)
   - A. is more likely to affect teens than adults.
   - B. is marked by mood changes tied to sunlight.
   - C. affects only those in northern parts of the country.
   - D. is a form of clinical depression that requires long-term treatment.

4. Which one of the following sentences from the article supports the fact that depression is common among teens?
   - F. Maybe you have known someone like Zack Greinke.
   - G. In addition, 1 in 10 teens will struggle with depression.
   - H. More young women than young men report being depressed.
   - I. Teens in both groups, though, often believe their feelings are "strange" or "weird," which only makes the problem worse.

5. Why does the author italicize the phrase "more likely" in the sentence in paragraph 6 that begins, "Some other risk factors that mean teens might be more likely …"?
   - A. to emphasize that not all teens with these risk factors will suffer from depression
   - B. to suggest that most teens will experience depression at some point in their teen years
   - C. to reinforce the statistics in paragraph 2 showing that many teens suffer from depression
   - D. to compare Zack's experience with the likelihood that 1 in 10 teens will suffer from depression

6. What is the main idea of paragraph 5, which begins, "It is hard to identify the causes…"?
   - F. Depression cannot be treated until adulthood.
   - G. Parents often block treatment of teen depression.
   - H. Hormonal changes interfere with treatment plans.
   - I. Teen depression is hard to diagnose due to the growth patterns present during the teen years.

7. According to the article, young women may appear to suffer from depression more than young men because
    A. boys tend to isolate themselves.
    B. they are a larger segment of the population.
    C. they are more comfortable talking about their feelings.
    D. it has been proven that boys do not have the same hormonal changes as girls.

8. Dysthymia is most similar to major depression in that
    F. it happens only during the winter.
    G. it is generally a reaction to an event.
    H. its symptoms are generally much harder to deal with.
    I. those suffering from the disorder feel sad, hopeless, irritable, and moody.

9. What information from the article BEST supports the idea that depression in young people should involve a treatment plan with multiple approaches?
    A. Experts do not recommend any plan that uses only medication.
    B. It is difficult to determine the causes of depression during the teen years.
    C. Sometimes depression is the result of an upsetting event, such as a break-up or failure at school.
    D. It is important for teens to be aware of the things that cause depression so they will be comfortable asking for help.

10. According to the information in the text box,
    F. dreams of death indicate suicide is likely.
    G. bursts of energy are a symptom of depression.
    H. teens who suffer from depression often feel overwhelmed by life.
    I. the symptoms of depression in teenagers and adults are totally different.

11. Zack's own description of his life as just "another gray day"
    A. is a personal way of describing the same symptoms discussed in the article.
    B. shows that he didn't ask for the help he needed until his career was affected.
    C. indicates that his family and friends did not know that he suffered from depression.
    D. shows that he suffered from a severe form of depression known as seasonal affective disorder.

12. According to the article, why is teen depression often harder to treat than adult depression? Use facts from the article to support your answer.

> _____
>
> _____
>
> _____
>
> _____
>
> _____
>
> _____
>
> _____
>
> _____

TECHNICAL WRITING PROMPT

13. You are the leader of a high school support group for teens suffering from anxiety disorders and depression. Create a pamphlet for other students overviewing teen depression, including risk factors, types, symptoms, and treatments. The goal is to help students identify and become familiar with how depression presents in teenagers. Use bullet points or paragraph form, and be concise.

Technical Writing

VOCATIONAL EXTENSION

Has your doctor ever asked about your spiritual practices when you had an upset stomach? How about questions about your emotional health?

HELP WANTED:

Holistic practitioner for local clinic. MD or DO degree required, with additional training in holistic medicine. Hours are 8 a.m. to 5 p.m., Monday through Friday, with occasional weekend on-call duty.

An appointment with a doctor who practices holistic medicine would look familiar at first. Your medical history would be taken. Then your blood pressure and temperature would be recorded, along with your weight and height. However, the holistic doctor might then ask questions about your emotional health, your diet, and your spiritual well-being as he or she tries to find the balance your body needs to regain its overall health.

The focus of this type of medical care is to find the true cause of a disease, not just treat the symptoms. The body is viewed as an interconnected web of systems that depend on one another to work.

Alternative forms of medicine within holistic practice often use herbs and plants to encourage healing. Complementary therapies like massage, acupuncture and acupressure, and chiropractic care are also offered as part of a well-rounded treatment plan. Holistic medicine emphasizes the negative effects of chemicals that pollute the body, including drugs, food additives, and alcohol.

Holistic practitioners have a wide range of training. Some have no formal training at all, relying instead on experience. Others have a formal medical degree from an accredited university, which requires a bachelor's degree plus an additional three years of medical school. Those seeking the highest level of credibility belong to organizations like the American Board of Holistic Medicine. All competent practitioners continue to study the latest research and methods in this area of medicine.

Most holistic practitioners work in clinics and offices as primary care doctors. Their hours often follow a regular 9-to-5 schedule, with occasional emergencies like any other doctor. Their income matches that of most other family practice doctors, with an average of around $100,000 per year. Benefits like paid vacation time and annual bonuses of $1,500 to $5,000 per year often increase the compensation a great deal.

Holistic medicine offers alternatives for people making decisions about their health care. Doctors in this field work hand in hand with traditional practitioners to keep us in the best health possible.

LOOKING FORWARD

14. Alternatives to traditional medicine are becoming increasingly popular. Imagine that you are pursuing a career in the field of holistic medicine. Choose a form of holistic medicine that interests you. Using personal knowledge and information from the article, explain why you believe this form could help someone with healing.

Looking Forward

ETHICAL DILEMMA

15. As the nurse in a holistic physician's office, you are responsible for coordinating the care requested by the doctor for all his patients. During a discussion with a patient (who is also a friend of your family), the patient asks you not to mention to the doctor that she had a problem with alcohol abuse over 20 years ago. The patient believes that it is no longer an issue, and she would prefer that people not know about it now. What are your choices in this situation? Should you respect her wishes, or should you tell the doctor?

Ethical Dilemma

UNIT VOCABULARY ASSESSMENT

Matching
Match each word in Column I to its definition in Column II.

Column I
_____ 1. episode
_____ 2. debilitating
_____ 3. psychiatric
_____ 4. acupuncture
_____ 5. chiropractic

Column II
A. relating to mental disorders
B. event in a person's life
C. piercing the body with needles to relieve pain
D. causing a loss of strength or energy
E. therapy that focuses on the spine and nervous system

Multiple Choice
Choose the word that MOST NEARLY replaces the underlined word in each sentence.

6. People who do not fit in often feel <u>isolated</u> from the majority.
    A. near
    B. humbled
    C. separated
    D. embarrassed

7. The politician gave a <u>candid</u> response to the tough question.
    A. open
    B. camera
    C. guarded
    D. restrained

8. Looking at footage of the tornado's damage was enough to <u>overwhelm</u> anyone.
    A. excite
    B. overlay
    C. comfort
    D. overcome

9. The troubled look on his face revealed the <u>agitation</u> he felt.
    A. ease
    B. calm
    C. sadness
    D. disturbance

Fill in the Blank
Choose a word from the word bank to fill in the blank in the sentence below.

10. After being accepted to several universities, the student had to _____ which college was the right choice for her.

11. The city was ecstatic to be awarded a new NFL _____.

12. Weightlifting can be beneficial by itself or _____ to other sports training programs.

13. Victims of crime can sometimes suffer serious _____ effects.

14. By practicing _____, the athlete was able to lower his blood pressure.

Word Bank

biofeedback
complementary
contemplate
franchise
psychological

AUTHENTIC ASSESSMENT

Students will create a public service announcement based on the unit "Pitching Anxiety."

Instructions for Public Service Announcement

1. **Definition.** A public service announcement (PSA) is an advertisement intended to convince the public of something or to raise awareness about a particular issue.

2. **Planning/questions.** Students will work in either assigned or self-chosen groups. Each group will create a PSA highlighting a specific anxiety disorder. Students may choose one mentioned within the unit (see Interpreting the Data for a list of specific disorders) or another disorder approved by the teacher. The PSAs should be informative. Groups should complete the following questions to begin planning.

   a. What is the purpose of an informative PSA?

   b. How will you introduce the issue?

   c. What information will you include about anxiety disorders?

   d. What support/data will you use?

3. **Storyboard.** After these questions have been answered, each group will complete a storyboard for the PSA, with details of what facts, graphics, etc. will be used for each scene. Groups should decide whether the message will be given by text, voice-over, pictures, or a combination.

4. **PSA product.** Groups will then create and record the PSAs on video camera, web cam, or software such as iMovie or PowerPoint. The PSAs will be either shown to the class or performed live, and they will be evaluated for factual accuracy and persuasiveness.

5. **Assessment.** Work will be assessed using the rubric that follows.

RUBRIC

Requirement	8–10 Points	4–7 Points	0–3 Points	Points Earned
Questions	The students answer the questions completely, using articles and facts from the unit.	The students answer most questions, using some articles and facts from the unit.	The students do not answer the questions completely or do not use articles and facts from the unit.	
Storyboard	The students draw out a storyboard with detail, including any text, graphics, and scripts needed.	The students draw out a storyboard with some detail but are missing some text, graphics, and scripts.	The students do not draw out a storyboard with detail or do not include text, graphics, and scripts.	
PSA Product	The PSA is well put together, complete, and has an informative message.	The PSA is mostly complete, but the message isn't fully informative.	The PSA is missing components or is not informative.	
Presentation	Work is neat, legible, and turned in on time.	Work is messy, hard to read, and/or late.	Work is incomplete or not turned in.	

— Unit 3 —
Online Communities

READING INSTRUCTIONAL GUIDE FOR HIGH-INTEREST ARTICLE

BEFORE READING

Looking at the Words

Determining How the Word Sounds (Phonics)

Using the Syllable Guide and the Reading Instructional Guide Template found in the beginning of the book, read the steps to learn how to break a word into manageable parts.

Determining What the Word Means (Vocabulary)

Words to Study	Breaking into Syllables	Short Definition
alias	a-li-as	(n.) false name
constructive	con-struc-tive	(adj.) serving to improve; helpful
conviction	con-vic-tion	(n.) the judgment of a jury or judge that a person is guilty
cryptic	cryp-tic	(adj.) using code
defame	de-fame	(v.) to damage the reputation of someone
provoke	pro-voke	(v.) to stir to action

Activating Background Knowledge

Anticipation Guide

Mark each of the following statements True or False:

1. ____ Social networking sites are losing popularity.

2. ____ Teenagers are the only people using social networking sites.

3. ____ Information posted on a person's social networking site can hurt his or her career.

4. ____ Information people post online about themselves is always true.

5. ____ Friends who have access to your networking webpage can post inappropriate images and comments for others to see.

Starter Questions

After completing the Anticipation Guide, participate in a group or class discussion using the following questions:

1. What are some differences between MySpace and Facebook?

2. How is YouTube different from MySpace and Facebook?

3. Why do you think so many people now use networking sites?

4. What are some positive and negative effects that social networking sites can have on friendships?

5. Have you heard of a mother named Lori Drew? If so, what was she accused of doing?

Make a prediction about what you think the article will be about.

DURING READING

- Skim the article for 45–60 seconds. Circle any words you don't know.

- When you are finished, decode and determine the meaning of unknown words.

- Skim the questions for 30–45 seconds.

- Predict what the article is about.

- Read the article.

- Reread to clarify as needed.

- Answer the questions.

AFTER READING

Discussion Starter Questions

1. Do you think Lori Drew should have been held legally responsible for her actions? Why or why not?

2. Do you think it is appropriate for college admissions officials to review social networking sites prior to admitting someone? Why or why not?

3. Do you have a social networking site? What measures do you take to protect your page?

4. According to the text box, what are some ways we can protect ourselves when using social networking sites?

5. What regulations should be in place to limit the access people have to sites such as YouTube?

The Dangers and Benefits
of Social Networking

"The world would be a better place without you." Tough words for a 13-year-old girl to hear from a boy she likes. We will never know exactly how Megan felt when she read these words from Josh Evans. All we know is that Megan committed suicide not long after receiving this online message. Police will never be able to question Josh to learn what would provoke him to send such a cruel message. The Josh Evans involved in this case does not exist. He is a made-up person created by the mother of one of Megan's former friends.

In 2006 Lori Drew believed that rumors were being spread about her daughter. Instead of talking to those involved, Drew took a different approach. According to prosecutors, she and her daughter created a MySpace page using an alias. She pretended to be a 16-year-old boy named Josh. Drew and others reportedly began to chat online with Megan, who they thought was gossiping about Drew's daughter. Drew posed as Josh when talking with Megan. As the communication increased, Megan was led to believe that "Josh" loved her. "Josh" later told Megan that he no longer wanted to be friends. He and others began to use cryptic messages to verbally attack Megan online. The last message to Megan was that the world would be better off without her.

Though Megan committed suicide, Drew couldn't be held responsible for her death. However, a jury did find her guilty of illegal computer access. A judge later overturned the conviction, but Drew was the subject of a great deal of negative news.

Keeping Facebook Private

Facebook overhauled its privacy settings in December 2009, with mixed reviews. Facebook's creators said they were trying to give individuals more control over their personal information, but they actually gave less control over other aspects. For example, items like name, profile picture, gender, geographic location, and networks are now considered public knowledge and have no privacy settings. The only way to stop people from finding this information is to limit their access through the "search privacy settings," a more complicated approach.

At the same time, Facebook gave users more specific control (and the ability to easily change default privacy settings) than most other social networking sites. Users can also add specific privacy controls to individual updates or pictures, choosing to allow viewing only by certain friend groups or networks, or even choosing the "Only Me" option.

The privacy settings of a social networking site can never be perfect, though. Ultimately, Facebook can't protect its users if they don't protect themselves. If in doubt about the safety of an update or image, the easiest thing to do is not to post it.

MySpace, Facebook, and Twitter are just a few of the online communities teens and adults join. We spend hours messaging, writing status reports, tagging friends, or posting photos and videos. These sites allow people to stay connected with friends and family. These are examples of constructive purposes. But sometimes they are used to cause harm, such as in the Drew case.

YouTube, a video-sharing site, has recently been criticized for allowing the posting of fight videos. In 2008 a video was posted showing the beating of a teen in Florida. The video soon caught the attention of officials. Five teenage girls were charged with a crime and punished. A similar video of another fight between two teenage girls in Florida came out on MySpace in 2009. The video clearly showed several adults watching

the violence. While police were concerned with the fight itself, they also wondered why the many onlookers did nothing to stop it. So, we may be held accountable not only for our action, but also for our failure to act in a situation.

Many people turn to social networking sites to learn more about someone. Even college admissions officers have recently used social networking websites to look for applicants. They are finding that some applicants have posted photos that hurt their character. While posting photos may begin as innocent fun, these same images can hurt an applicant's chances of getting into college. In some cases, the applicant doesn't know that inappropriate information has been posted. These sites can instantly be changed by others. In the case of Facebook, people can "tag" each other in photos. Once tagged, the photos

Tweeting Too Loudly

Twitter can be an influential marketing tool because of its networking potential. Stores use it to send exclusive offers to followers, and news organizations use it to make sure followers receive breaking news. Celebrities even use it to market themselves. However, with only 140 characters to use, many celebrities are realizing that their fast twittering fingers can cause more trouble than good.

The reason behind one of the most publicized Twitter exits—that of Miley Cyrus—was somewhat of a mystery, rumored to relate to her boyfriend's dislike of the site. Other celebrities have had defining moments in which their tweets harmed their image or career. Take these notable examples:

- Courtney Love was sued for defaming a fashion designer through tweets.

- A Michigan congressman tweeted his travels through Iraq and Afghanistan, causing a security breach.

- Dallas Mavericks owner Mark Coban was fined $25,000 by the NBA for tweeting about referees.

- Kansas City Chiefs player Larry Johnson tweeted negatively about his coach, leading to a tweet war with angry fans. He was ultimately cut by the Chiefs, becoming the poster boy for the celebrity Twitter meltdown.

then appear in personal profiles. Anyone who has access can easily view the photos. Status updates let people know what is happening in their lives, and others are welcome to comment. This information all sheds light on the lives of those applying for college.

Colleges aren't the only ones exploring social websites. Many employers today check Facebook, MySpace, and Twitter to acquire information about potential new hires. Employers critically study each page, and sometimes what they find can cost someone a job. A survey shows that 33% of employers who have visited the personal websites of job applicants have decided not to hire a candidate based on the sites. Companies are looking at character as well as experience and skill, and they are turning to these websites to learn more.

Once they land jobs, many employees admit to connecting to these social sites while they are supposed to be working. America Online recently learned that employees are browsing the Internet for an average of 2 hours per workday. This time-wasting costs companies billions of dollars. Many companies now block social networking sites to stop this problem. On the other hand, some companies have found that blogging can actually be used to benefit their companies. Cisco Systems recently created its own networking site that allows employees to blog about company policies and ideas. Employees of all levels provide creative input into the day-to-day practices of the company and how the company could improve.

An online community can be either valuable or harmful, depending on how it is used. So, what can be done to decrease harmful online activity? Many politicians are looking to create legislation to crack down on the harassment that happens through these websites. After the Lori Drew incident, Missouri joined other states to expand its anti-harassment laws to include cyberbullying. In these states, it is now against the law to harass someone online.

What can the rest of us do to stop the damaging material that floods social networks? Many sites allow viewers to mark content that is not suitable. To avoid being part of the problem, we can monitor our own comments and photos. Doing our part to ensure proper use of social networking sites will help us stay out of trouble—and might even save a life.

READING COMPREHENSION

After reading "The Dangers and Benefits of Social Networking," choose the options that best answer questions 1–14.

1. Read this sentence.
    YouTube, a video-sharing site, has recently been criticized for allowing the posting of fight videos.

    This sentence means that
    A. YouTube is in danger of being shut down.
    B. YouTube is receiving disapproval for its content.
    C. YouTube is increasing in popularity among teenagers.
    D. YouTube employees are losing their jobs for allowing posts of fight videos.

2. Read this sentence.
    So, we may be held accountable not only for our action, but also for our failure to act in a situation.

    What is the meaning of the word *accountable* as it is used in this sentence?
    F. unreliable
    G. responsible
    H. independent
    I. irresponsible

3. From this article, the reader can tell that
    A. social networking sites are popular and widely used.
    B. these networking sites are great ways for finding employment.
    C. MySpace is more commonly used by teens and adults than Facebook.
    D. legislation should ban the use of social networking sites during work hours.

4. Which of the following is an example of a way some companies are allowing employee use of social networking sites to benefit their companies?
    F. Some companies are allowing employees to advertise products on networking sites.
    G. Companies such as Cisco are encouraging employees to blog about company policies.
    H. The use of social networking sites during work hours is being permitted to increase morale.
    I. Employees are allowed to post reports about their jobs in an effort to increase employment.

5. With which statement would the author of the passage most likely agree?
    A. Cyberbullying is not a serious offense.
    B. Individuals should routinely monitor their networking sites.
    C. Social networking sites are great ways to meet new people.
    D. Employees should be able to access these sites during work hours.

6. The author organizes the article by
    F. comparing Facebook to MySpace.
    G. describing how online communities began in our society.
    H. presenting the negative and positive aspects of online communities.
    I. trying to persuade the reader of this article to create a social networking site.

7. Why does the author discuss Lori Drew?
   A. to show that cyberbullying can be dangerous
   B. to persuade the reader to fight for cyberbullying legislation
   C. to explain why social networking sites contain truthful information
   D. to compare Megan's story to that of the fights downloaded on YouTube

8. Which title BEST fits the article?
   F. Drew's Demise
   G. Business Blogging
   H. Making Friends One Click at a Time
   I. Safeguarding Social Networking Sites

9. Why did Lori Drew create a fictitious MySpace page?
   A. to look for a new job
   B. to build new friendships
   C. to learn more information about a teenager
   D. to become more involved in charitable events in her community

10. Why do some companies turn to social networking sites before hiring candidates?
    F. to adjust salaries
    G. to post job openings
    H. to learn more information about candidates
    I. to research the job-related skills of candidates

11. MySpace and Facebook are alike in that they both
    A. charge fees for personal use.
    B. allow individuals to stay in contact with others.
    C. prevent individuals from creating fictitious websites.
    D. allow access only to individuals who are over age 18.

12. Which fact from the article provides the BEST evidence that social networking sites affect work performance?
    F. Companies look for both character and experience.
    G. Some companies have decided to block these sites from work computers.
    H. People spend an average of 2 hours per day on networking sites while at work.
    I. Some college admissions officers research these sites prior to selecting applicants.

13. People who read this article will learn
    A. how to blog.
    B. how to download pictures to MySpace.
    C. tips for creating an attractive Facebook page.
    D. how to keep themselves safe when using social networking sites.

14. Based on information in BOTH the article and the text box, why should individuals continually monitor their social networking pages?
    F. to prevent identify theft
    G. to improve work performance
    H. to watch for unsuitable information or photos
    I. to keep track of what is happening in the lives of others

READING STRATEGY

Directions: Making a detailed list of the pros and cons of an issue can help put a debate in perspective. Use the graphic organizer to identify the pros and cons of social networking sites, using examples from the text. At the bottom of the page, give a summary of what you learned, including whether you believe the pros or cons ultimately "win."

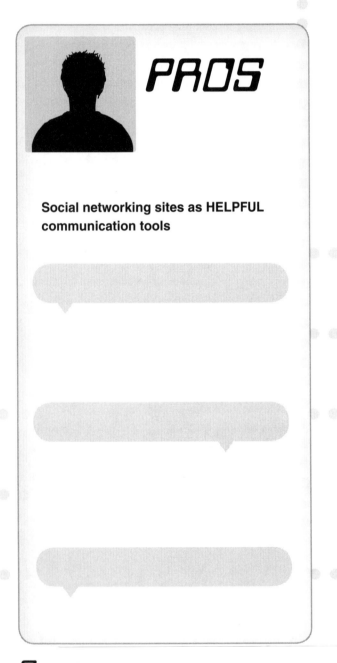

PROS

Social networking sites as HELPFUL communication tools

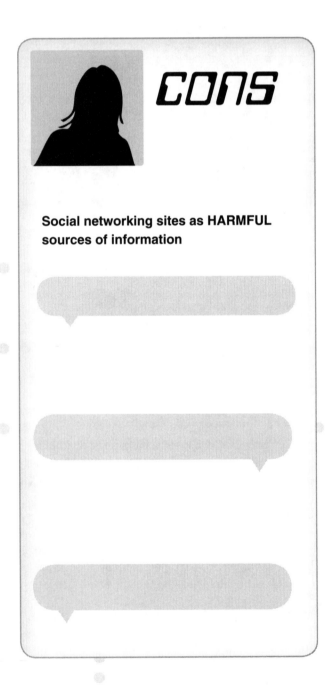

CONS

Social networking sites as HARMFUL sources of information

Summary:

INTERPRETING THE DATA

PART I

Who takes part in online social communities?

Fill in the missing numbers in Table 1 to answer questions 15–18.

Table 1. Demographics of Facebook users in 2008 and 2009

Gender	Users in 2008	Percentage in 2008	Users in 2009	Percentage in 2009	Growth
U.S. males	10,095,740	38.1%	17,747,880	42.2%	75.8%
U.S. females	12,520,760	**16.**	23,429,960	55.6%	87.1%
unknown	3,864,600	14.6%	911,360	**18.**	-76.4%
Total U.S. users	**15.**	100.0%	**17.**	100.0%	58.9%

Age	Users in 2008	Percentage in 2008	Users in 2009	Percentage in 2009	Growth
0-17	4,378,120	16.5%	5,674,780	13.5%	26.6%
18-24	14,258,160	53.8%	17,192,360	40.8%	20.6%
25-34	5,584,260	21.1%	11,254,700	26.7%	101.5%
35-54	1,856,680	7.0%	6,989,200	16.6%	276.5%
55+	324,420	1.2%	954,680	2.3%	194.3%
Unknown	79,460	0.3%	23,480	0.1%	-70.5%

19. According to Table 1, were there more females or males on Facebook in 2008 and 2009?

_____

20. Based on Table 1, what was the fastest growing age group from 2008 to 2009?

_____

21. A major part of Facebook is advertising. Based on Table 1, what age group(s) do you think advertisers would have the most success reaching on Facebook, according to the number of users and rate of growth?

> **ANALYZE EVALUATE EXPLAIN**
>
> _____
> _____
> _____
> _____
> _____
> _____
> _____
> _____

PART II

What role does Facebook play in its users' lives?

Consider the following statistics:

- _About half of Facebook's 300 million users log on every day._
- _More than 6 billion minutes are spent on Facebook daily._
- _There are more than 40 million status updates each day._

Social networking is a social phenomenon that is a major part of the lives of not only teens and college-aged students, but increasingly of adults in the workforce (ages 35-54), as shown in Part I.

Table 2. Top 5 global parent websites, October 2009

Rank	Parent website	Unique users	Time per person (HH:MM:SS)
1	Google	353,880	2:52:53
2	Microsoft	317,671	3:13:13
3	Yahoo!	237,342	2:20:27
4	Facebook	199,961	5:47:04
5	eBay	159,424	1:51:02

22. According to Table 2, what website had the most unique users?

23. Based on Table 2, on which website did the average user spend the most time in October 2009, and how much time was spent?

_____

24. What does Table 2 say about how people are using social networking sites like Facebook, as compared to search engines like Google? Based on this information, compare the benefits of using Facebook and Google for advertising.

ANALYZE EVALUATE EXPLAIN

REFLECT AND RESPOND

25. What are the pros and cons of using social networking sites such as Facebook? Using examples from the article and facts learned through Interpreting the Data, discuss ways in which social networking sites are beneficial and ways in which they could possibly be harmful.

Reflect & Respond

READING INSTRUCTIONAL GUIDE FOR TECHNICAL EXTENSION

BEFORE READING

Looking at the Words

Determining What the Word Means (Vocabulary)

Words to Study	Breaking into Syllables	Short Definition
interconnected	in-ter-con-nect-ed	(adj.) mutually joined or related
investment	in-vest-ment	(n.) the act of spending money to make money
merchandising	mer-chan-dis-ing	(n.) the promotion of sales by organized advertising
modest	mod-est	(adj.) limited; ordinary
networking	net-work-ing	(n.) a system of sharing information among people
statistics	sta-tis-tics	(n.) numerical facts or data
tap	tap	(v.) to reach into or begin to use

Activating Background Knowledge

Graphic Organizer

Either individually or in groups, brainstorm about online marketing, recalling anything previously learned and any prior experience with the subject. Next, complete the KWS chart to demonstrate what you already know about how social networking sites are used to market products.

What I **K**now	What I **W**ant to Learn	Possible **S**ources of Information

Starter Questions

After completing the Graphic Organizer, participate in a group or class discussion to come up with questions about the subject, a prediction about the article, and at least one learning goal. The first question has been provided for you.

Question: What are some ways companies market their products?

Question: _____

Prediction: _____

Goal: _____

DURING READING

- Skim the article for 45–60 seconds. Circle any words you don't know.

- When you are finished, decode and determine the meaning of unknown words.

- Skim the questions for 30–45 seconds.

- Predict what the article is about.

- Read the article.

- Reread to clarify as needed.

- Answer the questions.

AFTER READING

After reading, you may do the following:

- Review, paraphrase, and summarize

- Participate in main-idea discussions by describing the information in their own words

- Reflect on concept maps and generate additional discussion starter questions based on the mappings

- Participate in small-group discussions using discussion starter questions

Discussion Starter Questions

The first question has been provided for you.

1. Would you pay to have access to social networking sites such as MySpace or Facebook? Why or why not?

2. _____

3. _____

TECHNICAL EXTENSION

Show Me the Money!

Did you ever stop to wonder who pays to provide social networking sites like Facebook and MySpace? Users don't provide a credit card number every time they log on, so where is the money coming from? You and your friends post pictures and videos and trade hundreds of messages with one another for free, don't you?

Our economic system is based primarily on profit. Businesses are built on the money made from sales of either products or services; therefore, businesses fail if no money is coming in. So, what provides the money that allows almost 850 web-based communities to exist? It's not coming from you and your hundreds of online "friends." Or is it?

Facebook, the biggest of the social networking sites, claims about 175 million active users. As those millions of people sign on every day, advertising immediately begins popping up on the screen. Many of us don't even notice these product ads. However, companies pay big money to place online commercials in front of us. They are hoping that we will "click through" an advertisement if we are interested in their products.

Recent figures show that this advertising revenue came to about $50 billion last year. All that money is produced in several ways. Companies using a site like Facebook can build their profits through those "banner" ads on your page. Facebook says that a business can reach 300,000,000 people every day.

Businesses like Toyota and Coca-Cola build their own pages on many sites. These pages market directly to other users. Smaller companies with modest budgets use the sites to get the most from their advertising budgets. The following testimonial appears on Facebook's advertising page:

"[Our company] generated nearly $40,000 in revenue directly from a $600 advertising investment on Facebook. Of the Facebook users who were directed to [our] website from the ads, 60% became qualified leads and actively expressed interest in more information."

Not a bad return for a $600 investment!

Advertisers can get important statistics from the site to show who is clicking on their ads. This gives them valuable marketing information. It also tells Facebook which ads to show on each user's page. This means that every time you sign on to Facebook, different ads pop up on your screen based on the ads you have clicked on before.

So how much money is involved in this type of advertising? In 2006 MySpace made a deal with Google for $900 million. The site also has agreements with several large companies like Sony BMG Music Entertainment to sell ring tones and artist merchandising. Experts believed that MySpace would make between $700 and $800 million in 2008 from deals like these. Facebook hoped to increase its income to nearly $440 million by its fourth year in existence. The creators of social networking sites are also looking for ways to tap into international markets.

As we can see, this interconnected world makes a lot of money for the companies that use it. However, the future might not stay "free." Some social networking sites are thinking about charging us for access to our pages. MySpace, for one, is "definitely looking into subscription services," says CEO Chris DeWolfe. It will be interesting to see if teens will agree to pay in order to sign on to their pages in the future.

"Show me the money!" has proven to be true for more and more advertisers in today's online marketplace. Now when you sign on to your favorite site, you will have a better idea of how much money is behind the world of social networking.

Top 10 Social Networks, January 2009

Rank	Site	Monthly Visits	Previous Rank
1	facebook.com	1,191,373,339	2
2	myspace.com	810,153,536	1
3	twitter.com	54,218,731	22
4	fixster.com	53,389,974	16
5	linkedin.com	42,744,438	9
6	tagged.com	39,630,927	10
7	classmates.com	35,219,210	3
8	myyearbook.com	33,121,821	4
9	livejournal.com	25,221,354	6
10	imeem.com	22,993,608	13

READING COMPREHENSION

After reading "Show Me the Money!" answer questions 1–12.

1. Read this sentence.
    The following testimonial appears on Facebook's advertising page.

    What is the meaning of the word *testimonial* as it is used in this sentence?
    - A. denial
    - B. demand
    - C. criticism
    - D. recommendation

2. Read this sentence.
    "[Our company] generated nearly $40,000 in revenue directly from a $600 investment on Facebook."

    What does the word *revenue* mean as it is used in this sentence?
    - F. income
    - G. payments
    - H. outstanding debt
    - I. international investment

3. According to the article, social networking sites will probably fail
    - A. once there are too many sites.
    - B. if they charge users to sign on.
    - C. unless money is being made in some way.
    - D. unless they branch out to international markets.

4. The businessperson quoted in the article probably believes that
    - F. his advertising money was spent wisely.
    - G. the $600 spent on advertising was a risky investment.
    - H. pop-up ads on sites like Facebook probably don't benefit his business.
    - I. revenue generated through advertising on Facebook wasn't a wise investment.

5. What writing strategy does the author of the article use to quickly create reader interest in the topic?
    - A. The author quotes a business.
    - B. The author ranks social networking sites.
    - C. The author uses a question as the first sentence.
    - D. The author compares the advertising programs for Facebook and MySpace.

6. What is the main idea of paragraph 2?
    - F. There are many social networking sites available.
    - G. The economic system in this country is based on product sales.
    - H. The users of sites like MySpace will soon have to pay to sign on.
    - I. Social networking sites must be making money from some source, or they could not stay in business.

7. The ads that appear on your social networking page are determined by
    A. the advertisers' budgets.
    B. your previous use of the site.
    C. which sites have the largest number of advertisers.
    D. large product deals that have been negotiated with advertisers.

8. The similarity noted between Facebook and Twitter is that
    F. both are older than MySpace.
    G. both are thinking about charging users.
    H. both are competing for the same international advertisers.
    I. both have risen in the rankings of social networking sites.

9. Which fact from the article BEST supports the idea that social networking sites are not completely satisfied with their current revenue?
    A. All sites are climbing in the rankings.
    B. The sites are beginning to tap into international markets.
    C. Click-through advertising creates a database of information for advertisers.
    D. Businesses can create increased sales through their use of pop-up and banner ads.

10. Which information from the article would probably be most convincing to a potential advertiser on a social networking site?
    F. the numbers of users
    G. the ranking of all the networking sites
    H. the quote from a successful business advertiser
    I. the information about large deals between the sites and huge companies

11. According to the article and the text box, the reader can see that
    A. Facebook and MySpace are highly competitive.
    B. Twitter will soon take over first place in the rankings.
    C. the sites that charge subscription rates have dropped in the rankings.
    D. some businesses will not be able to compete with international advertisers.

12. What facts from the article *might* support the idea that social networking sites use our personal information without our knowledge?

TECHNICAL WRITING PROMPT

13. As part of the advertising team for Facebook, you have been asked by the company to make a presentation about how advertising on Facebook can increase revenues. Based on the information you learned in the article, create a clear and persuasive PowerPoint presentation explaining the advantages of advertising on Facebook.

Technical Writing

VOCATIONAL EXTENSION

Advertising is a type of marketing that is all about persuading consumers to buy products or services. The people who write all the catchy jingles and slogans that we hear on television and radio are usually employed by advertising companies or are freelancers who work on their own.

HELP WANTED:

Copywriter for small advertising agency. Will report to marketing manager in two-person department. Duties include writing ads for multiple clients. Degree in journalism or marketing desired. No experience necessary.

Advertising copywriters must listen to customers, research the company and its product, and then let their imaginations run wild! An advertising campaign strives to make the client's product a brand. The goal is that the public will immediately identify a slogan, song, or visual cue with that product. You can probably think of several such products right now, whether it is a design on a shoe or a caveman who bowls or walks through airports. Those campaigns might have sounded extreme while in production, but many have become successful. And they started with a copywriter who had an unusual idea.

Besides copywriting, below are many other career possibilities in the world of advertising:

- client servicing
- photography
- media
- film
- event management
- market research
- television
- production
- promotion
- direct marketing

No matter what type of advertising appeals to you, one personality trait necessary to succeed is the ability to handle rejection. Clients will often have very specific ideas about their advertising and might not like a new idea that the copywriter has spent a great deal of time on. Sometimes last-minute changes can result in stopping the ad campaign. The copywriter cannot take these changes personally. It is all part of the job.

Besides being creative thinkers with the ability to handle rejection, those seeking a career in advertising must be good writers. Taking an old idea and making it fresh and interesting is important to success. One expert says that "advertising is salesmanship in print." A degree in journalism, marketing, or advertising is usually necessary, although art schools often offer similar training.

If you are considering a career in this field, do not expect to work a normal 40-hour week. Advertising is a whirlwind of activity, depending on the needs and budgets of the clients. Clients with huge advertising budgets can demand a great deal from their advertising agency. The copywriters are the ones who sometimes have to work long hours to meet those demands.

Incomes for those in advertising are often a combination of a base salary plus commission of ad revenue. Starting salaries range from $25,000 to $40,000 a year. However, those who have been in the field for a while and have proven themselves can sometimes earn $100,000 or more.

The digital age has opened some new areas of advertising, too. Many companies are branching into the Internet, trade shows, conferences, and custom publishing.

Lance Kinney, an associate professor of advertising and public relations for the College of Communication at the University of Alabama-Tuscaloosa says, "Careers in advertising can be a great deal of fun. Ad professionals often work with very creative people on the newest technologies available....My advice is to commit yourself to this demanding field, get involved early, and set professional goals."

Are you ready to get started?

LOOKING FORWARD

14. Being creative is important in the advertising industry. If you were to pursue a career in advertising, you would need to market a product in order to increase a company's revenue. Using personal experience and information from the article, select a product and create an advertising plan for the product. Be sure to include how your plan differs from the existing advertising for that product.

Looking Forward

ETHICAL DILEMMA

15. As the newest person hired at a large advertising agency, you have been working with small clients with small budgets. One morning the boss assigns you to replace a copywriter who has been fired. Your new team works solely for the agency's largest client, and they have been searching for a new ad concept. You find a folder in your new desk with a great idea in it, obviously created by the copywriter who was fired. Do you present it to the team and claim it as your own? What are your options?

Ethical Dilemma

UNIT VOCABULARY ASSESSMENT

Matching

Match each word in Column I to its definition in Column II.

Column I

_____ 1. provoke
_____ 2. defame
_____ 3. conviction
_____ 4. investment

Column II

A. judgment of guilt
B. to damage someone's reputation
C. stir into action
D. spending money to make money

Multiple Choice

Choose the word that MOST NEARLY replaces the underlined word in each sentence.

5. Networking is a great way to make contacts that could lead to employment.
   A. wiring
   B. sharing
   C. lecturing
   D. separating

6. After watching the practice, the coach provided constructive criticism and assistance to the athlete.
   A. vague
   B. helpful
   C. negative
   D. impractical

7. Prior to making a decision, the councilman wanted to review the statistics regarding the issue.
   A. data
   B. editorials
   C. arguments
   D. regulations

8. Though she is very wealthy, she chooses to live in a modest home.
   A. neat
   B. ordinary
   C. extravagant
   D. sophisticated

Word Bank

alias
cryptic
interconnected
merchandising
tap

Fill in the Blank

Choose a word from the word bank to fill in the blank in the sentence below.

9. The celebrity used an _____ to protect her identity while traveling.

10. The team had to have her _____ message translated by a detective.

11. The World Wide Web is full of _____ networks that are open to the public.

12. The art classes inspired students to _____ into their creativity.

13. _____ involves promoting sales through advertisements in order to gain attention and customers.

AUTHENTIC ASSESSMENT

Students will create an advertisement based on the unit "Online Communities."

Instructions for Advertisement

1. **Planning/questions.** Students will work in either assigned or self-chosen groups. Each group will create a Facebook advertisement for a product of their choice. Students may choose either an existing product or one that they invent. The advertisements should be informative and/or persuasive. Groups should complete the following questions to begin planning.

   a. What is the purpose of your advertisement?

   b. What do you want people to know about your product?

   c. What support will you use to back up your advertising claims?

   d. Who is your target audience?

2. **Design.** After these questions have been answered, each group will complete the advertisement design for Facebook. Each ad should include the following:

   a. A creative title (up to 25 characters)

   b. Content for the body of the advertisement (up to 135 characters)

   c. A clear, relevant photo accurately depicting the product

3. **Target audience.** Facebook allows advertisers to target their ads to a specific audience, based on many different demographics. Groups will narrow down their audience by filling in these demographic categories:

   a. Age:

   b. Gender:

   c. Location:

   d. Keywords:

   e. Education:

   f. Workplace:

   g. Languages:

4. **Assessment.** Advertisements should be printed in a finished format and presented to the larger group. Work will be assessed using the rubric that follows.

RUBRIC

Requirement	8–10 Points	4–7 Points	0–3 Points	Points Earned
Questions	The students answer the questions completely.	The students answer most questions.	The students do not answer the questions completely.	
Design	The students produce an advertisement based on the three criteria listed.	The students produce an advertisement that is missing some of the required elements.	The students do not produce an advertisement, or it does not address the required criteria.	
Target Audience	The demographics for the advertisement are clearly thought out and appropriate for the product.	The demographics for the advertisement are present but not completely thought out or appropriate.	The demographics are missing or not appropriate.	
Presentation	Work and presentation are neat, legible, and turned in on time.	Work and presentation are messy, hard to read, and/or late.	Work and presentation are incomplete or not turned in.	

BEATING THE ODDS

READING INSTRUCTIONAL GUIDE FOR HIGH-INTEREST ARTICLE

BEFORE READING

Looking at the Words

Determining How the Word Sounds (Phonics)

Using the Syllable Guide and the Reading Instructional Guide Template found in the beginning of the book, read the steps to learn how to break a word into manageable parts.

Determining What the Word Means (Vocabulary)

Words to Study	Breaking into Syllables	Short Definition
eligibility	el-i-gi-bil-i-ty	(n.) qualification
essential	es-sen-tial	(n.) something necessary
nurture	nur-ture	(n.) upbringing; training
prowess	prow-ess	(n.) superior ability
sibling	sib-ling	(n.) a brother or sister
testimony	tes-ti-mo-ny	(n.) proof

Activating Background Knowledge

Anticipation Guide

Mark each of the following statements True or False:

1. _____ Michael Oher is famous because of his talent on the basketball court.

2. _____ Oher played for the University of Tennessee.

3. _____ The left tackle is an offensive line position.

4. _____ Oher won many awards and honors for his football accomplishments.

5. _____ In addition to being an excellent athlete, Oher is known for his determination.

Starter Questions

After completing the Anticipation Guide, participate in a group or class discussion using the following questions:

1. Who is Michael Oher?

2. What is the job of the offensive tackle in football?

3. What professional football team does Michael Oher play for?

4. What types of adversities did Michael Oher overcome in his life?

5. Who is Donald Driver?

Make a prediction about what you think the article will be about.

DURING READING

- Skim the article for 45–60 seconds. Circle any words you don't know.
- When you are finished, decode and determine the meaning of unknown words.
- Skim the questions for 30–45 seconds.
- Predict what the article is about.
- Read the article.
- Reread to clarify as needed.
- Answer the questions.

AFTER READING
Discussion Starter Questions

1. How do you think the difficulties Michael Oher faced early in life might have affected his character?

2. As students, what can you do in the community to help those who are less fortunate than you?

3. How do you think Michael Oher's life might have been different if he had not met the Tuohy family?

4. What role do you think our government should have in ensuring an equal education for all students?

5. If you were the Tuohy Family, would you have welcomed Michael Oher into your home? Why or why not?

BEATING THE ODDS
THE MICHAEL OHER STORY

As a child, Michael Oher never had a bed of his own. He had an absent father and a mother who was addicted to crack cocaine. He and his 12 siblings constantly searched for places to live, sleeping on friends' couches, on porches, and on the streets. Not a typical life for a teenager. Michael, however, is not a typical individual. And that's the key. Despite being homeless for most of his life, Oher never gave up.

Fortunately for Michael, he met some extraordinary people who shared the same resolve and helped him change his life forever. They opened up their home to Michael and paved the way for him to receive an excellent high school education. At the age of 16, after being homeless and alone for much of his life, Oher was spotted at a bus stop by Sean and Leigh Anne Tuohy, a wealthy couple whose children attended school with Oher. Sean Tuohy recalls that upon seeing Oher, his wife grabbed the wheel, made a U-turn, and "cried the second she met him." Oher had been admitted to the private school as a special-needs student. Otherwise, he would never have been given the opportunity to attend a school like Briarcrest. But thanks to generous donors who paid for his education, and an administration that saw something special in Oher, he was given the chance. Then the Tuohys brought Oher home. They gave him shelter, his first bed, a tutor to help him succeed academically, and all the essentials he could possibly need. It was there that Michael eventually learned how to give and receive love.

Academics did not come easy for Michael. After all, he spent his first 9 years in school in 11 different schools. Once at Briarcrest, he constantly had to work toward improving his grades in order to be eligible for football. Thanks to the nurture and support from his caretakers and teachers, Michael was able to increase his academic performance. He went from barely passing to making the honor roll during his senior year. Michael never dreamed that an education like this was possible for him.

Being Homeless

In today's economy, being homeless is more common than people realize. Following are some of the reasons why people are turning to living on the streets and/or in shelters:

- Foreclosure – Inability to pay for the home one is living in. In many cases the banks will foreclose on a home and evict the residents.

- Poverty – Being unable to earn enough money to pay for the cost of living.

- Decline in employment

- Rising cost of homes and the cost of living

- Health issues

While attending Briarcrest, his size became an asset when he pursued football. With continued guidance from his coaches and teachers, he continued to improve both on and off the field. Oher earned such honors as being selected the "Best Player in Tennessee" by a local newspaper and was chosen as "Mr. Football." Although Oher had improved his grade point average, it was still too low for him to meet NCAA eligibility requirements. So Oher enrolled in online grade forgiveness classes at Brigham Young University following high school graduation. His GPA quickly improved, and he was admitted to the University of Mississippi. It was the effort of all of those who cared about him, along with his own hard work, that allowed him to develop the academic skills he needed to attend college.

Once at Ole Miss, Oher helped the Rebels improve their record and become a football team to be reckoned with. Oher played left tackle for Ole Miss and was selected as an All-American player. As left tackle, he had the important responsibility of protecting the quarterback's weak side, also known as "the blind side."

Overcoming the Odds

Michael Oher is not the only NFL star athlete to overcome adversity. Donald Driver, who now plays for the Green Bay Packers, grewe up without a permanent residence for many years. Like Oher, Driver perservered and went on to become a star football athlete. Recognizing that inadequate education often comes with homelessness, Driver has now created the Donald Driver Foundation to provide aid to homeless families and scholarships for students.

Michael Oher graduated from Ole Miss with a degree in criminal justice and entered the NFL in 2009 as a first-round draft pick. He was drafted by the Baltimore Ravens and started at right and left tackle during his first NFL season. However, it isn't Oher's football prowess that really makes him stand out, but rather his story. Oher is more than a successful athlete. He has proven that with perseverance and determination, anything is possible. Michael Oher had to continually work to achieve his goals and never took his gifts for granted. Regardless of his early hardship, Oher takes pride in being "very determined in everything" he does. He also credits his new family with making his path much easier.

Oher's story inspired a book, *The Blind Side: Evolution of a Game*, by Michael Lewis. The book was later made into a very successful movie. Oher obviously no longer worries about having a place to lay his head. He is indeed a testimony that even the most difficult circumstances can be overcome with perseverance and the loving support of others who care.

READING COMPREHENSION

After reading "Beating the Odds: The Michael Oher Story," choose the options that best answer questions 1–14.

1. Read this sentence.
    Fortunately for Michael, he met some extraordinary people who shared the same resolve and helped him prevail over his circumstances.

    What is the meaning of the word *resolve* as it is used in the sentence?
    - A. greed
    - B. indecision
    - C. puzzlement
    - D. determination

2. Read this sentence.
    While attending Briarcrest, his size became an asset when he pursued football.

    What is the meaning of the word *asset* as it is used in the sentence?
    - F. loss
    - G. pride
    - H. benefit
    - I. obstacle

3. From this article, the reader can tell that
    - A. Oher is a talented track and field star.
    - B. Oher always shined in both academics and sports.
    - C. Oher is ungrateful for his second chance in life and all that others did for him.
    - D. had it not been for those who helped him, Oher's talent may have never been noticed.

4. What exception did Briarcrest make for Oher?
    - F. The school provided a tutor to help Oher with his studies.
    - G. The school admitted Oher even though his grades were not up to par.
    - H. The school created a special diploma track for Oher to allow him to graduate.
    - I. The athletic department waived the required GPA for football so Oher could play.

5. The author of this article would most likely make the statement that
    - A. everyone should take in foster care children.
    - B. Oher is a model of determination and perseverance.
    - C. Oher should have played for the University of Tennessee.
    - D. The offensive line is more important in football than the defensive line.

6. What method of organization does the author use to introduce Oher to the reader?
    - F. providing data
    - G. presenting chronological information about Oher's life
    - H. comparing the effects of private school and public school education
    - I. explaining the differences in the admission requirements for various colleges

7. What was the author's main purpose for writing this article?
   A. to teach the reader the fundamentals of football
   B. to introduce the reader to Oher's life and the obstacles he overcame
   C. to illustrate the many differences between Michael Oher and Donald Driver
   D. to entertain the reader by presenting a fictional story with a positive outcome

8. What is the main idea of the first paragraph?
   F. Oher had a difficult childhood.
   G. Oher had a large family of 12 siblings.
   H. Oher's mother was addicted to cocaine.
   I. The Tuohys wanted to increase the size of their family.

9. Leigh Anne Tuohy originally attempted to help Oher because
   A. she saw someone who needed help.
   B. she wanted to do something good for the community.
   C. she thought Oher could serve as a strong role model for her son.
   D. she believed Oher would be a wonderful asset to the Briarcrest football team.

10. Why did Oher take classes at Brigham Young University?
    F. The university offered more electives than Briarcrest.
    G. Oher needed to improve his grades so he could graduate from high school.
    H. The Tuohys both graduated from Brigham Young and encouraged Oher to do the same.
    I. Oher wanted to obtain his associate's degree before enrolling at the University of Mississippi.

11. What is true of BOTH Oher and Driver?
    A. They played football for the same team.
    B. They attended the University of Mississippi.
    C. They overcame difficult childhoods to become strong individuals.
    D. Their stories have inspired best-selling autobiographies and successful movies.

12. Which of the following statements provides the BEST support for the argument that private individuals can help fight homelessness?
    F. Despite being homeless, Oher never gave up.
    G. The Tuohys helped Oher overcome being homeless.
    H. County-run homeless shelters help provide food and shelter for the homeless.
    I. The government provides medical care and mental health services to the homeless.

13. People who read this article will
    A. learn more about the beginning of the NFL.
    B. learn more about factors that lead to homelessness.
    C. gain understanding about various NCAA recruiting rules.
    D. be able to compare and contrast college football and the NFL.

14. What conclusion may the reader draw based on information in BOTH the article and the second text box?
    F. Oher didn't put much effort into his studies.
    G. A family like the Tuohys helped Donald Driver.
    H. Homelessness is too big of a problem to try to fix.
    I. An education can be the first step in climbing out of homelessness.

READING STRATEGY

Directions: Michael Oher experienced a series of events in his life that ultimately led to success on and off the football field. At each 10-yard marker, starting with the 50, record each event that led to his success, including what he did to gain that success. The first event has been listed as a starting point. In the end zone, write a summary of how Oher's life was changed by circumstances and his own actions.

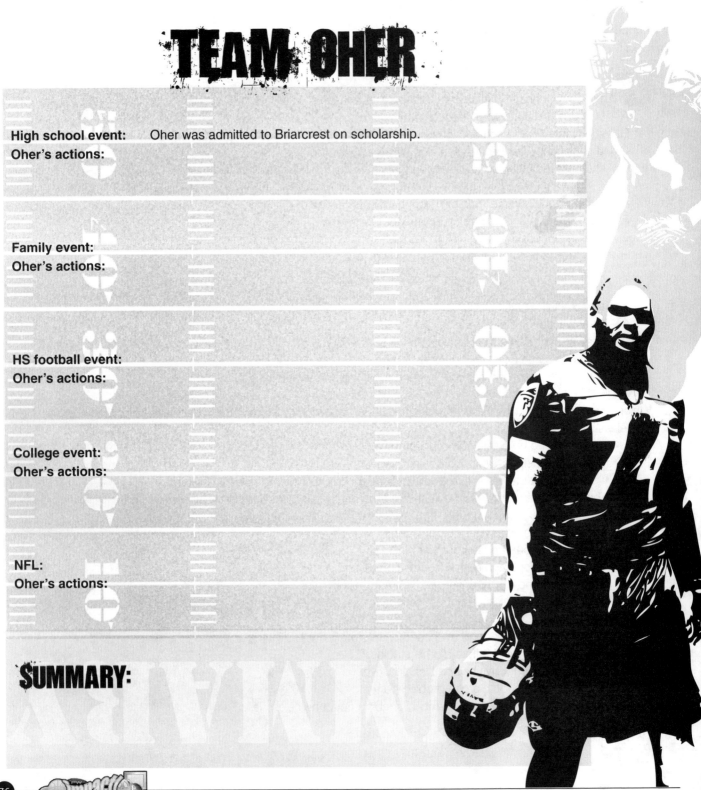

TEAM OHER

High school event: Oher was admitted to Briarcrest on scholarship.
Oher's actions:

Family event:
Oher's actions:

HS football event:
Oher's actions:

College event:
Oher's actions:

NFL:
Oher's actions:

SUMMARY:

INTERPRETING THE DATA

PART I

Who struggles with homelessness?

Complete the pie chart to answer questions 15–17. Use the information in the table to help you fill in the pie chart.

Figure 1. Occurrence of homelessness by family status

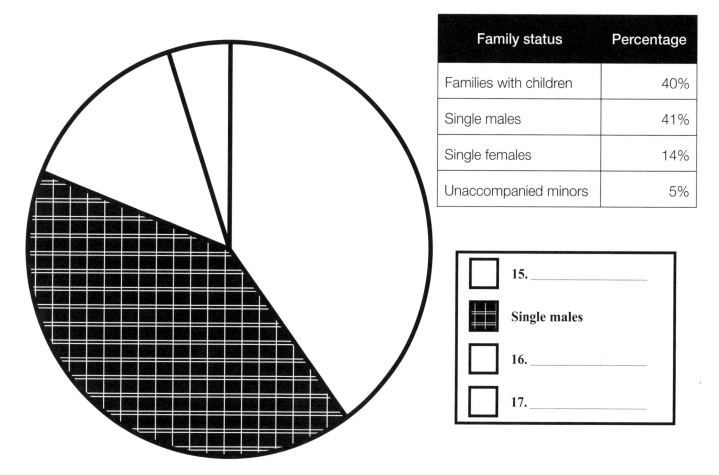

Family status	Percentage
Families with children	40%
Single males	41%
Single females	14%
Unaccompanied minors	5%

☐ 15. _____

▦ **Single males**

☐ 16. _____

☐ 17. _____

18. What is the smallest segment of the homeless population?

_____

19. The fastest growing segment of the homeless population is families with children. Based on the data, who would probably be the second biggest segment once families with children take over the top position?

_____

20. The chronically homeless population (those with repeated episodes or those who have been homeless for long periods) fell from 175,914 in 2005 to 123,833 in 2007.

    The number of chronically homeless in 2007 is what percent of what it was in 2005?

    _____

21. If the chronically homeless population decreased at the same rate in the two years after 2007, how many people would be chronically homeless in 2009?

    _____

22. Data on homelessness is difficult to accurately collect. This is based on many factors, including the changing economy and the difficulty in determining a constant number of the homeless (in part because they move often). Why does this make it harder to combat homelessness in our society?

ANALYZE EVALUATE EXPLAIN

_____

_____

_____

_____

_____

_____

_____

_____

PART II

What is the connection between foster care and homelessness?

The Runaway and Homeless Youth Act defines homeless youth as "individuals under age 18 who are unable to live in a safe environment with a relative and lack safe alternative living arrangements, as well as individual ages 18 to 21 without shelter." The exact number of homeless youth is unknown because of their mobility and because of unstandardized methods of determining the population. There is a large correlation between youth labeled homeless and those labeled runaways.

In addition, youth in foster care have strong ties to the homeless community. Not all children get the opportunities that Michael Oher did; in fact, most don't. Approximately 11,000 children in the American foster care system run away each year. An additional 24,000 youth "age out" (turn 18 or 21, depending on the state) without being provided a place to live or the means to find a place to live.

Look at the following timeline, outlining the history of the Federal Runaway and Homeless Youth Policy, to answer the questions in this section.

Figure 2. Evolution of federal runaway and homeless youth policy, 1912-2003

1912	1935	1954	1958	1968	1972	1977	1994	2003
Children's Bureau established to investigate and report on all matters related to children's welfare.	Social Security Act is passed, and for the first time, the federal government provides grants to states for child welfare.	Division of Juvenile Delinquency is established in the Children's Bureau.	Social Security Act is amended to provide federal funds for the return of a runaway child under the age of 18.	Congress passes the Juvenile Delinquency Prevention and Control Act, which provides funding to four runaway youth centers.	Senate Subcommittee to Investigate Juvenile Delinquency holds two-day hearings in problems facing runaway youth.	Congress reauthorizes the Runaway Youth Act and broadens its scope to include "otherwise homeless youth."	Street Outreach Program is established by the Violent Crime and Law Enforcement Act.	Runaway, Homeless, and Missing Children Protection Act reauthorizes the Runaway and Homeless Youth Act.

1933	1950	1955	1961	1970	1974	1988	1999
Federal Transient Bureau assists states in developing aid for homeless children and adults. Civilian Conservation Corps establishes camps for more than one million older youth.	Social Security Act is amended to permit use of federal child welfare funds for the return of a runaway child under the age of 16.	Senate Subcommittee to Investigate Juvenile Delinquency first examines problem of runaway youth.	Congress enacts the Juvenile Delinquency and Youth Offenses Control Act, drawing on the recommendations of the President's Committee on Juvenile Delinquency and Youth Crime regarding the basis of delinquency.	The Youth Development and Delinquency Prevention Administration is created within HHS to provide leadership in youth issues.	Congress enacts the Runaway Youth Act as Title III of the Juvenile Justice and Delinquency Prevention Act. The legislation established what is now referred to as the Basic Center Program.	Runaway and Homeless Youth Act is reauthorized. A provision is added to establish the Transitional Living Program.	The Runaway and Homeless Youth Act is reauthorized. Funding and administration of the Basic Center Program and Transitional Living Programs are merged under the Consolidated Runaway and Homeless Youth Program.

23. In what year was the Transitional Living Program established?

_____

24. How did the government attempt to solve the issue of runaway youth in the 1950s?

_____

25. How many times was the Runaway Youth Act (also called the Runaway and Homeless Youth Act) reauthorized after it was first enacted in 1974?

_____

26. Based on the information in Figure 2, do you believe the government has made a difference in improving the lives of homeless youth and preventing homelessness in youth under 18? Include specific evidence to back up your claim.

**ANALYZE
EVALUATE
EXPLAIN**

ALONE
RUNAWAY

REFLECT AND RESPOND

27. What services do you think could be provided to foster children in order to better equip them to arrange for a place to live after they "age out" of the foster care system? Be specific, using examples from the text and experiences from real life.

READING INSTRUCTIONAL GUIDE FOR TECHNICAL EXTENSION

BEFORE READING

Looking at the Words

Determining What the Word Means (Vocabulary)

Words to Study	Breaking into Syllables	Short Definition
alter	al-ter	(v.) to change
inflict	in-flict	(v.) to impose or bring
overwhelming	o-ver-whelm-ing	(adj.) crushing; overpowering
profound	pro-found	(adj.) deep
supplement	sup-ple-ment	(v.) to add to or complete
virtually	vir-tu-al-ly	(adv.) nearly

Activating Background Knowledge

Graphic Organizer

Either individually or in groups, brainstorm about homelessness, recalling anything previously learned and any prior experience with the subject. Next, complete the inverted triangle to demonstrate what you already know about the needs of the homeless.

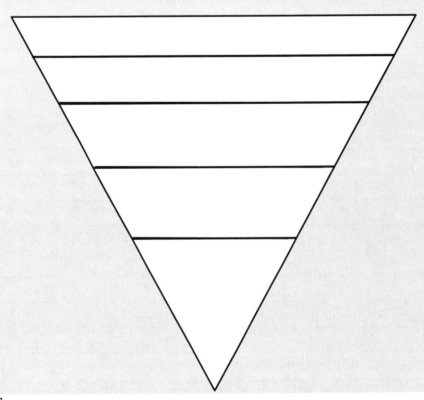

Starter Questions

After completing the Graphic Organizer, participate in a group or class discussion to come up with questions about the subject, a prediction about the article, and at least one learning goal. The first question has been provided for you.

Question: How can a chain of events result in a person becoming homeless?

Question: _____

Prediction: _____

Goal: _____

DURING READING

- Skim the article for 45–60 seconds. Circle any words you don't know.

- When you are finished, decode and determine the meaning of unknown words.

- Skim the questions for 30–45 seconds.

- Predict what the article is about.

- Read the article.

- Reread to clarify as needed.

- Answer the questions.

AFTER READING

After reading, you may do the following:

- Review, paraphrase, and summarize

- Participate in main-idea discussions by describing the information in their own words

- Reflect on concept maps and generate additional discussion starter questions based on the mappings

- Participate in small-group discussions using discussion starter questions

Discussion Starter Questions

The first question has been provided for you.

1. What effects can homelessness have on children?

2. _____

3. _____

TECHNICAL EXTENSION

HOMELESS CHILDREN IN AMERICA

*"It is virtually impossible to reclaim the life of a child
who has spent his childhood without a home."*
-State Report Card on Child Homelessness

Michael Oher was homeless for much of his early life and things must have looked dismal to him. His childhood was marked by moving from place to place just to stay out of the heat and cold. However, he now plays football in the NFL and is the subject of *The Blind Side*. The movie is about his struggles with homelessness and learning. According to statistics, he has beaten the odds by climbing out of his desperate situation. As he says, "It's unbelievable."

Children like Oher find themselves homeless through no fault of their own. The economy in America in the past few years has gone into a downward spiral, which means that many adults are losing their jobs. The price of gas has risen, which means the cost of transportation and food also goes up. Without a dependable income, parents can't pay the rent or mortgage on their homes. They don't have gas money to get to job interviews or money to pay for child care. And landlords won't wait for too long to get their rent, so families find themselves out on the street. It is like watching dominoes fall.

When we think of "the homeless," we often picture a single person sitting on a corner asking for a handout. The facts are quite different. Over 3 million people become homeless every year in our country. 1.3 million of those people are children. And 42% of those children are younger than age 6. One study found that 1 in 50 children is homeless in the United States every year.

The picture for children who become homeless is painted with hunger and illness. Many are unable to read, and many never graduate from high school. These young people do not have basic safety, privacy, comfort, or routine in their lives. Many of their relationships are constantly broken. According to the Campaign to

Housing and Income

- In all 50 states, the cost of housing outpaces wages.

- One minimum-wage earner in a family does not earn enough to move into designated HUD* housing for a 2-bedroom apartment. (*United States Department of Housing and Urban Development)

- In most states, the necessary hourly wage needed to rent a 2-bedroom apartment is 2-3 times the minimum wage.

- Vouchers to supplement income for housing meet only one-quarter of those needed in America.

- Most minimum-wage earning families are one unexpected expense away from homelessness.

Min Wage bought this cardboard sign.

Another goal is that job training programs be funded and available to those who need to climb out of homelessness. Finally, more social service programs, like health care, child care, mental health care, and substance abuse treatment could provide needed support.

The problem seems overwhelming, doesn't it? There are ways to help, though. Homeless shelters and local food pantries are the first places to start. Families staying in the shelters need many things, like toiletries, snacks, books, and money for transportation. Both shelters and food pantries are always in need of volunteers of any age to lend a hand, too.

Students at school can organize clothing and school supply efforts. School districts often have an office assigned to help homeless students and can get the donations to those who need them. Cash donations would also help organizations who work with homeless children.

However, the most meaningful thing we can do is spread the word about the causes and effects of being homeless. It has been called "virtually impossible" for a child to do well in life after being homeless. But Michael Oher was one of the lucky ones who proved that it *is possible*. There are millions of other young people who could become doctors, lawyers, teachers, construction workers, and professional athletes— if only they could find a helpful hand to hold onto like Michael did.

End Child Homelessness, "These factors combine to create a life-altering experience that inflicts profound and lasting scars." We can see how Michael Oher feels that his life is "unbelievable" today.

But what about all the other kids who don't find a helping hand like Oher did? The National Law Center on Homelessness and Poverty is one of several groups that suggest realistic solutions to this problem in America. First on nearly every list is the need to make affordable housing more available. Many government programs have been cut due to lack of funding; however, these programs help those who are homeless or about to become homeless. These programs provide subsidies (a contribution of money) so that families can move into affordable housing.

Working people are also homeless. So, a second goal is making sure that those who work minimum-wage jobs earn enough to actually pay rent and buy food for their families. Incomes for those living in poverty have not kept up with the increase in housing prices, food, transportation, and other necessities.

READING COMPREHENSION

After reading "Homeless Children in America," answer questions 1–12.

1. Read the following sentence from the first paragraph of the article.
   Michael Oher was homeless for much of his early life, and things must have looked dismal to him.

   What is the meaning of the word *dismal* as used in the sentence?
   - A. joyful
   - B. upbeat
   - C. hopeless
   - D. optimistic

2. Which of the following phrases from the article best describes how being homeless affects a child?
   - F. job-training
   - G. life-altering
   - H. realistic solutions
   - I. affordable housing

3. According to the article, the reader can tell that
   - A. fuel prices do not affect homelessness.
   - B. homelessness has little effect on children.
   - C. moving from place to place has little to do with success in school.
   - D. many working families in America no longer earn enough to afford housing.

4. Why does Michael Oher describe his life today as "unbelievable"?
   - F. He believes he was not worthy of the help he received.
   - G. Most children who are homeless do not get the chances he did to succeed.
   - H. Oher does not think enough government programs exist to help homeless children.
   - I. Job-training programs were not available to Oher and his family to help them get out of their situation.

5. The author organizes the article by
   - A. comparing Oher to other homeless children.
   - B. arguing the need for government assistance for the homeless.
   - C. using Oher's life to outline homelessness, its causes, and solutions.
   - D. comparing the facts for homeless children in America with the facts for homeless adults.

6. What is the main idea of the final paragraph?
   - F. Most children will find their way out of homelessness.
   - G. Adults who help homeless children are not likely to make much difference.
   - H. Education on homelessness can help more children succeed like Oher did.
   - I. There are only a limited number of careers available to those who are homeless.

7. Why does the author use the sentence, "It is like watching dominoes fall" to describe how some families find themselves homeless?
    A. Many families have no control over their lives.
    B. Once parents lose their jobs, there is no way to stop the loss of their homes.
    C. The government programs to help the homeless are like watching a game play out.
    D. One event that leads to homelessness often causes a chain of events that is hard to stop.

8. According to the article, how do the facts about homelessness contrast with most people's ideas about the homeless in America?
    F. Millions of homeless people are children and families.
    G. There are more government programs today to assist the homeless.
    H. The numbers of those arrested for being homeless have recently gone down.
    I. Housing subsidies have been increased due to the failing economy in the United States.

9. Which statement below is BEST supported by the data presented in the article?
    A. Raising minimum wage could help the homeless.
    B. Federal programs must replace state programs to assist the homeless.
    C. School systems should offer housing to homeless families and their children.
    D. Individual efforts to help the homeless are not enough to improve the lives of the homeless.

10. Based on the information in the article and the text box, which of the following is MOST accurate?
    F. Those that are homeless often cause it themselves.
    G. Many Americans work hard and still become homeless.
    H. Homeless children make up over 50% of the homeless in America.
    I. Programs like health care and substance abuse help are always available to all who need them.

11. How does the quote under the title of the article relate to Michael Oher's life?
    A. Oher found it impossible to live at home.
    B. He finds his life "unbelievable" due to the help he received.
    C. Michael did not experience hunger, illness, or problems at school.
    D. He is an exception to what most children experience in life after being homeless.

12. What information from the article could you use to respond to a classmate who says, "There is nothing people our age can do to help the homeless"?

TECHNICAL WRITING PROMPT

13. You are a leader in your local branch of Homeless Children in America, an organization committed to raising awareness and creating solutions for homeless children. You have been asked to write a one-page sheet outlining the problem of homelessness in America and practical steps that can be taken to help overcome it. Design this sheet so that it can be easily used by a speaker during oral presentations on homelessness. Be concise and use bullet points to aid the speaker.

Technical
Writing

VOCATIONAL EXTENSION

Does your heart melt when you see a dog wandering along the roadside? Or photographs of children who are hungry? Do you wish you could help?

If so, non-profit work might be for you. A non-profit, or charitable, organization is created to carry out a specific mission, such as finding homes for unwanted animals or feeding the hungry. As the term "non-profit" implies, the goal is not to make money, other than what is needed to help others.

There are thousands of non-profit organizations, each focused on an issue that needs attention. Some of the largest charitable groups in the United States include familiar names like the American Red Cross, American Cancer Society, and Volunteers of America. Although less well known, agencies such as Food for the Poor and the Nature Conservancy are huge, too. In addition, there are many small local organizations, called "grass roots" agencies, which work on important issues in their area.

So how do you find the cause and possible career that you are most passionate about? You can volunteer. Young people can do many important tasks at a non-profit. Some volunteers bathe and groom rescued dogs. Others cook and serve meals for people who come to shelters. Volunteers offer valuable help while also deciding whether non-profit work might be for them.

When you are in college, you can contact a non-profit agency and offer to work as an intern. This might be a paid position, or you might be working as a volunteer. In either case, you are gaining experience and making valuable contacts for future jobs. It also gives the agency a chance to evaluate your skills. If you have proven yourself and your commitment, they might come to you first when paid positions become available,

But how about later, when you need a paying job? Charitable organizations usually cannot afford to hire highly specialized employees for each individual task like large profit-driven companies can. Non-profits need people who can do multiple jobs well. If you want to work at your local humane society, for example, you might be responsible for greeting people, supervising volunteers, or raising money for the organization.

People who work in the non-profit sector understand that they will probably not make a great deal of money. Office workers might start out near minimum wage, with small raises over time. The highest salaries are made by the chief executive officers of large non-profits. However, those positions are few.

Mahatma Gandhi, a political and spiritual leader of India during the last century, once said that "you must be the change you want to see in the world." If there is a change that you would like to see, a career in a non-profit agency that works toward that change might be the right fit for you.

LOOKING FORWARD

14. In the article about non-profit organizations, you have learned how groups such as the American Red Cross and the American Cancer Society are designed to help others in need. In order for a non-profit agency to succeed, it needs organized and qualified professionals who are passionate about its cause. Using personal experience and information from the article, explain why you are qualified to work for a non-profit organization. What qualities do you have that would allow you to help those who are less fortunate or have a life-threatening illness?

Looking Forward

ETHICAL DILEMMA

15. As a student volunteer at a homeless shelter, you learn that a mother needs additional services for her children. These services are provided by the shelter, but the mother won't ask for fear that her abusive husband will find out where she and the children are staying. Must you keep her need for services confidential, even though it means her children might not have things like medical attention or warm clothing? How do you handle this situation?

Ethical Dilemma

UNIT VOCABULARY ASSESSMENT

Matching
Match each word in Column I to its definition in Column II.

Column I

_____ 1. essential

_____ 2. eligibility

_____ 3. profound

_____ 4. testimony

Column II

A. deep

B. qualification

C. something necessary

D. proof

Multiple Choice
Choose the word that MOST NEARLY replaces the underlined word in each sentence.

5. Some people give dogs vitamins to <u>supplement</u> their diet.
    A. miss
    B. lower
    C. change
    D. complete

6. When the entrepreneur was forced to resign from his company, he passed control to his <u>sibling</u>.
    A. son
    B. friend
    C. brother
    D. grandfather

7. When the nurse gave the flu shot, the goal was not to <u>inflict</u> pain but to guard against illness.
    A. bring
    B. prevent
    C. increase
    D. decrease

Fill in the Blank
Choose a word from the word bank to fill in the blank in the sentence below.

Word Bank

alter

nurture

overwhelming

prowess

virtually

8. Though the student's responsibilities seemed _____ at times, she continued on to graduation.

9. Many animals are born with the natural ability to _____ their young.

10. Though best known for their football _____, the school also excels in other sports.

11. Although I enjoy _____ all sports, my favorite sport to watch is basketball.

12. The rainy weather forecast caused us to _____ our plans for a beach vacation.

AUTHENTIC ASSESSMENT

Students will write a journal entry based on the unit "Beating the Odds."

Instructions for Journal Entry

1. **Choice of subject.** Students will choose a person who has had to endure homelessness. It can be a person from the article or someone else from popular culture whose story is researched or already known. Some choices include (but are not limited to) the following:

   Halle Berry, Jim Carrey, Charlie Chaplin, Ella Fitzgerald, Harry Houdini, Lil' Kim, Tupac Shakur, William Shatner, Hillary Swank, Chris Gardner (story told in the movie *The Pursuit of Happyness*)

2. **Synopsis.** Students will write a one-paragraph synopsis about how being homeless affected the person's life, including job, social life, family, etc.

3. **Research.** Students will then research further, using newspapers, magazines, and the Internet to determine any unknown information about the person and/or homelessness. A minimum of three sources should be used to support the writing.

4. **Journal entry.** Students will write a one-page journal entry about a real or hypothetical event in the person's life as it relates to homelessness. Students should write in first person point of view. The entry should include the following components:

   a. Details of one hypothetical event that clearly shows how homelessness affected the person's daily life.

   b. A hypothetical description of emotions that the person feels about the event, his or her state of homelessness, and how the two interact with one another.

   c. A well-written account, using appropriate writing conventions.

5. **Assessment.** Work will be assessed using the rubric that follows.

RUBRIC

Requirement	8–10 Points	4–7 Points	0–3 Points	Points Earned
Sources	The student uses at least three sources, one of which is the assigned text. Facts are gathered from each source and used accurately in the entry.	The student uses between one and two sources. Facts are gathered from each source and used somewhat accurately in the entry.	The student fails to list sources or makes up facts with no basis.	
Event Details	The student provides a detailed account of the event.	The student provides a somewhat detailed account of the event.	The student provides little detail of the event.	
Emotional Description	The student provides a detailed emotional description, clearly showing the effect of homelessness.	The student provides a somewhat detailed emotional description, generally showing the effect of homelessness.	The student provides little detail of emotional reaction or does not show the effect of homelessness.	
Quality of Writing	The writing is clear and follows appropriate writing conventions.	The writing is somewhat clear, and most conventions are correct.	The writing is unclear, and the conventions are incorrect or misused.	

— Unit 5 —

THE SOUND OF SUCCESS

READING INSTRUCTIONAL GUIDE FOR HIGH-INTEREST ARTICLE

BEFORE READING

Looking at the Words

Determining How the Word Sounds (Phonics)
Using the Syllable Guide and the Reading Instructional Guide Template found in the beginning of the book, read the steps to learn how to break a word into manageable parts.

Determining What the Word Means (Vocabulary)

Words to Study	Breaking into Syllables	Short Definition
dissect	dis-sect	(v.) to examine part by part; analyze
eloquent	el-o-quent	(adj.) characterized by powerful, persuasive speech
optimism	op-ti-mism	(n.) the belief that good will occur
preceding	pre-ced-ing	(adj.) previous
proclaim	pro-claim	(v.) to announce or declare
prodigious	pro-di-gious	(adj.) immense; huge
secure	se-cure	(v.) to get possession of; to obtain

Activating Background Knowledge

Anticipation Guide
Mark each of the following statements True or False:

1. _____ Repeating phrases can make speeches easier to remember.

2. _____ Tim Tebow played quarterback for the University of Mississippi.

3. _____ Leadership and religion play a huge role in Tim Tebow's life.

4. _____ The University of Florida won a National Championship in 2009.

5. _____ The UF football team went undefeated during the 2008-2009 season.

Starter Questions

After completing the Anticipation Guide, participate in a group or class discussion using the following questions:

1. Who is Tim Tebow?

2. What do UF fans refer to as "The Promise"?

3. Why do you think people look up to Tim Tebow as a role model?

4. What event changed Tim Tebow's regular football season in 2008?

5. How does Tim Tebow demonstrate leadership on the football field?

Make a prediction about what you think the article will be about.

DURING READING

- Skim the article for 45–60 seconds. Circle any words you don't know.

- When you are finished, decode and determine the meaning of unknown words.

- Skim the questions for 30–45 seconds.

- Predict what the article is about.

- Read the article.

- Reread to clarify as needed.

- Answer the questions.

AFTER READING
Discussion Starter Questions

1. Why is Tim Tebow's "Promise" speech significant?

2. What key elements are represented in Tebow's speech?

3. Which one of the common elements of great speeches do you think is most important? Why?

4. Can you identify how specific parts of the famous quotations are similar to parts of "The Promise"?

5. What promise can you make to yourself? How can you accomplish the goal?

THE SOUND OF SUCCESS

When the University of Florida's undefeated football season ended with a loss to the University of Mississippi during the 2008-09 season, Gators quarterback Tim Tebow took the blame for the loss. He put the team on his shoulders and made a statement that is now engraved on a plaque outside of the Gators' stadium. The quote, which came to be known as "The Promise," came true when Florida delivered on it.

Tim Tebow has been known for his abilities as quarterback of one of the nation's most successful football programs over the past few years. He's also been known for his work off the field, showing his religious beliefs and desire to set an example in a sport in need of role models.

The speech that Tebow gave after that game has been held up as an example of the kind of leadership organizations need for success. Is it possible for that type of speech to be repeated by other teams, companies, politicians, and military leaders looking to inspire others? The answer can be found in history books.

When one dissects great speeches and quotes over the course of history, the same elements can be found time and time again: HOPE, CONFIDENCE, DESIRE, LEADERSHIP, REPETITION, and a PROMISE. Tebow's quote seems to come from that same playbook.

THE PROMISE

"To the fans and everybody in Gator Nation, I'm sorry. I'm extremely sorry. We were hoping for an undefeated season. That was my goal, something Florida has never done here.

I promise you one thing, A lot of good will come out of this. You will never see any player in the entire country play as hard as I will play the rest of the season. You will never see someone push the rest of the team as hard as I will push everybody the rest of the season.

You will never see a team play harder than we will the rest of the season. God bless."

-Tim Tebow, September 27, 2008

HOPE

"Believe you can and you are halfway there."
-Teddy Roosevelt, former president of the United States and great adventurer

CONFIDENCE

"You can run, but you cannot hide."
-Ronald Reagan, former president of the United States, after terrorists hijacked a cruise ship, killed a passenger, and attempted escape

"I have not yet begun to fight."
-John Paul Jones, one of the U.S. Navy's most famous commanders, after a British commander asked him if his battered ship and crew were ready to surrender

DESIRE

"Winning isn't everything, but wanting to win is."
-Vince Lombardi, one of the most successful professional football coaches in the history of the sport

LEADERSHIP

"Always do everything you ask of those you command."
-General George S. Patton, a U.S. military leader during WWII who defended our country's freedom from the attacks of the German and Axis forces

REPETITION

"And so let freedom ring from the prodigious hilltops of New Hampshire. Let freedom ring from the mighty mountains of New York. Let freedom ring from the heightening Alleghenies of Pennsylvania. Let freedom ring from the snow-capped Rockies of Colorado. Let freedom ring from the curvaceous slopes of California."
-Martin Luther King, the great champion of civil rights

PROMISE

"You ask, what is our aim? I can answer with one word: Victory—victory at all costs, victory in spite of all terror, victory however long and hard the road may be; for without victory there is no survival."
-Winston Churchill, the prime minister of Britain during WWII, when England was facing almost certain defeat by the German and Axis forces

HOPE is all that most people need in life. A spirit of optimism is enough for anyone, from little league players to soldiers on the front lines, to believe that success is possible. Any amount of success begins with hope.

CONFIDENCE is Pride's first cousin. It is the drive in us that says, "I will use all of my given talents to the best of my ability, and I will be successful." Confidence in oneself is important. People who are confident they will win don't always win. But people who are confident they will lose will always find themselves at a disadvantage.

DESIRE is that hunger we feel when we see something worth going after. It makes us want to be successful. Without desire, nothing is seen as worth having, and life lacks purpose.

LEADERSHIP requires the ability to take the "team" on one's shoulders and bust through walls before them. True leaders are born in moments of personal brilliance out of the spotlight. When they build a following, they begin to realize that others count on them. They then demand more of themselves, not for personal glory but for the success of their followers.

REPETITION can be used in a speech simply to make it more powerful and memorable. The more we hear the same thing, the more we remember it. Think about the chorus to a song. Those are the words we typically remember the most because repetition has driven the words into our heads. In Martin Luther King's "I Have a Dream" speech, he repeats some of his main points so that people will more easily remember them. Due to the repetition, anyone who has heard his speech may recall some of his most eloquent phrases.

PROMISE is what most Americans want to hear. They want to know that some sort of reward awaits them. They will work hard and put forth their best efforts when they know they will get something in return. In Tebow's case, his promise is built on all of the preceding elements. He had hope that he could turn his team around and the leadership skills to get them there. He had confidence to proclaim that the team could and would do it.

When you find yourself down and out, delivering a promise to yourself and staying focused on it may be the best way to guide yourself to success.

Support for this approach can be found in history as we look at the outcomes of some of the situations described in the beginning of this article. John Paul Jones went on to defeat the British Navy in the American Revolution. Martin Luther King changed the face of civil rights in our country. Ronald Reagan saw his military capture those terrorists. General Patton and Winston Churchill went on to secure freedom for the allied countries.

And though small in comparison, Tim Tebow helped turn his team around, and on January 9, 2009, his Florida Gators delivered on The Promise and were crowned college football's national champions.

READING COMPREHENSION

After reading "The Sound of Success," choose the options that best answer questions 1–14.

1. Read the following words from the article.
   When one dissects great speeches and quotes over the course of history, the same elements can be found time and time again: HOPE, CONFIDENCE, DESIRE, LEADERSHIP, REPETITION, and a PROMISE. Tebow's quote seems to come from that same playbook.

   What is the meaning of the word *playbook* as used in these words from the article?
   A. script for a play
   B. strategy for success
   C. notebook of football plays
   D. famous football quotations

2. Read this sentence.
   LEADERSHIP requires the ability to take the "team" on one's shoulders and bust through walls before them.

   What would be another way of saying "bust through the walls before them"?
   F. break a wall
   G. rebuild a team
   H. practice stronger
   I. overcome obstacles

3. The reader can tell from Tim Tebow's "Promise" speech that
   A. Tebow gave the speech after winning the Heisman Trophy.
   B. Tebow is a player who has both the hunger and the confidence to win.
   C. Tebow believed that his mistakes led to his team's loss to the University of Mississippi.
   D. Tebow used this speech to motivate his players prior to the start of every football game.

4. The goal of "The Promise" was to
   F. recruit more players for the University of Florida.
   G. foster a sense of respect and friendship among the players.
   H. encourage others to admit their weaknesses in order to achieve greatness.
   I. apologize to the fans and players and dedicate himself to leading his team to work hard.

5. What element of Tim Tebow's college football career does the author seem to admire the most?
   A. his knowledge
   B. his leadership
   C. his aspirations
   D. his composure

6. The author organizes the article by
   F. providing statistics on Tebow's college career.
   G. comparing Tebow's speech to famous quotations of other individuals.
   H. starting with memorable flashbacks of the national championship game in 2009.
   I. listing the reasons why Tebow will go on to have a successful career as a coach for UF.

7. What is the author's main purpose in writing this article?
    A. to tell the reader about Tim Tebow's life
    B. to explain the importance of focusing on a goal
    C. to compare and contrast various famous quotations
    D. to introduce the reader to famous individuals with inspiring stories

8. If the article were published in a newspaper, which would be the most informative headline?
    F. Teaching Tebow
    G. Quotable Quotes
    H. The Power of a Promise
    I. The Journey of the 2009 UF Football Team

9. Which event led Tebow to give his famous speech?
    A. winning the national championship
    B. a desire to serve as a role model for others
    C. the goal of one day having a career in the NFL
    D. the regular season loss to The University of Mississippi

10. Tebow attempted to turn the 2009 football season around for UF because
    F. he wanted to be recognized.
    G. he believed that a win would allow him to do more for the community.
    H. he believed that he and his team owed it to the fans to work as hard as they could.
    I. he wanted to show that he shared some of the same qualities as other famous public figures.

11. What is true of both Tebow and Lombardi?
    A. Both knew the importance of having a desire to win.
    B. They both played football for the University of Florida.
    C. They are both known for their famous coaching tactics.
    D. Tebow has influenced the way Lombardi thinks about football.

12. Which of the following facts from the article BEST supports the idea that Tim Tebow is a team player who puts the interest of others ahead of his desire for personal glory?
    F. Tim Tebow took the blame for the loss to Mississippi.
    G. Tim Tebow has been known as an excellent quarterback for a strong football program.
    H. Tim Tebow's "Promise" speech is displayed outside of the University of Florida's stadium.
    I. Tim Tebow has also been known for the charitable work he has done outside of playing football.

13. Which of the following elements is illustrated by quotations from Reagan and Jones?
    A. hope
    B. desire
    C. leadership
    D. confidence

14. In his speech, Tim Tebow said, **"You will never see someone push the rest of the team as hard as I will push everybody the rest of the season."** General Patton said, **"Always do everything you ask of those you command."**

    Which of the following conclusions can be drawn from the two statements?
    F. Patton and Tebow found joy in directing others.
    G. Patton and Tebow were optimistic about winning.
    H. Patton and Tebow believed that hard work always leads to winning.
    I. Patton and Tebow believed that leaders should work hard along with those they lead.

READING STRATEGY

Directions: Fill in the chart below. Next to each element of Tim Tebow's speech, write a definition of the element as you understand it from the article. Then record how Tebow used this element in his speech and/or in leading the Gators through the rest of the season. Finally, write a summary of how the elements combined to make good on Tebow's promise.

ELEMENT	DEFINITION	HOW TEBOW USED THE ELEMENT
Hope		
Confidence		
Leadership		
Desire		
Repetition		
Promise		

SUMMARY:

INTERPRETING THE DATA

PART I

Which pronouns are most commonly used in powerful speeches?

Time magazine recently named the top ten speeches of all time. Table 1 includes a brief synopsis of five of those ten. You will analyze the use of words in each of these five speeches to draw your own conclusions about the value of certain types of words in great speeches.

Table 1. Five of the top ten speeches of all time according to *Time* magazine

Speaker	Speech	Total # of words in speech
John F. Kennedy (JFK)	*Inaugural Address, 1961*– Kennedy stressed the importance of national service during his inaugural address as he was named the 35th president of the United States.	1,347
Martin Luther King Jr. (MLK)	*I Have a Dream, 1963* – In King's speech delivered from the steps of the Lincoln Memorial, he declared his faith in the American people to come together and live in racial harmony.	1,666
Lyndon B. Johnson (LBJ)	*The American Promise, 1965* – This speech was delivered after much racial violence in Selma, Alabama. President Johnson called for Americans to put an end to racial discrimination.	3,708
Winston Churchill (WC)	*Blood, Toil, Tears, and Sweat, 1940* – In this speech, known as one of the greatest war-time motivational speeches ever delivered, Britain's prime minister declared to the British people that the survival of Britain rested on their ability to fight off the Nazis.	627
Ronald Reagan (RR)	*Tear Down This Wall, 1987*– In President Reagan's speech, he issued a challenge to the leader of the Soviet Union to tear down the wall between East and West Berlin as a symbolic gesture to allow democracy to begin its reign over communism.	2,752

15. Complete Table 2 by determining how many times each of the listed pronouns appears in the five speeches combined. Write the totals in the shaded boxes.

Table 2. Number of times given pronouns appear in the top speeches

Pronouns	JFK	MLK	LBJ	WC	RR	Total
I	3	15	51	19	34	
me	0	0	7	0	3	
my(self), mine	4	5	8	3	11	
he	0	1	18	0	1	
she	0	0	0	0	0	
we	30	33	45	5	27	
our, ours	21	17	34	6	10	
him(self)	0	1	1	0	0	
her (object form)	0	0	0	0	0	
us	12	4	12	4	4	
you	10	9	24	2	26	
his	3	3	23	2	2	
her, hers (possessive form)	0	1	0	0	0	
your, yours	3	1	9	0	6	

COMPLETE ADDITION HERE FOR GIVEN PRONOUNS

16. Use the numbers from Table 2 to complete Table 3. Compute how many times in total each of the pronouns appears in the five speeches in the following categories. The first group (I, me) has been completed as an example.

Table 3. Categorization of total number of pronouns used in top speeches

Singular pronouns	vs.	Plural pronouns	
I, me: 122 + 10 = 132	vs.	We, us:	
My, mine:	vs.	Our(s):	

Gender-Specific pronouns		
He, him, his:	vs.	She, her, her(s):

17. What might Table 3 suggest about the overall message intended by those who wrote these powerful speeches? Consider the number and types of pronouns used.

ANALYZE
EVALUATE
EXPLAIN

I SPEAK TONIGHT FOR THE DIGNITY OF MAN AND THE DESTINY OF DEMOCRACY

PART II

Does the use of positive or negative words set the tone of powerful speeches?

18. Complete Table 4 by computing the totals for the listed positive and negative words used in the five speeches. The total for the first column has been completed for you. Write your answers in the shaded boxes.

Table 4. Positive and negative words used in five powerful speeches

Positive words	JFK	MLK	LBJ	WC	RR	Negative words	JFK	MLK	LBJ	WC	RR
victory/triumph/win	1	0	0	5	1	burden	4	0	0	0	1
freedom	4	20	5	0	17	struggle	2	2	2	1	0
change	1	1	1	0	3	foe	2	0	0	0	0
power(s)(ful)	9	0	2	0	2	enemy	0	0	1	0	0
life/ live(s)	4	5	12	0	5	oppose	2	0	0	0	0
friend	3	1	1	1	2	fear	2	0	2	0	1
new (anew)	9	2	1	2	4	divide	2	0	0	0	1
proud/ pride(ful)	1	1	2	0	2	defeat	2	0	0	0	1
liberty	1	2	3	0	5	oppress(ed)(ion)	1	1	1	0	0
faith(ful)	2	5	2	0	1	protest(ed)	0	1	5	0	3
help	4	0	10	0	4	denial	0	0	3	0	0
good	3	0	4	0	2	kill(ed)	0	0	1	0	0
courage	0	0	1	0	2	wrong	0	1	4	0	0
strong(ly)	2	0	0	0	3	depression	0	0	1	0	0
pledge	7	1	1	0	2	fail(ed)(ure)	1	0	1	1	1
peace(ful)	5	0	7	0	5	deny/ denial	0	0	10	0	0
strength(en)	2	0	1	2	4	dishonor	0	0	1	0	0
begin(ning)	4	1	1	0	2	dead/die/death	1	1	4	0	1
unite(d)	2	0	0	2	0	discrimination	0	1	1	0	0
success	2	0	0	0	0	restriction	0	0	1	0	1
lead(s)(ers)(ership)	1	2	6	0	4	hesitation	0	0	1	0	0
believe	1	3	3	0	2	bigotry	0	0	1	0	0
loyalty	2	0	0	0	0	injustice	0	3	4	0	0
prosperity	0	1	1	0	4	ignorance	0	0	2	0	0
dignity	0	2	3	0	0	violence	0	1	3	0	1
promise/promissory	0	4	6	0	0	hunger	0	0	1	0	1
hope	4	4	8	3	5	sick(ness)	0	0	1	0	0
commit	2	0	0	0	1	poverty	3	1	6	0	1
TOTAL	76					TOTAL					

19. Complete Tables 5 and 6 to compare the number of positive and negative words used in the five speeches. Gather your data from Table 1 and Table 4. Compute the percentages and the totals. Table 5 has been started for you.

Table 5. Total positive words used in the five speeches

POSITIVE						
	JFK	**MLK**	**LBJ**	**WC**	**RR**	**TOTAL**
# of positive words	76					309
# of words in speech	1,347					
% (rounded to the hundredth)	5.64%					

Table 6. Total negative words used in the five speeches

NEGATIVE						
	JFK	**MLK**	**LBJ**	**WC**	**RR**	**TOTAL**
# of negative words						
# of words in speech						
% (rounded to the hundredth)						

20. What do Tables 4, 5, and 6 suggest about the overall message intended by those who wrote these powerful speeches? Consider the number and types of positive and negative words used.

**ANALYZE
EVALUATE
EXPLAIN**

REFLECT AND RESPOND

21. Think about your personal goals and what you would like to improve about yourself in order to reach those goals. Consider what you want to be in the future. Use those ideas to write a powerful "Promise" speech to yourself. Choose five or six powerful, positive words. Use repetition with a few of those words to set the tone for the speech.

Reflect & Respond

READING INSTRUCTIONAL GUIDE FOR TECHNICAL EXTENSION

BEFORE READING

Looking at the Words

Determining What the Word Means (Vocabulary)

Words to Study	Breaking into Syllables	Short Definition
capacity	ca-pac-i-ty	(n.) ability
critique	cri-tique	(n.) a critical evaluation
empathy	em-pa-thy	(n.) identifying with and understanding another's situation
humility	hu-mil-i-ty	(n.) the condition of being modest
passionate	pas-sion-ate	(adj.) showing intense feelings
podium	po-di-um	(n.) a stand for holding the notes of a public speaker
vision	vi-sion	(n.) an anticipation of what could happen

Activating Background Knowledge

Graphic Organizer

Either individually or in groups, brainstorm about leadership, recalling anything previously learned and any prior experience with the subject. Next, complete the word web to demonstrate what you already know about the characteristics of a strong leader.

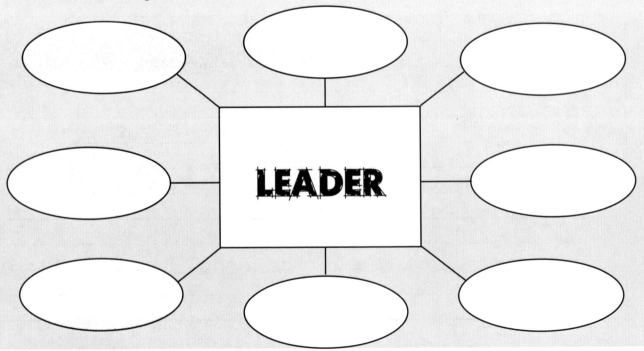

Starter Questions

After completing the Graphic Organizer, participate in a group or class discussion to come up with questions about the subject, a prediction about the article, and at least one learning goal. The first question has been provided for you.

Question: What qualities does a leader possess?

Question: _____

Prediction: _____

Goal: _____

DURING READING

- Skim the article for 45–60 seconds. Circle any words you don't know.

- When you are finished, decode and determine the meaning of unknown words.

- Skim the questions for 30–45 seconds.

- Predict what the article is about.

- Read the article.

- Reread to clarify as needed.

- Answer the questions.

AFTER READING

After reading, you may do the following:

- Review, paraphrase, and summarize

- Participate in main-idea discussions by describing the information in their own words

- Reflect on concept maps and generate additional discussion starter questions based on the mappings

- Participate in small-group discussions using discussion starter questions

Discussion Starter Questions

The first question has been provided for you.

1. What qualities of emotional intelligence do you possess? Which qualities would you like to develop or strengthen, and how can you do so?

2. _____

3. _____

TECHNICAL EXTENSION

LEADERSHIP 101

"Managers are people who do things right, while leaders are people who do the right thing."

- Warren Bennis, Ph.D. "On Becoming a Leader"

Tim Tebow stepped to the podium on Sept. 27, 2008, and did the right thing for his team when he made "The Promise." As their leader, he shared his vision and then committed to making it happen.

We can name other leaders who have done the same in a variety of ways: George Washington, Abraham Lincoln, Thomas Jefferson, Rosa Parks, Martin Luther King Jr. You can probably think of others to add to this list. Leaders can be any age and can hold any position in a company, organization, or community. Leadership comes from people who have a purpose in life. They want to create a better world.

But what are the qualities that cause these names to rise to the top? A leader is someone who has a vision, is passionate about that vision, and motivates others to join the cause. *USA Today* reporter Hilary Owen put it this way: "Management is based on order and control....Leadership, on the other hand, is about expressing the human spirit— the real source of greatness."

Qualities like creativity, a thirst for new information, confidence, and humility go along with the leader's passion and vision. True leaders are more concerned with providing encouragement to the team than they are with getting any recognition for themselves. They seek to make others great while improving the world around them.

Of course, their followers must also be able to understand the vision and know how to get there. So leaders must be good communicators and planners. Martin Luther King Jr., for example, had the ability to touch his audience through his speeches and writing. He also had a plan to reach the goal of equality in our country. His

followers identified with the view he had for America and were willing to help him as he worked to achieve that view.

Another interesting aspect of leadership is the concept of "emotional intelligence." Psychologist and author Daniel Goleman believes that some specific personal qualities are necessary for true leadership. These qualities are self-awareness, self-regulation, motivation, empathy, and social skills. More traditional traits, like intelligence, toughness, determination, and vision, are still necessary for leadership. But Goleman believes that those traits are not enough to allow us to reach our highest potential.

It is encouraging to know that we can learn those characteristics. First we must want to change the way we deal with others. Then we must be committed to practicing new habits that will cause us to connect with others more successfully. Finally, we must be willing to receive honest feedback on our progress from trusted advisors. It is also believed that our EQ increases as we grow and mature. This is good news for all of us!

The 21st century requires some other leadership traits—global experience and understanding, and diversity in the workplace. *New York Times* columnist Thomas Friedman has written about doing business in a global economy. Based on his research of the modern business community, he states that today's leaders must learn to be global citizens. They must also be preparing for the next generation of technology *before* our current tools are outdated.

Tim Tebow had a vision for his team and his school. He then communicated that vision to his team and led them to achieve that vision. His actions provide a blueprint for other young people who want to improve their lives in some way. British General Bernard Montgomery describes leadership like Tebow's as "the capacity and the will to rally men and women to a common purpose and the character which inspires confidence."

TRAITS OF AN EMOTIONALLY INTELLIGENT LEADER

Trustworthy	Shows good judgment
Fair	Broad-minded
Unassuming	Flexible, adaptable
Good listener	Makes timely decisions
Sensitive to others	Motivates others
Sensitive to situations	Has a sense of urgency
Takes initiative	Culturally sensitive

READING COMPREHENSION

After reading "Leadership 101," answer questions 1–12.

1. Read this sentence from the article.
    Another interesting aspect of leadership is the concept of "emotional intelligence."

    What is the meaning of the word *aspect* as it is used in this sentence?
    A. plan
    B. feature
    C. organization
    D. communication style

2. Read this sentence from the article.
    His actions provide a blueprint for other young people who want to improve their lives in some way.

    Which of the following words can be used instead of *blueprint*?
    F. goal
    G. record
    H. characteristic
    I. a model or plan of action

3. According to the article, good management skills and control
    A. are qualities of a leader.
    B. are both based on vision.
    C. are different from leadership.
    D. are not necessary for someone to be successful.

4. Daniel Goleman believes that
    F. emotional intelligence sets leaders apart from managers.
    G. emotional intelligence is an inherited trait that cannot be lost or changed.
    H. leaders must teach emotional intelligence to everyone in their workplace.
    I. traits like toughness and determination are all that are necessary to be successful.

5. The author organizes the article by
    A. comparing leaders from our history.
    B. describing Tebow's path as a leader.
    C. discussing why managers are not good leaders.
    D. defining leadership and then expanding that definition.

6. What is the main idea of the second paragraph?
    F. Elected officials are always leaders.
    G. Leaders are usually historical figures.
    H. Anyone with a vision can be a leader.
    I. Young people are not mature enough to be true leaders.

7. In order to convince others to follow their vision, leaders must also be
    A. effective communicators.
    B. more mature than their followers.
    C. followers at some point in the process.
    D. at the upper levels of their companies or organizations.

8. According to the article, one difference between managers and leaders is that
    F. leaders are usually business owners.
    G. managers are more concerned with order.
    H. good managers are required to inspire the people they manage.
    I. leaders often have the educational background to advance quickly in their companies.

9. Which of the following statements from the article provides the BEST evidence that leadership is a trait that can be learned and cultivated over time?
    A. Tim Tebow had a vision for his team and his school.
    B. Leaders can be any age and can hold any position in a company, organization, or community.
    C. Leadership emerges from people who have a purpose in life and want to create a better world.
    D. Those who support the idea of emotional intelligence believe that EQ increases as we mature.

10. According to the article, including the text box and quotes, it can be said that
    F. leaders are born.
    G. managers focus on companies, while leaders focus on people.
    H. one's confidence has nothing to do with the ability to lead successfully.
    I. business owners who resist the use of technology will not be able to lead successfully.

11. According to one website, a person in business will face many difficult challenges. The site states, **"Some of these may involve the coordination of many different people, the completion of many tasks in a precise sequence, and the expenditure of a great deal of time and money."**

    Based on what you have learned about leaders and managers, which of the following statements BEST describes this statement?
    A. This is a description of management tasks.
    B. It is an outline of the organizational structure of a global company.
    C. The paragraph describes the sole responsibilities of a business owner.
    D. The description provides a blueprint of how to become an effective leader.

12. Could Tim Tebow best be described as a good leader or as a good manager of his team? Use the information from "Leadership 101" and "The Sound of Success" to support your answer.

TECHNICAL WRITING PROMPT

13. You are applying for a leadership position in an organization at your school. Part of the application is to prove yourself to be an emotionally intelligent leader. Look at the traits of emotionally intelligent leaders listed on the second page of the "Leadership 101" article. Choose three traits that describe you. Then concisely explain how you possess those three traits, using relevant examples.

Technical Writing

VOCATIONAL EXTENSION

"If your actions inspire others to dream more, learn more, do more and become more, you are a leader."
– John Quincy Adams

Leadership can be learned. But exactly where do we get these skills? Not everyone likes to join clubs or be involved in extracurricular activities, and many teens must work after school. Some also have family responsibilities that take a great deal of time.

According to one writer, "Good leaders are made, not born. If you have the desire and willpower, you can become an effective leader." So, the first step is to decide that you want to learn the skills to "inspire others to dream more, do more, and become more." Next, you must assign some time to developing leadership skills. You will still have time for things you enjoy, but learning leadership skills will benefit you for the rest of your life.

The process will be ongoing. You will move from one experience to the next, all of which will add to your leadership skills. Professor Boyd at Texas A & M University states that developing leadership requires experiencing an activity, discussing it, identifying common themes, and then coming up with guidelines that can be used in other settings. Following these steps with many experiences will take time, self-evaluation, education, and training. But you can start out small and build from there.

So, begin by looking at where you spend time now. If you have a job, you can seek out leadership there. Ask your supervisor if you can be given more responsibility in your duties. (It might also lead to more money!) Most business people are glad to help young people in this way; they just need to be asked.

Are you involved in a church or other faith-based group? If so, do the same thing there. Ask if there are other ways you can help that require more responsibility. For example, younger children sometimes need a mentor or role model. This is a great way to practice being a leader.

HELP WANTED:

Director of Creative Services. Requirements include a sense of vision and excellent leadership skills. No specific technical skills necessary. College degree in any field of study or five years of successful work experience considered. Fax current resume.

Your school has opportunities to develop as a leader, too. Sports, band, chorus, newspaper, and other similar activities are perfect places to learn these skills. Some groups, such as student council, lend themselves naturally to building leaders. Other examples might be clubs for art, photography, writing, and peer mediation. Once involved, seek out experiences that will develop leadership. These types of groups often offer formal leadership training through conferences and workshops. It might take a while to find the right group for you, but the effort will be worth it.

Your community also provides a chance to flex your leadership muscle. Your neighborhood might have a homeowners association that can use volunteer help. Or you might check with organizations like animal shelters, food banks, or retirement and nursing homes. Call or visit one that is convenient to your daily routine and ask if they can use your help as a volunteer.

Once you find the right place for you, it will be important to take your duties seriously and follow through on everything you are given to do. Ask the adults who supervise you to assess your progress and give constructive suggestions. You will be building your reputation as a responsible, effective worker first, and leadership will follow naturally after that. The people supervising your efforts will take notice and can help you climb the ladder of leadership success into your future.

LOOKING FORWARD

14. Becoming a strong leader begins by strengthening leadership skills while doing something you enjoy. Select an extracurricular activity that you currently participate in (or would like to) and explain what strengths you bring to this activity and how you might use this activity to develop your leadership skills. Using personal experience and information from the article, explain how building leadership skills now will help you make a difference in whatever you choose as your future career.

Looking Forward

ETHICAL DILEMMA

15. You are responsible for documenting the volunteer hours of all the students in your leadership program. A friend who mentors at an elementary school has asked you to add half an hour to his latest report so that he will qualify for a grant to pay for his trip to a national leadership conference. How will you respond when he asks you to do this? Do you think you will change your mind either way after you have time to consider his request? Defend your answer.

Ethical Dilemma

UNIT VOCABULARY ASSESSMENT

Matching

Match each word in Column I to its definition in Column II.

Column I

_____ 1. humility
_____ 2. preceding
_____ 3. podium
_____ 4. proclaim
_____ 5. empathy
_____ 6. prodigious

Column II

A. immense
B. to announce or declare
C. condition of being modest
D. understanding of another
E. previous
F. stand for holding the notes of a public speaker

Multiple Choice

Choose the word that MOST NEARLY replaces the underlined word in each sentence.

7. The politician gave an <u>eloquent</u> speech that was designed to make the listeners see his perspective.
   A. weak
   B. gracious
   C. powerful
   D. disappointing

8. In addition to making good decisions on the field, the quarterback has the <u>capacity</u> to run the ball.
   A. ability
   B. strength
   C. athleticism
   D. determination

9. The forensic detectives had to <u>dissect</u> the evidence to determine the cause of death.
   A. collect
   B. connect
   C. analyze
   D. organize

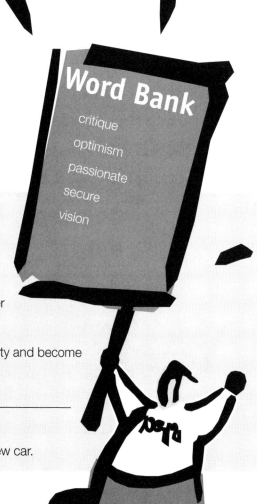

Word Bank

critique
optimism
passionate
secure
vision

Fill in the Blank

Choose a word from the word bank to fill in the blank in the sentence below.

10. He is _____ about helping orphaned children, and his commitment shows.

11. Part of her personality is an underlying _____ based on her belief that people are basically good.

12. My _____ is that the country will one day rise above poverty and become an economic powerhouse.

13. Because I want to improve my writing, I will ask the teacher for a _____ of my essay.

14. She is going to the bank to try to _____ a loan to buy a new car.

AUTHENTIC ASSESSMENT

Students will create a biographical poem based on the unit "The Sound of Success."

Instructions for Bio Poem

1. **Planning.** A bio poem is a poem written about one's life, personality traits, future, and ambitions. Students will examine the six elements from Tim Tebow's speech and determine what they reveal about his character. This planning may take place individually or in group discussion

2. **Brainstorming.** Students will then work individually to write aspects of those elements that exemplify or describe themselves. The following prompts may be used:

   a. I HOPE that…

   b. I have CONFIDENCE that/when…

   c. I DESIRE…

   d. I show LEADERSHIP by…

   e. The phrase that I want REPEAT is…

   f. My PROMISE to myself or others is…

3. **Product.** Students should work individually on poems with the guidance of the teacher. The poem may be in any format that the teacher supports, directly naming the elements or not, as long as it fits into the focus of a bio poem.

4. **Presentation.** Each student will choose a creative way to present the poem, either orally or visually.

5. **Assessment.** Work will be assessed using the rubric that follows.

RUBRIC

Requirement	8–10 Points	4–7 Points	0–3 Points	Points Earned
Planning	The student fully participates in planning for the poem.	The student partially participates in planning for the poem.	The student does not participate or participates very little in planning for the poem.	
Brainstorming	The student exhibits much detail in brainstorming use of the elements.	The student uses some detail in brainstorming use of the elements.	The student uses little detail in brainstorming use of the elements or does not brainstorm.	
Product	The poem is well-written, thoughtful, and meets the teacher's requirements.	The poem meets most of the teacher's requirements.	The poem is incomplete and/or carelessly written.	
Presentation	Work is neat, legible, and turned in on time.	Work is messy, hard to read, and/or late.	Work is incomplete or not turned in.	

HOME FRONT

READING INSTRUCTIONAL GUIDE FOR HIGH-INTEREST ARTICLE

BEFORE READING

Looking at the Words

Determining How the Word Sounds (Phonics)
Using the Syllable Guide and the Reading Instructional Guide Template found in the beginning of the book, read the steps to learn how to break a word into manageable parts.

Determining What the Word Means (Vocabulary)

Words to Study	Breaking into Syllables	Short Definition
convoy	con-voy	(n.) a group of military vehicles traveling together
deployment	de-ploy-ment	(n.) a military assignment away from home
exaggerate	ex-ag-ger-ate	(v.) to magnify beyond limits of truth; overstate
rampage	ram-page	(n.) behavior that is violent and reckless
sustain	sus-tain	(v.) to experience or suffer (injury, loss, etc.)
validate	val-i-date	(v.) to give approval to; affirm

Activating Background Knowledge

Anticipation Guide
Mark each of the following statements True or False:

1. _____ Kimberly Munley is a famous politician.

2. _____ Men and women have equal respect in the military.

3. _____ The roles women play in the military are limited.

4. _____ Our military soldiers put their lives on the line for us every day.

5. _____ Soldiers are permitted to board airplanes before other passengers.

Starter Questions

After completing the Anticipation Guide, participate in a group or class discussion using the following questions:

1. What is post-traumatic stress disorder (PTSD)?

2. What is a civilian police officer?

3. What is an IED?

4. What difficulties does a soldier face when returning home from war?

5. What has our military done in the past to preserve our freedom?

Make a prediction about what you think the article will be about.

DURING READING

- Skim the article for 45–60 seconds. Circle any words you don't know.
- When you are finished, decode and determine the meaning of unknown words.
- Skim the questions for 30–45 seconds.
- Predict what the article is about.
- Read the article.
- Reread to clarify as needed.
- Answer the questions.

AFTER READING
Discussion Starter Questions

1. What are the effects of post-traumatic stress disorder (PTSD)?

2. What is the main idea behind House Resolution 868?

3. Do you think male and female civilian employees should be treated equally? Why or why not?

4. Do you think it is fair that women have limited roles in the military? Why or why not?

5. Do you think women in the military should be permitted to serve in combat? Why or why not?

THE HOME FRONT

On November 5, 2009, police Sergeant Kimberly Munley received a call about gunfire at Fort Hood, a military base in Texas. She and her partner responded within three minutes. When they arrived, a gunman was wildly shooting an automatic weapon. Munley turned a corner and took aim at him. She shot at him four times even as she was shot in return. Many have credited Munley for heroically stopping his deadly rampage.

Munley joined the police force on the military base after serving several years in the Army. Women like her have been a respected part of police forces for many years. Their service is considered just as important as that of male civilian officers. The service of American military soldiers is also valued. Everyday Americans usually respect soldiers. When thinking about how they put their lives on the line to ensure our freedom, it is hard to feel anything but respect. It is tradition to walk up and shake the hands of soldiers in uniform, thanking them for their service. They are allowed to board airplanes first and are applauded once on board for all they do to keep our country safe. Though small actions can never repay soldiers for the cost of their service, they show our appreciation.

Often these gestures of thanks are saved primarily for the traditional male soldier. It seems that many people still aren't sure how to honor female soldiers and veterans. Ashley Pullen used her body as a shield against enemy fire to help another soldier. Monica Brown rescued five injured soldiers. Yet it's likely you've never heard their stories. This is partly because their actions are occurring oceans away, but also because of the invisibility that seems to trouble women in the military.

Female soldiers and veterans can feel left out when they return home. Often they never receive the "hero's welcome" that every soldier dreams of while at war. Research shows that when any soldier feels like his or

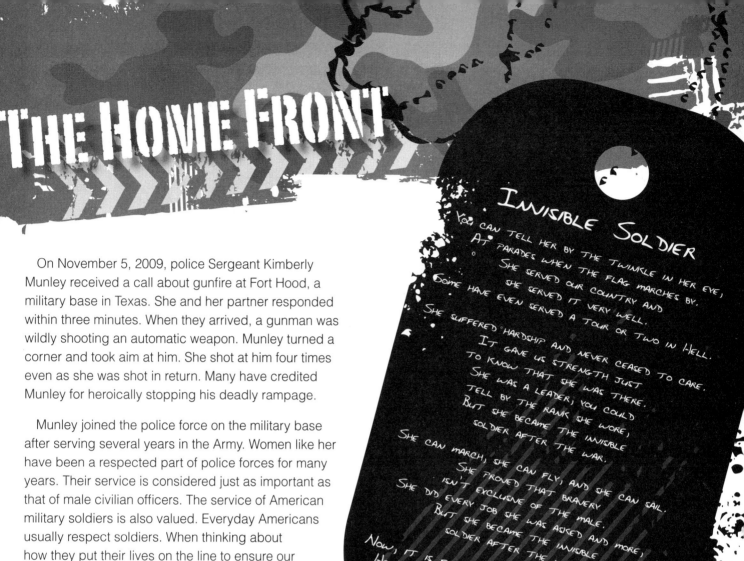

INVISIBLE SOLDIER

You can tell her by the twinkle in her eye
At parades when the flag marches by.
She served our country and
She served it very well.
Some have even served a tour or two in Hell.

She suffered hardship and never ceased to care.
It gave us strength just to know that she was there.
She was a leader, you could
Tell by the rank she wore,
But she became the invisible
Soldier after the war.

She can march, she can fly, and she can sail.
She proved that bravery
Isn't exclusive of the male.
She did every job she was asked and more,
But she became the invisible
Soldier after the war.

Now, it is finally time to right a wrong.
Honor our sister soldier; hear her song.
It's very clear that
She's a patriot to the core.
Don't let her be the
Invisible soldier anymore.
—Sarge Lintecum, 1995

her service isn't validated, the transition home is more difficult. Female veterans say their desires are simple: to be recognized, respected, and understood by Americans. As one sergeant put it, "You want to feel like you're coming home to open arms, rather than to a public that doesn't acknowledge you for what you've just done and what you just sacrificed."

One of the major issues for female veterans is injuries from combat. Sometimes females' injuries are made out to be less severe than they really are. Doctors may think that women exaggerate their conditions more than

Women in the U.S. Military

Females have served in the United States military for over 200 years, dating back to the Revolutionary War. At that time, women had to pretend to be men in order to become soldiers. Today women can participate openly in the armed forces. The places in which they can serve are limited. Women cannot serve in direct combat situations or Special Forces programs such as Navy SEALs. However, because of the open-ended battlefields of today's wars, women see more "front-line" action than ever before.

male soldiers would. Consider the story of Casey Elder, who served in Baghdad as a military police officer. Her position was dangerous and unusual for a woman. Elder was an expert shot, so she served as a gunner. Her job was to protect a moving convoy. When her convoy was hit by an IED (improvised explosive device), Elder was slammed into the truck and her left shoulder separated. By the next day, her arm was numb from shoulder to fingers. A medical examination determined that the injury was only a sprain. She made it through her deployment but sought medical attention at the veteran's hospital when pain led to muscle spasms and numbness. Army

doctors questioned whether she was faking her injury. Finally, an orthopedist diagnosed her with a displaced bone. She continues to suffer from permanent joint and nerve damage, which surgery has helped to correct. Elder entered Montana State University, where she found it difficult to fit in. But after about 6 months, she began to readjust to life as a civilian. And after 4 ½ years of paperwork, she was finally awarded a purple heart for the injuries she sustained. Elder comments, "I'm proud of my service, and all I hope is that other women don't have to face the same struggles I have to get the recognition that we all deserve."

While physical war injuries can sometimes be hard to prove, psychological injuries are just as common and twice as hard to identify and treat. Post-traumatic stress disorder (PTSD) is a common result of the trauma suffered in war. Women are especially susceptible to it. The severity of PTSD is difficult to determine. Many women find that doctors are unable or unwilling to recognize the symptoms as a disorder rather than simply emotions. Air Force veteran Aimee Sherrod was medically discharged in 2005 with a diagnosis of PTSD. She believes that her disability rating was too low when she was discharged. Her PTSD is so severe that she can't function to work or attend school, and she wakes up with nightmares in which she is under attack.

Another female veteran, Angela Peacock, describes how PTSD affects her life, contributing to an addiction, a divorce, and facing homelessness. "You're sitting on your couch and you hear a car go down the street, and you think it's going to come through your house," Peacock said. "That's stuff normal people don't do, but if you're in a combat zone on convoys all the time, you can't help but do that." Female veterans have higher rates of divorce, are more likely to be single parents, and have a greater chance of homelessness.

Medical issues can be overwhelming, but many veterans say that everyday misunderstandings are just as hard to take. People often assume that female soldiers new to the base are simply wives or girlfriends of male soldiers. They aren't thanked for their service. Military units in the field often yield strong friendships among soldiers, so a female veteran's friends may all be men. However, these friendships often must end when soldiers return home to their families.

One female veteran who felt cut off after returning from the field organized a gathering of female veterans. What started as a get-together led to the foundation of American Women Veterans, an organization with 2,000 online supporters. Organizations such as this and Female Veterans Resource Connection have helped VA leadership understand the need for female veteran advocates. They've asked for changes to recognize the unique needs of female soldiers. On November 5, 2009, House Resolution 868 was passed, supporting female soldiers with the following, a major step in recognizing the service and commitment of female soldiers to our country.

Resolved, That the House of Representatives—

(1) *honors and recognizes the service and achievements of current and former female members of the Armed Forces;*

(2) *encourages all people in the United States to recognize the service and achievements of women in the military and female veterans on Memorial Day;*

(3) *encourages all people in the United States to learn about the history of service and achievements of women in the military; and*

(4) *supports groups that raise awareness about the service and achievements of women in the military and female veterans through exhibitions, museums, statues, and other programs and activities.*

Perhaps we can all take this as a cue to honor the service of our female soldiers. The next time you meet a female soldier or veteran, pause to consider what she has given for your freedom.

Unit 6

READING COMPREHENSION

After reading "The Home Front," choose the options that best answer questions 1–14.

1. Read this sentence.
    Many have credited Munley for heroically stopping his deadly rampage.

    Which of the following has nearly the same meaning as the word *credited* as it is used in the sentence?
    A. scolded
    B. applauded
    C. mistrusted
    D. compensated

2. Read this sentence.
    Military units in the field often yield strong friendships among soldiers, so a female veteran's friends may all be men.

    Which of the following has nearly the same meaning as the word *yield* as it is used in the sentence?
    F. crop
    G. create
    H. honor
    I. withhold

3. From this article, the reader can tell that
    A. women will lose their desire to join the military.
    B. women will learn to ignore the lack of respect they receive.
    C. respect for women in the military will increase as awareness increases.
    D. women in the military will encourage other females to join the armed forces.

4. What is the primary purpose of the American Women Veterans organization?
    F. to assist and support female veterans
    G. to recruit new members to the military
    H. to financially support female veterans' families
    I. to provide support to women who are new to the military

5. Why does the author conclude the article with, "pause to consider what she has given for your freedom"?
    A. to point out that women have always supported men in the military
    B. to prove that women in the military do not deserve the same respect as men
    C. to encourage the reader to honor the women who have sacrificed for our freedom
    D. to emphasize that women cannot fight in combat, so they are forced to work behind the scenes

6. The author organizes the article by
    F. quoting experts
    G. answering a series of questions
    H. discussing various issues faced by female soldiers and veterans
    I. analyzing the pros and cons of female soldiers serving in the military

7. What is the purpose of the poem entitled "Invisible Soldier"?
    A. to support the military
    B. to encourage the reader to join the military
    C. to inform the reader about the roles women play in the military
    D. to encourage the reader to honor female soldiers who return home from war

8. What is the main idea of the first paragraph?
    F. Munley acted with record speed.
    G. Munley should receive a medal of honor.
    H. Munley has chosen to pursue a career in the military.
    I. Munley put her life on the line to stop a dangerous situation.

9. According to the article, post-traumatic stress disorder is one of the most common effects of
    A. losing a job.
    B. serving in a war.
    C. joining the military.
    D. completing boot camp.

10. Why did the House of Representatives pass Resolution 868?
    F. to raise awareness of the military service of women
    G. to encourage all women to pursue careers in the armed forces
    H. to demonstrate the role that women play in the United States Navy
    I. to increase the financial compensation women in the military receive

11. What was true of both soldiers Aimee Sherrod and Angela Peacock?
    A. Both were Navy Seals.
    B. Both have become homeless.
    C. Both served in the Vietnam War.
    D. Both have suffered from post-traumatic stress disorder.

12. Which statement from the article BEST supports the idea that female soldiers today are limited in the roles they can play in the military?
    F. "At that time, women had to pretend to be men in order to become soldiers."
    G. "Often, though, these gestures of thanks are saved primarily for the traditional male soldier."
    H. "Women are barred from serving in direct combat situations and Special Forces programs such as Navy SEALs."
    I. "Residents in military bases often assume that female soldiers new to the base are simply wives or girlfriends of male soldiers."

13. According to the second text box titled "Women in the U.S. Military,"
    A. military service is not suitable for women.
    B. women today can serve more openly than in the past.
    C. women are more likely than men to be injured in combat.
    D. the military needs to employ more women for front-line positions.

14. Based on BOTH the article and the second text box, which of the following conclusions might be drawn?
    F. Women do not easily get hurt while fighting in combat.
    G. It has become easier for women to serve in the military, but female soldiers still face many difficulties.
    H. Women in the United States military face difficulties because they have only recently begun serving in the military.
    I. Today women openly serve in the United States military without any limits or restrictions on where or how they can serve.

READING STRATEGY

Directions: Many issues affect female military members and veterans. On each medal, write a supporting point of the main idea. In the center, write about what has been done to remedy the challenges women face.

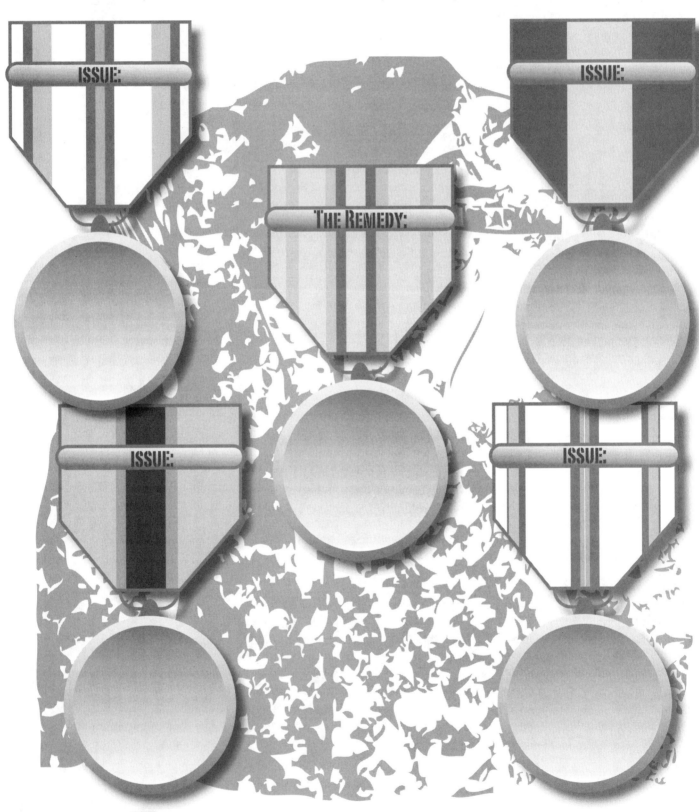

INTERPRETING THE DATA

PTSD and Military Veterans

Military veterans are at an increased risk for developing post-traumatic stress disorder (PTSD), an anxiety disorder that occurs after a person has been through a traumatic event.

Table 1. Incidence of post-traumatic stress disorder (PTSD) in veterans serving in major U.S. wars

War	Percentage of veterans suffering from PTSD
WWII	5%
Korean War	30%
Vietnam War	30%
Persian Gulf War	10%
Afghanistan	18%
Iraq	11%

15. Based on Table 1, which war(s) had the highest percentage of veterans suffering from PTSD?

16. Research has found that rates of PTSD are higher among veterans who spent the most time in combat situations. Based on this fact, what does the percentage of veterans suffering from PTSD in the Persian Gulf War (see Table 1) tell you about the war itself?

17. Much more is known about PTSD today than in past years, which has led to more diagnoses of PTSD. In light of that information, do you think the percentage of WWII veterans suffering from PTSD is accurate?

ANALYZE EVALUATE EXPLAIN

_____
_____
_____
_____
_____
_____
_____
_____

Table 2. Rates of post-traumatic stress disorder (PTSD) over time in Persian Gulf War veterans

	Immediately after return	18–24 months after return
Male veterans	3%	7%
Female veterans	8%	16%

18. Explain what the data in Table 2 reveals about how PTSD presents itself over time.

ANALYZE EVALUATE EXPLAIN

_____
_____
_____
_____
_____
_____
_____
_____

19. Taking into account both Tables 1 and 2, why do you think the most recent U.S. Wars (Persian Gulf, Afghanistan, and Iraq) have lower instances of PTSD than the two wars preceding them?

**ANALYZE
EVALUATE
EXPLAIN**

20. What might Table 2 lead one to believe about the differences in males and females when it comes to PTSD?

**ANALYZE
EVALUATE
EXPLAIN**

REFLECT AND RESPOND

21. Statistics show that 7–8% of the U.S. population will struggle with PTSD at some point in their lives. Imagine that a friend or family member is showing signs of PTSD, including hopelessness and reliving a traumatic event. What would you say to convince that person to seek help?

Reflect
&
Respond

READING INSTRUCTIONAL GUIDE FOR TECHNICAL EXTENSION

BEFORE READING

Looking at the Words

Determining What the Word Means (Vocabulary)

Words to Study	Breaking into Syllables	Short Definition
consultant	con-sult-ant	(n.) a person who gives professional advice
discrimination	dis-crim-i-na-tion	(n.) treatment based on category rather than individual merit
enlist	en-list	(v.) to join or enroll
foundation	foun-da-tion	(n.) the basis or groundwork
objection	ob-jec-tion	(n.) an argument presented in disagreement
pursuit	pur-suit	(n.) an effort to attain
substantial	sub-stan-tial	(adj.) truly existing; real

Activating Background Knowledge

Graphic Organizer

Either individually or in groups, brainstorm about women in the military, recalling anything previously learned and any prior experience with the subject. Next, complete the T-chart to demonstrate what you already know about the pros and cons of women playing an active role in the military.

PROS: CONS:

Starter Questions

After completing the Graphic Organizer, participate in a group or class discussion to come up with questions about the subject, a prediction about the article, and at least one learning goal. The first question has been provided for you.

Question: What is meant by the term "equality"?

Question: _____

Prediction: _____

Goal: _____

DURING READING

- Skim the article for 45–60 seconds. Circle any words you don't know.

- When you are finished, decode and determine the meaning of unknown words.

- Skim the questions for 30–45 seconds.

- Predict what the article is about.

- Read the article.

- Reread to clarify as needed.

- Answer the questions.

AFTER READING

After reading, you may do the following:

- Review, paraphrase, and summarize

- Participate in main-idea discussions by describing the information in their own words

- Reflect on concept maps and generate additional discussion starter questions based on the mappings

- Participate in small-group discussions using discussion starter questions

Discussion Starter Questions

The first question has been provided for you.

1. How might work conditions be changed to make joining the military more appealing to women?

2. _____

3. _____

TECHNICAL EXTENSION

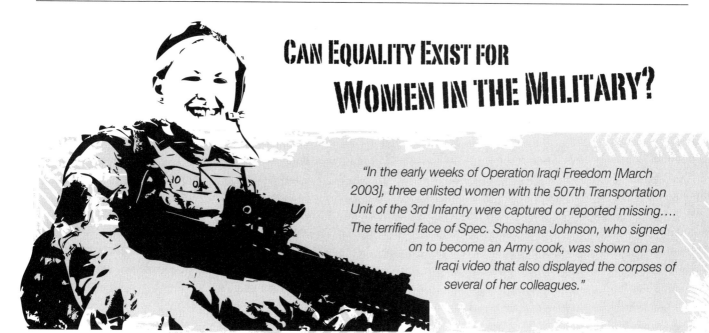

CAN EQUALITY EXIST FOR
WOMEN IN THE MILITARY?

"In the early weeks of Operation Iraqi Freedom [March 2003], three enlisted women with the 507th Transportation Unit of the 3rd Infantry were captured or reported missing.... The terrified face of Spec. Shoshana Johnson, who signed on to become an Army cook, was shown on an Iraqi video that also displayed the corpses of several of her colleagues."

Shoshana Johnson joined the Army because she had a dream to become a chef. She enlisted and was trained as a cook attached to a unit at Fort Bliss, Texas. By 2003 she was a single mother. So, how did she get close enough to be attacked and captured on the front lines of combat in Iraq?

The issue of women serving on the front lines is not a new one. There are many who believe there are important factors to consider before sending women into danger. But the concept of equality is at the foundation of our democracy. How can these two views be resolved?

Women have been instrumental in times of war since our country's beginning. Margaret Corbin fought alongside her husband during the Revolutionary War. She later received a pension equal to half a soldier's pay for her service. Deborah Samson enlisted in the Continental Army, although she served under a man's name. It was 3 years before it was discovered that she was a woman and she was honorably discharged.

The history of service by women has been defined by what the military needs during times of conflict. Female nurses served on the front lines during World War II. Some were even captured and spent time as prisoners of war. During the 1950s and 1960s in Korea and Vietnam, women again provided medical assistance and support services.

In 1991 the United States entered the First Gulf War in the Middle East. It was during this conflict that Americans became aware of how many women were serving in the military. They also realized that women were fulfilling almost all the roles that were available to men. And it might be a surprise to many Americans to learn that there are no laws that prohibit women from serving in combat roles.

In 1994 Secretary of Defense Aspin made changes in the rules about the role of women in the U.S. military. The main change involved assigning women where there might be a *"substantial risk of capture."* Many units that had previously been closed to women were opened. Today, the only areas not open to women are on submarines; in Special Forces programs like the Navy Seals; and in the Infantry, Artillery Armor, and Forward Air Defense. And those areas are closed to women only because of military regulations, not because of any laws prohibiting it.

You might ask why this is an issue at all. Our Declaration of Independence states that all Americans have the right to "life, liberty, and the pursuit of happiness." If a woman wants to be in the military to pursue her definition of happiness, why can't she be treated as a full member, even if she is in harm's way? Many people feel that she should be the one to make that decision.

MILITARY WOMEN

Some Military Female "Firsts"

Mary Walker
Civil War: First Medal of Honor

Annie Fox
WW II: First Purple Heart

Barbara Dulinsky
Vietnam: First female Marine ordered into combat zone

Kara Hultgreen
1994: First female combat pilot to die in service

Darlene Iskra
1994: First female commander of a Navy Ship

Many others agree. Madeline Morris, a professor at Duke University and an Army consultant, says that not only do women belong in the military, but the military needs to change to make it easier for them. As a traditionally male organization, Morris feels that today's military contributes to discrimination and sexual harassment against women.

There are many who disagree, though. Life in the military is characterized by working in close quarters over long stretches of time. According to those who believe women should not serve in all areas of the military, this situation can lead to many negative experiences for women. They point to things like sexual harassment, including rape; romantic jealousies; and unwanted pregnancies. They say that this reality needs to be faced rather than ignored.

There is also the problem of mothers leaving their children when they must report for duty far from home. Alexis Hutchinson knows first hand about this issue. She refused to leave with her Army unit for Afghanistan in December 2009 because there was no one to care for her 10-month-old son. It is a fact that most children in the United States are cared for on a daily basis by women. When a mother enlists and is then deployed away from home, who takes care of her children?

The Army's policy is that soldiers who are parents can be disciplined if they are unable to find caregivers for their children. Hutchinson was briefly arrested and put in jail, and her son was put under the care of child services. The facts in this case are still being debated, but the question remains: Should mothers be allowed to serve in the military?

There are no easy answers. Maybe it is better for society as a whole that women are not allowed to pursue their dreams in the military. However, Americans are used to "pursuing happiness" with few restrictions. There could be many creative solutions to the objections raised.

What do *you* think?

READING COMPREHENSION

After reading "Can Equality Exist for Women in the Military?" answer questions 1–12.

1. Read this sentence from the article.
   Women have been instrumental in times of war since our country's beginning.

   What is a synonym for the word *instrumental* as used in this sentence?
   A. useless
   B. important
   C. unnecessary
   D. unimportant

2. Read this sentence from paragraph 10 in the article.
   When a mother enlists and is then deployed away from home, who takes care of her children?

   What is the meaning of the word *deployed* as used in this sentence?
   F. not used
   G. gathered
   H. sent out
   I. withheld

3. From reading this article, the reader can infer that the role of women in the military today
   A. has been one marked by the abuse of all women.
   B. changes over time, often based on the needs of the military.
   C. creates disagreement over whether women can command men.
   D. will lead to a military force that in the future does not include women.

4. According to the article, a woman who wants to enlist and serve in a combat role might argue that
   F. the military draft is unfair to women.
   G. there are not enough men to fill the positions.
   H. Congress has passed too many laws limiting how they serve.
   I. our country believes in individuals' rights to follow their own paths to happiness.

5. The author organizes the article by
   A. naming famous women in the military.
   B. presenting issues for and against women serving in the military.
   C. listing the reasons why women should serve in many roles in the military.
   D. comparing the roles of women in the military with their roles as parents to their children.

6. If an article about Alexis Hutchinson were published in a newspaper, which of the following would be the BEST headline to use?
   F. "Single Mothers in the Army: Kids or Country?"
   G. "Unfit Army Mother Jailed for Neglecting Her Child"
   H. "Army Says That Soldiers Must Choose Military Over Children"
   I. "Single Mothers in the Army Find Themselves Dishonorably Discharged"

7. Why are there no women serving on submarines in the U.S. military?
    A. U.S. law forbids it.
    B. The public won't support it.
    C. Military regulations forbid it.
    D. The Declaration of Independence does not support it.

8. Madeline Morris disagrees with those who want to restrict the role of women in the military because
    F. she advises the Army on their policies.
    G. women have already served honorably.
    H. sexual harassment has not proven to be a problem in today's military.
    I. she believes the military should change instead of limiting the role of women.

9. Why might young women today be encouraged about their careers in the military?
    A. There are no laws restricting where women serve.
    B. Americans are now aware of how many women are in the military.
    C. Life in the military often leads to negative situations for women who serve.
    D. The laws restricting how women can serve in the armed forces cannot be re-evaluated.

10. Using all the information presented, the reader knows that
    F. women have served in several branches of the military.
    G. women have never died in combat in the history of the U.S. military.
    H. Shoshana Johnson enlisted in the Army in order to become an officer.
    I. parents who are also soldiers must resign their positions in the military as soon as possible.

11. Read the following statement taken from a news article.

    I would not want to be in a war zone and be depending on her to protect my life. How many thousands of men would love not to have to be deployed because they are fathers?

    Using information from the article, which of the following people is the statement probably referring to?
    A. Annie Fox
    B. Darlene Iskra
    C. Alexis Hutchinson
    D. Deborah Sampson

12. What are some of the reasons presented in the article for limiting the role of women in the military?

TECHNICAL WRITING PROMPT

13. You are a military recruiter specifically trained to work with women who are thinking of enlisting in the military. Write the text for a pamphlet that outlines the benefits and drawbacks of women serving in the military. Clearly and briefly address the following topics and any others you think are relevant.

- History of female military service
- Jobs of females in the military
- Limitations/obstacles for females in service
- Military moms

Technical Writing

VOCATIONAL EXTENSION

Do you think a career in the military might be for you? Here are the basic enlistment requirements for both men and women.

High school graduates ages 18 to 34 will be considered; however, you may enlist at 17 with a parent's written permission. Only a limited number of enlistees are accepted with a GED. You must also be a permanent resident of the United States. Those married with more than two children and those who are single parents are not eligible to enlist.

A vocational aptitude exam is required for all applicants. The results determine qualification as well as job placement if accepted. You must pass a physical and meet height and weight standards. A detailed drug history will be taken, along with ongoing drug tests.

The military also considers moral fitness. Those with convictions for crimes like assault, burglary, kidnapping, murder, rape, or robbery are not accepted.

Financial qualifications will be checked, too. If you have children, are younger than 23, or have had credit problems, the military will verify your ability to handle money.

What about basic training? Many young people want to know what to expect before they sign up for a career in the military. The Army, Navy, Marines, and Air Force have some training differences that you should consider.

The Air Force requires 6 weeks of basic training. Days begin at about 4:45 a.m. with physical training. This is followed by courses in discipline, fitness, financial management, ethics, marksmanship and field training.

Phrase created in 1917 to recruit soldiers, beginning in WW I

The Navy's boot camp is at Great Lakes Naval Training Center on Lake Michigan. It lasts 8 weeks. Training covers the same topics as the Air Force, and enlistees must be able to swim by the end of the camp.

Basic combat training for the Army is 9 weeks long. Recruits' days begin before dawn and last into the evening. Some of the instruction includes nuclear, biological, and chemical defense; landmine defense; rappelling; marksmanship; enemy awareness; hand grenades, night vision equipment; and weaponry.

Marine recruits must complete 12 long weeks of training. Training sites are located in San Diego, California, and Parris Island, South Carolina. All women, however, train at Parris Island.

Recruits who meet certain requirements can earn large bonuses. The Army will pay up to $40,000 in enlistment bonuses. Recruits with college degrees or credits can earn additional bonuses. Bonuses of less than $10,000 are paid in full when the entry training is over. Higher bonuses are paid in yearly payments.

What about regular pay? Some people believe that our military men and women are not paid enough for their service to country. Here is a quick look: Over half of military pay is made up of basic pay. The rest consists of allowances for food and housing, and these allowances are not taxed. In 2006, for example, regular military pay ranged from $29,700 per year to $89,600, depending on grade, years of service, and size of family. Officers, of course, earn more.

Interested? Head on down to a local recruiting office and start asking questions!

LOOKING FORWARD

14. Uncle Sam wants YOU to join the military, but do you have what it takes to devote yourself to this line of work? Using your personal experience and information from the articles in this unit, discuss whether the military seems to be the place for you, and why or why not. If it does suit you, which branch of the military and what job best fits your interests?

ETHICAL DILEMMA

15. Several friends seated with you in the school auditorium are loudly making fun of a female soldier who is part of a group of military recruiters visiting your school to answer questions about a career in the military. All the recruiters served in the Persian Gulf War. How do you handle this situation? Do you say anything to your friends?

UNIT VOCABULARY ASSESSMENT

Matching
Match each word in Column I to its definition in Column II.

Column I
_____ 1. foundation
_____ 2. convoy
_____ 3. discrimination
_____ 4. pursuit
_____ 5. objection

Column II
A. treatment based on a category rather than merit
B. the basis or groundwork
C. a group of military vehicles traveling together
D. an argument presented in disagreement
E. an effort to attain

Multiple Choice
Choose the word that MOST NEARLY replaces the underlined word in each sentence.

6. The young woman wants to <u>enlist</u> in the military after she graduates from college.
   A. quit
   B. stay
   C. enroll
   D. describe

7. The socialite always felt the need to <u>exaggerate</u> her importance.
   A. exit
   B. contract
   C. magnify
   D. aggravate

8. Would you <u>validate</u> the truth of this research for me?
   A. affirm
   B. explain
   C. disprove
   D. contradict

Fill in the Blank
Choose a word from the word bank to fill in the blank in the sentence below.

9. Auto accident victims often _____ broken bones.

10. In just one short month, the young Marines will begin their _____ to Iraq.

11. Hearing the bad news sent him on a violent _____.

12. The company hired a _____ to help them identify ways they could improve.

13. There is _____ evidence that smoking causes cancer.

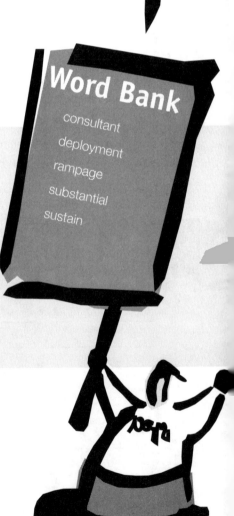

Word Bank

consultant
deployment
rampage
substantial
sustain

AUTHENTIC ASSESSMENT

Students will create a technology research project based on the unit "Home Front."

Instructions for Technology Research Project

1. **Research question.** Students write a research question about the possible relationship between the number of females serving in the military (especially combat situations) and the occurrence of post-traumatic stress disorder (PTSD). The question should ask about the relationship between the two variables.

2. **Hypothesis.** Students write a hypothesis predicting whether there will be a correlation between the two variables (females serving and PTSD occurrence).

3. **Data collection.** Students collect and record online data addressing the research question. The following websites may be good starting points:

   - Healthy Place, http://www.healthyplace.com
   - Department of Defense, http://www.defense.gov

4. **Analysis.** Students analyze the collected data. Following are some questions that might help guide the analysis:

   a. How long have women been serving in combat situations?

   b. How has the role of women in the military changed over time?

   c. How has the occurrence of PTSD changed over time?

   d. Do the two seem to be related?

   e. What are some other factors that might contribute to the relationship?

5. **Conclusion.** Students write a conclusion statement that discusses the trends of both variables and the possible relationship between the two.

6. **Assessment.** Work will be assessed using the rubric that follows.

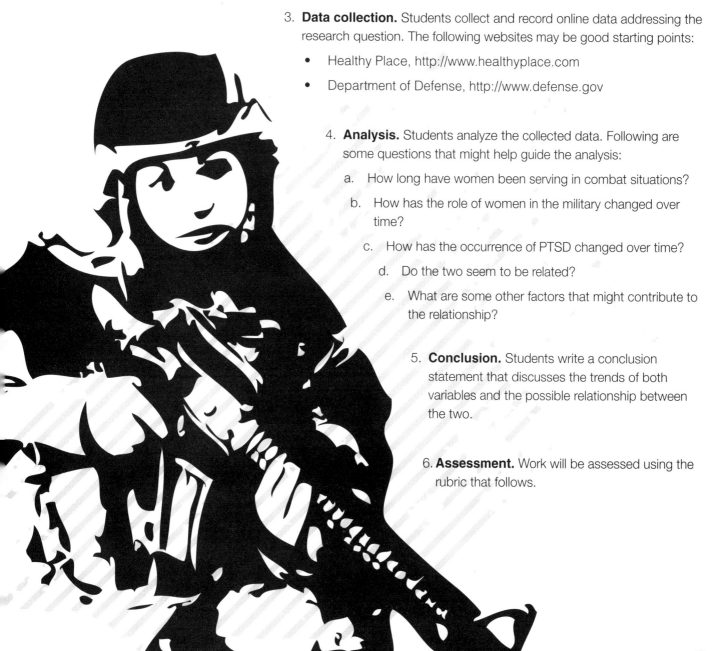

RUBRIC

Requirement	8–10 Points	4–7 Points	0–3 Points	Points Earned
Research Question and Hypothesis	The student writes a clearly stated research question and hypothesis with correctly identified variables.	The student writes a research question and hypothesis that are somewhat unclear.	The student does not write a research question or hypothesis.	
Technology Use	The student uses appropriate technology to collect data and complete the assignment.	The student uses somewhat appropriate technology to collect data and complete the assignment.	The student does not use appropriate technology to collect data or complete the assignment.	
Data Collection and Analysis	The student collects a proper amount of data and correctly interprets it.	The student collects some data and attempts to correctly interpret it.	The student does not collect data or interprets it completely incorrectly.	
Conclusion Statement	The student writes a clearly stated conclusion statement based on the data collected.	The student writes a conclusion statement that is somewhat unclear and/or not entirely based on the data collected.	The student does not write a conclusion statement or writes a statement that is not based on data.	

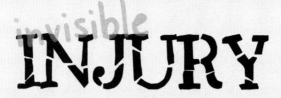

READING INSTRUCTIONAL GUIDE FOR HIGH-INTEREST ARTICLE

BEFORE READING

Looking at the Words

Determining How the Word Sounds (Phonics)

Using the Syllable Guide and the Reading Instructional Guide Template found in the beginning of the book, read the steps to learn how to break a word into manageable parts.

Determining What the Word Means (Vocabulary)

Words to Study	Breaking into Syllables	Short Definition
ascertain	as-cer-tain	(v.) to determine with certainty
dementia	de-men-tia	(n.) loss of intellectual ability
discount	dis-count	(v.) to brush off or treat as unimportant
revamp	re-vamp	(v.) to revise or redo
sensitivity	sen-si-tiv-i-ty	(n.) the state of being easily affected by something
severity	se-ver-i-ty	(n.) seriousness

Activating Background Knowledge

Anticipation Guide

Mark each of the following statements True or False:

1. _____ Brett Favre is a quarterback for the Pittsburgh Steelers.

2. _____ Concussions are easy to diagnose.

3. _____ The symptoms of a concussion are the same for every person.

4. _____ Concussions are serious injuries that should not be taken lightly.

5. _____ Concussions can occur both during practice and while playing in a contact game.

Starter Questions

After completing the Anticipation Guide, participate in a group or class discussion using the following questions:

1. What is a concussion?

2. What are the most common symptoms of a concussion?

3. Have you ever had a concussion? If so, what were your symptoms?

4. Why are professional football players inclined to suffer multiple concussions?

5. How can a concussion impact memory?

Make a prediction about what you think the article will be about.

DURING READING

-   Skim the article for 45–60 seconds. Circle any words you don't know.
-   When you are finished, decode and determine the meaning of unknown words.
-   Skim the questions for 30–45 seconds.
-   Predict what the article is about.
-   Read the article.
-   Reread to clarify as needed.
-   Answer the questions.

AFTER READING

Discussion Starter Questions

1. What are the long-term effects of suffering a concussion?

2. How have retired NFL players influenced the way athletes and coaches view concussions?

3. What precautions do you think athletes could take to avoid serious head injuries such as concussions?

4. Why is it crucial to get plenty of rest after suffering a concussion?

5. Why is it more difficult to diagnose a concussion than a broken bone?

HOW DO YOU FIX A BROKEN BRAIN?

...quarterback is running...

...defensive tackle...

...knocks to the turf...

...woozy ...

...on the sideline...

..."are you okay?"..."yeah, coach..."

...back in the game...

...fans cheer...   ...good pass...

...TOUCHDOWN!

...after the game...

...he doesn't remember...

Brett Favre suffered a concussion when a 315-pound defensive lineman knocked him to the ground in a game in 2004. His coach asked him if he was okay. Favre said he could still play. The coach didn't seek the opinion of the medical staff. He just sent Favre back in. Doctors would have discouraged him from allowing Favre to get back on the field. But it was a time when football coaches often discounted head injuries. The attitude was, "Concussion? Get back out there. We don't want to hear it." Three plays after re-entering the game, Favre threw a 28-yard touchdown pass, leading his team to victory. But when he talked with the opposing team's quarterback after the game, Favre couldn't remember the play.

In 2009, quarterback Ben Roethlisberger decided to sit out a game after suffering a concussion. He had suffered concussions before, both in football and in a motorcycle accident. He was aware of the danger of playing with a concussion. Unfortunately, one of his teammates publicly criticized Roethlisberger for taking time off to heal. The teammate's comment likely came from a lack of information concerning the cost of choosing to return too soon after a concussion.

The National Football League has recently revamped its policy on how teams should deal with concussions. Some of its highest-profile players, including Clinton Portis, Brian Westbrook, Ben Roethlisberger, DeSean Jackson, and Kurt Warner, have been affected by head injuries. Concussions awareness has increased since some retired NFL players have begun reporting long-term problems such as memory loss, mood swings, depression, and difficulty concentrating. There have even been a couple of cases of suicide among players who suffered from major depression after multiple concussions.

Several former NFL players have donated their brains to medical research after their deaths. Scientists at the Sports Legacy Institute have found that the brains of players who have sustained multiple concussions show damage similar to those of much older people who suffered from dementia later in life. This leads doctors to conclude that multiple hits to the head can lead to serious damage. A football player with an injured knee might be able to repair the knee or even have a knee replacement later in life. However, there is no such thing as a "brain replacement."

Athletes in sports ranging from cheerleading to biking need to know the dangers of returning to any athletic activity after a concussion. At present, the ever-popular NFL seems to be raising awareness and setting the standard for how athletic organizations should deal with the dangers of concussions. *leading the way*

What is a concussion?

Concussions are invisible injuries. Injuries like a broken leg, a badly bruised hand, and a sprained ankle are easy to see. The injuries can be seen through swelling, bleeding, or x-rays. But concussions can't be seen. The symptoms are also hard to ascertain. And the symptoms may vary depending on the person, the severity of the injury, or the length of time that has lapsed since the injury occurred.

According to the Centers for Disease Control (CDC), a concussion is a brain injury that

- is caused by a bump or blow to the head,
- can change the way your brain normally works,
- can occur during practices or games in any sport,
- can happen even if you haven't been knocked out,
- can be serious even if you've just been "dinged."

The symptoms of a concussion might include a headache or pressure in the head. In addition, there may be nausea or vomiting, balance problems or dizziness, double or blurry vision, and sensitivity to light and noise. An injured person may also feel sluggish, hazy, or groggy. He may have trouble paying attention, memory problems, and confusion.

Here is one example of the bewilderment one could experience with a concussion. Imagine this scenario.

It is Monday morning. You played a great game Friday night, but you remember it being rough. You had a slight headache all Saturday morning. You are in a fog. You are sitting at your desk in school, fiddling with your pencil. Your friend Mike says something to you. You look across the aisle to your right. Mike is sitting there. Then you look back to your pencil. It is gone. You are confused about where it is. You try to focus. Where did it go? Did you drop it? You look back over to Mike. He's busy at work…with your pencil. "How did you get my pencil?" you ask. "Dude," he replies, "you just gave it to me."

You just look away. You wonder, what just happened? Did I give him my pencil? I just don't remember.

The CDC recommends that you *always* tell your coaches and parents whenever you take a bump or blow to the head, no matter the other symptoms. You must also get the opinion of a medical professional to determine when you may return to play. Medical experts stress taking time to rest and get better. They warn that you are much more likely to sustain a second concussion or brain damage when your brain is still healing.

One of the most important things to remember is not to be swayed by peer pressure. Remember, your health is at risk. Professional athletes admit that they often return to the action much too early because they feel like their team needs them or they are afraid they will lose their position. The risk just isn't worth taking. Remember, a broken bone can heal—but what happens to a "broken" brain?

title

READING COMPREHENSION

After reading "How Do You Fix a Broken Brain?" choose the options that best answer questions 1–14.

1. Read this sentence.
    Here is one example of the bewilderment one could experience with a concussion. Imagine this scenario.

    After reading the scenario that follows this sentence in the article, what does the word *bewilderment* mean?
    A. confusion
    B. excitement
    C. amazement
    D. peacefulness

2. Read this sentence.
    But when he talked with the opposing team's quarterback after the game, Favre couldn't remember the play.

    What is the meaning of the word *opposing* as it is used in the article?
    F. same
    G. equal
    H. facing
    I. unbalanced

3. From this article, the reader can infer that
    A. concussions are easy to see.
    B. most athletes have a good understanding of the need to rest after a concussion.
    C. athletes who participate in non-contact sports are equally likely to suffer concussions.
    D. Favre and Roethlisberger would be candidates to participate in a research study on the effects of concussions.

4. According to the article, which of the following is one of the possible symptoms of a concussion?
    F. hearing loss
    G. loss of appetite
    H. memory problems
    I. flu-like symptoms, which may include fever

5. From the author's point of view,
    A. symptoms of a concussion should not be ignored.
    B. many professional athletes exaggerate the effects of concussions.
    C. Favre and Roethlisberger should be inducted into the Hall of Fame.
    D. athletes should not waste their time participating in research studies.

6. The author organizes the article by
    F. comparing and contrasting the careers of NFL quarterbacks.
    G. discussing why football players should wear better-designed helmets.
    H. using an NFL game as a starting point for discussing the serious effects of concussions.
    I. analyzing the technology that is available to diagnose and treat athletes with concussions.

7. Why does the author mention the long-term effects of concussions?
  A. to encourage the reader to avoid playing football
  B. to persuade the reader to wear a helmet when playing football
  C. to inform the reader about the dangers of suffering concussions ✓
  D. to explain why professional football players seek retirement at an early age

8. If this article were published in a newspaper, which would be the most informative headline?
  F. Consequences of Concussions ✓
  G. The Impact of Football Injuries
  H. Retiring from the National Football League
  I. Medical Advances in Treating Head Injuries

9. According to the article, the NFL has decided to tighten its policy on concussions because
  A. former players are reporting long-term health concerns. ✓
  B. they fear that retired players will bring lawsuits against the NFL.
  C. of the serious complaints they are receiving from professional coaches.
  D. professional football athletes are getting more aggressive with each other.

10. Why have some retired players decided to participate in research studies?
  F. to earn extra money
  G. to learn how to do research
  H. to discourage others from playing football
  I. to allow scientists to see the damage to the brain ✓

11. What is the main advantage of resting after a concussion?
  A. to prevent vision loss
  B. to avoid extreme exhaustion
  C. to prevent an athlete from experiencing headaches
  D. to allow time for healing and lower the risk of another concussion ✓

12. Which fact from the article provides the BEST evidence that concussions are difficult to diagnose?
  F. Doctors still have much to learn about concussions.
  G. Concussions are "invisible injuries" that cannot be seen. ✓
  H. Athletes often hide their symptoms from coaches and medical staff.
  I. The number of concussions suffered every year is minimal compared to other injuries.

13. Based on the information in the article, what would be a good way to determine if someone has had a concussion?
  A. Schedule an X-ray. ✓ ?
  B. Watch carefully for symptoms. ✓
  C. See if the person can count to 20 without forgetting any numbers.
  D. Encourage the person to sleep for 8 hours followed by an X-ray the next day.

14. Based on the information in the article, along with the opening lines about Brett Favre's game, the reader may conclude that
  F. athletes who suffer concussions may not remember getting hit. ✓
  G. professional athletes intentionally endanger their long-term health.
  H. quarterbacks are more likely to suffer concussions than other football players.
  I. research on concussions is a waste of time and will not likely make a difference in the long run.

READING STRATEGY

Directions: Use the cluster map to record facts about concussions learned from the article. In the center box, write a summary sentence about why it is important to rest and fully heal from a concussion before returning to physical activity.

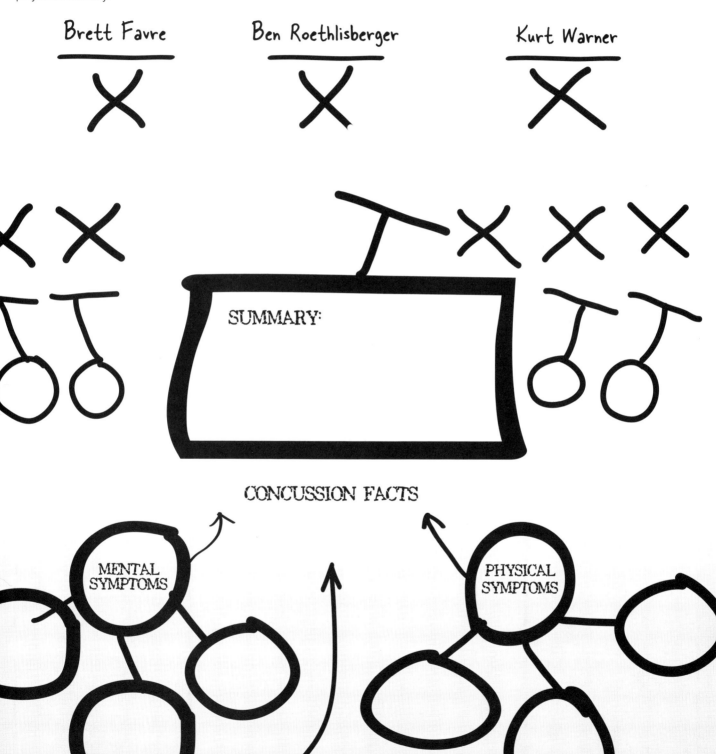

Brett Favre · Ben Roethlisberger · Kurt Warner

SUMMARY:

CONCUSSION FACTS

MENTAL SYMPTOMS

PHYSICAL SYMPTOMS

INTERPRETING THE DATA

PART I

Table 1.

Number of head injuries reported

Week	Head injuries
1	0
2	4
3	3
4	3
5	6
6	6
7	5
8	4
9	4
10	10
11	15
12	12
13	22
14	19
15	12
16	13
17	12

How do head injuries measure up to the worst injuries in the NFL?

This page illustrates data on four types of injuries that were reported to the NFL's injury report list each week of the 2009-10 season.

15. Look at the data on this page and complete the line graph in Figure 1 for each type of injury.

Table 3.

Number of hamstring injuries reported

Week	Hamstring injuries
1	22
2	21
3	29
4	22
5	27
6	23
7	14
8	25
9	9
10	17
11	17
12	15
13	16
14	23
15	23
16	25
17	18

Table 2.

Number of knee injuries reported

Week	Knee injuries
1	43
2	52
3	66
4	48
5	44
6	58
7	49
8	46
9	47
10	66
11	68
12	74
13	77
14	74
15	75
16	69
17	67

Figure 1. Number of main injuries reported to the injury list during the 2009-10 NFL season

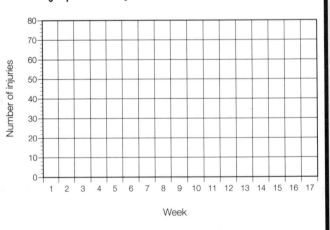

Head   Ankle   Hamstring   Knee

Table 4.

Number of ankle injuries reported

Week	Ankle injuries
1	23
2	21
3	46
4	32
5	31
6	37
7	42
8	35
9	43
10	46
11	51
12	49
13	47
14	41
15	43
16	43
17	40

INJURY

Table 5. 2009-10 NFL Schedule

Week		Week	
1	Sept. 10-14	10	Nov. 12-16
2	Sept. 20-21	11	Nov. 19-23
3	Sept. 27-28	12	Nov. 26-30
4	Oct. 4-5	13	Dec. 3-7
5	Oct. 11-12	14	Dec. 10-14
6	Oct. 18-19	15	Dec. 17-21
7	Oct. 25-26	16	Dec. 25-28
8	Nov. 1-2	17	Jan. 3
9	Nov. 8-9		

On December 2, 2009, the NFL commissioner issued a new policy for the way teams have to handle concussions. The rules require players who show certain signs of a concussion to be immediately removed from the game or practice. The player would not be allowed to play again until cleared to play by an "outside" independent neurological consultant (a doctor not employed by the team).

Figure 2. Total injuries (excluding head injuries) reported to the injury list during the 2009-10 season

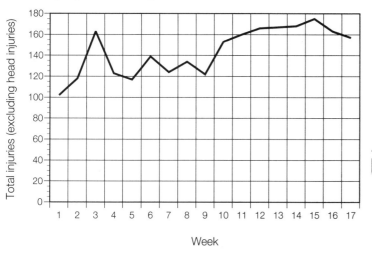

16. According to the preceding information, did the new NFL policy appear to have an effect? Use data to explain your answer.

ANALYZE
EVALUATE
EXPLAIN

PART II

Which recreational activities cause the most concern regarding traumatic brain injuries (TBIs) among people ages 5–18?

Figure 3. Number of injuries in children ages 5–18 that resulted in hospitalization (2001-2005)

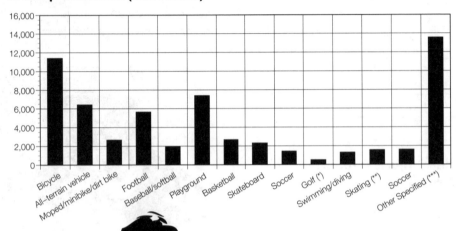

Figure 4. Number of traumatic brain injuries (TBIs) in children ages 5–18 that resulted in hospitalization (2001-2005)

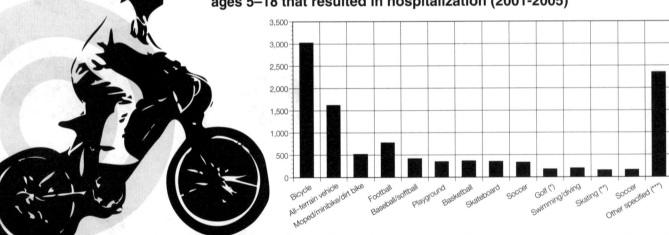

Figure 5. Percentage of all injuries in children ages 5–18 that resulted in hospitalizations that were traumatic brain injuries (TBIs) (2001-2005)

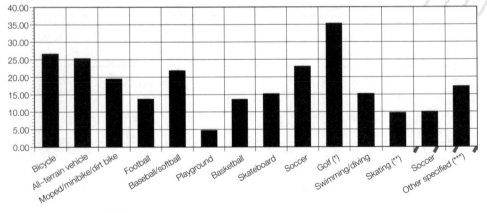

Notes for Figures 3-5:
*"Golf" includes injuries involving golf carts.
**"Skating" includes injuries involving ice, in-line, and roller skating.
***"Other specified" includes trampoline, toboggan/sled, go-cart, gymnastics, bowling, hockey, racquet sports, volleyball, miscellaneous ball games, track/field, combative, exercise, amusement attractions, water skiing, surfing, personal watercraft, snow skiing, snowmobile, snowboarding, camping, fishing, archery, darts, table tennis, non-powder/BB guns, and billiards.

17. Look carefully at Figures 3–5. Decide what some of the activities with higher numbers have in common. Explain what types of activities are most often associated with TBIs among youth. Use data to support your answer.

ANALYZE EVALUATE EXPLAIN

18. Study Figures 3–5. What might the data suggest about the importance of bicycle helmet laws? Compare the numbers for bicycle injuries to other activities to support your answer.

ANALYZE EVALUATE EXPLAIN

REFLECT AND RESPOND

19. If you were a trainer for a high school sports team, what rules would you set for players concerning concussions and head injuries? Make a list of four or five rules or statements you might print on a sign that would be hung in the locker room.

Reflect
&
Respond

_____

_____

_____

_____

_____

_____

_____

_____

_____

_____

_____

_____

_____

_____

_____

_____

_____

_____

_____

_____

_____

_____

_____

_____

READING INSTRUCTIONAL GUIDE FOR TECHNICAL EXTENSION

BEFORE READING

Looking at the Words

Determining What the Word Means (Vocabulary)

Words to Study	Breaking into Syllables	Short Definition
amnesia	am-ne-sia	(n.) partial or total loss of memory
degenerative	de-gen-er-a-tive	(adj.) tending to lose functional activity (as a tissue or organ)
deteriorate	de-te-ri-o-rate	(v.) to grow worse
diagnose	di-ag-nose	(v.) to identify a disease or condition
gravity	grav-i-ty	(n.) critical or serious nature
probation	pro-ba-tion	(n.) a suspended prison sentence of freedom under supervision

Activating Background Knowledge

Graphic Organizer

Either individually or in groups, brainstorm about brain injuries, including concussions, recalling anything previously learned and any prior experience with the subject. Next, complete the tic-tac-toe chart of true/false statements to demonstrate what you already know about brain injuries. The place an "X" or "O" in the box for each statement correctly identified as true or false.

There are no long-term effects of a concussion.	Education and prevention are key for athletes.	A headache is not an effect suffered after a concussion.
Once a football player has suffered a concussion, the player can return to the game after sitting out one quarter.	The Sports Legacy Institute was created to research brain injuries.	Concussions are rare among NFL players.
A brain injury is a common injury suffered in the military.	A concussion occurs when a person suffers an injury to the spleen.	Dementia can occur following a concussion.

Starter Questions

After completing the Graphic Organizer, participate in a group or class discussion to come up with questions about the subject, a prediction about the article, and at least one learning goal. The first question has been provided for you.

Question: What is dementia?

Question: _____

Prediction: _____

Goal: _____

DURING READING

- Skim the article for 45–60 seconds. Circle any words you don't know.

- When you are finished, decode and determine the meaning of unknown words.

- Skim the questions for 30–45 seconds.

- Predict what the article is about.

- Read the article.

- Reread to clarify as needed.

- Answer the questions.

AFTER READING

After reading, you may do the following:

- Review, paraphrase, and summarize

- Participate in main-idea discussions by describing the information in their own words

- Reflect on concept maps and generate additional discussion starter questions based on the mappings

- Participate in small-group discussions using discussion starter questions

Discussion Starter Questions

The first question has been provided for you.

1. What safety advice would you give a friend who is considering playing a contact sport?

2. _____

3. _____

TECHNICAL EXTENSION

Willie Baun is a high school senior who worries about the same things most young men his age do: girls, school, and his future. It's the last item on that list that caused him to give up football when he was in the 7th grade.

"The kid was helmet to helmet with me while I was covering the ball, and that gave me the first concussion," Willie said. He had a headache for a few days, but things got better, and he headed out on the field again. Three weeks went by until he was hit in the head again.

"I dropped down to a second grade level, and I didn't know my parents, none of my friends," he said. "If I did continue, I may not be here right now."

Willie didn't want to be another Mike Webster, former Pittsburgh Steelers player who died in 2002 at age 50. "Iron Mike" was known for his robustness on the field. However, after leaving the NFL with four Super Bowl rings, he was diagnosed in 1999 with brain damage. The damage is believed to be the result of repeated blows to the head on the football field. Webster even went through a time when he was homeless after he was placed on probation for forging prescriptions.

To deal with this issue among athletes, the Sports Legacy Institute was started in 2007. There is more scientific information about head injuries available now, thanks to former players who have died and donated their brain tissue for medical research. The SLI uses this information to educate coaches, athletes, and parents about the long-term results of repeated head injuries.

The SLI believes that their work will also help the military. Brain trauma is often called "the signature injury" to U.S. service men and women fighting around the globe. The scientific name for this neurodegenerative disease is Chronic Traumatic Encephalopathy, or CTE. As the name suggests, the condition deteriorates over time.

Steelers Quarterback Ben Roethlisberger knows this first-hand. He sustained two concussions in 2006—one in a game and another in a motorcycle accident. Then in 2008 he was then was knocked out for 15 minutes during a game against the Cleveland Browns. He experienced the common symptoms of concussion: confusion, amnesia, headache, dizziness, and a lack of coordination. Roethlisberger and his coaches decided that he would sit on the sidelines for several weeks.

But not everyone takes these injuries as seriously. Even though his teammates knew Roethlisberger's physical condition, some of them criticized him for sitting out. Receiver Hines Ward said, "These games, you don't get back."

The answer is education and prevention. Young athletes in any contact sport must always use the proper protective gear. Their coaches and parents must be aware of the dangers of repeated hits to the head. If there is an injury, everyone must cooperate by following the guidelines for rest afterward. A player or coach might be tempted to rush back onto the field to help the team. Experts say that this temptation must be ignored.

It is easy to think that dementia, a condition often caused by concussions, won't happen to you. However, there is too much evidence to ignore the gravity of concussions any longer. Dementia can happen at any age; it isn't just an "old people's disease." A head injury, a stroke, or a brain tumor can destroy brain cells in anyone, young or old.

Mood and personality changes also occur with dementia. At first, these things bother only the person experiencing them. As the condition gets worse, their care falls on family and friends when they can no longer care for themselves.

In his free time today, Willie Baun speaks to young people and their parents about the dangers of concussions. He says he knows that the effects of hits to the head can start small, but the situation only gets worse.

"I've tried golf, and I'm not a big fan of that, but I'm doing tennis now," he added. At least he knows he did the right thing for his future when he walked off the football field for the last time.

Some NFL Players Affected by Head Injuries

Merril Hoge: Sued the NFL after fourth concussion ended his career; has experienced significant health problems

Ted Johnson: Believes repeated concussions caused memory loss and emotional problems

Andre Waters: Committed suicide

Terry Long: Committed suicide

John McKay: Started NFL Player's Association "88 Plan" to provide financial assistance to ex-players suffering from dementia

READING COMPREHENSION

After reading "Who Wins? Who Loses?" answer questions 1–12.

1. Read these sentences.
    Even with Roethlisberger's physical condition widely known, some of his teammates criticized him for not playing as soon as they thought he should. Teammate Hines Ward said, "These games, you don't get back."

    Which of the following words best describes Ward's attitude toward Roethlisberger in this situation?
    A. helpful
    B. approving
    C. supportive
    D. condemning

2. Read the sentence below.
    "Iron Mike" was known for his robustness on the field.

    What does the word *robustness* mean as used in the sentence?
    F. weak
    G. strength
    H. thinness
    I. frailness

3. Based on the article, the reader can infer that
    A. dementia is always a result of head trauma.
    B. the NFL took care of Mike Webster after he retired.
    C. Willie Baun is sorry that he gave up football when he was younger.
    D. head injuries are among the most common war injuries suffered today.

4. One primary focus of the Sports Legacy Institute is
    F. prevention.
    G. training sports referees.
    H. funding medical research.
    I. supporting injured players.

5. Which writing strategy does the author use to make the article interesting to young people?
    A. using low-level vocabulary
    B. inserting the NFL policy on concussions
    C. beginning and ending the article with a teenager's story
    D. providing a lot of data about medical research carried out on players' brains

6. What is the main idea of this article?
    F. A teen speaks out about concussions.
    G. Head injuries can lead to long-term disability.
    H. Mike Webster's life took a downward turn after retirement.
    I. The Sports Legacy Institute joins in partnership with Boston University Medical School.

7. According to this article, dementia
    A. can be caused by concussions.
    B. is a result of two or more concussions.
    C. is a condition that can be reversed if diagnosed in time.
    D. has no long-term effects on the person who experiences it.

8. One factor that has improved medical research on brain injuries is
    F. donations of brain tissue.
    G. more NFL players being injured.
    H. an improved NFL policy on concussions.
    I. Willie Baun's speaking about brain injuries.

9. Which statement below BEST supports the idea that Willie Baun personally understood the dangers of having any more concussions?
    A. Willie described his first concussion as "helmet to helmet."
    B. He encourages others to switch to non-contact sports like golf or tennis.
    C. He had his first concussion when in the 7th grade, but he recovered quickly.
    D. Willie said he knows that the effects of hits to the head can start small, but the situation only gets worse.

10. People who read this article will learn
    F. to avoid all contact sports.
    G. that all sports are too dangerous.
    H. that increased information has led to better prevention.
    I. that the Sports Legacy Institute has influenced the NFL to loosen their policies.

11. The NFL stopped its own study into concussions and offered $1 million to a leading research group to take over the study. This suggests that
    A. the NFL couldn't afford its own research.
    B. the NFL is finally ready to accept the facts about concussions.
    C. players forced the NFL to donate funds to take care of players injured during their careers.
    D. players like Ted Johnson, Merril Hoge, and John McKay were threatening the NFL with lawsuits.

12. After reading this article, what facts could you present to players like Hines Ward who do not seem to understand the seriousness of concussions suffered during sports?

TECHNICAL WRITING PROMPT

13. Imagine that you are a retired football player who has experienced many head injuries. You believe that these injuries have led to memory loss and other cognitive (relating to reasoning, judgment or awareness) problems. Write an editorial column for a newspaper that defends the new NFL policy on concussions and explains why brain injuries can have dangerous, long-term effects on quality of life. Defend your position clearly and concisely.

Technical Writing

VOCATIONAL EXTENSION

HELP WANTED:

Occupational therapist for large rehab center. Will work with clients with traumatic brain injuries. Master's degree in occupational therapy, minimum 3 years of experience, and certification required. Salary dependent on experience. E-mail current resume with references to Clarkson Rehabilitation Center at humanresources@clarkson.com.

Millions of Americans face disabilities every day as a result of brain trauma, stroke, disease, or tumors. They don't give up, though. They learn new ways to do the ordinary tasks we often take for granted.

One professional who helps them deal with their new lives is the occupational therapist.

Occupational therapists do more than get patients ready to go back to work. They help people get back to all their normal routines after an injury. They re-teach people to dress and feed themselves, bathe safely, and use wheelchairs and other special equipment.

Occupational therapists teach exercises that will strengthen their clients' bodies and improve coordination. They also work on problem solving, decision making, and improving memory. Many brain injuries severely affect these skills, all of which are necessary for independent living.

Many people return to work after a brain injury. The therapist might evaluate and suggest changes to the person's workplace. The therapist sometimes even arranges for employment so the client can feel productive again.

Some occupational therapists work with particular age groups or disabilities. These therapists help children with special needs succeed at school. The therapist might work with children individually or in small groups in the classroom.

The elderly also need help recovering from injuries, such as falls. The therapist tries to help them stay active and independent as long as possible. They evaluate clients' homes for safety and sometimes assess clients' driving skills.

Occupational therapists who work in hospitals usually work a regular 40-hour work week. School-based therapists might have to attend meetings with parents after normal work hours. Therapists who work in large rehabilitation centers usually have pleasant work environments with lots of equipment, but the work involves a great deal of time standing and bending to assist clients. Home health therapists drive from one client to the next, so they spend a lot of time on the road.

If therapy sounds like the career for you, start preparing now by taking classes in biology, chemistry, physics, health, art, and social sciences. Then go to college and get a bachelor's degree, followed by a master's degree in occupational therapy. Finally, you must pass a national certifying exam.

Jobs in this field are good and are expected to get better. A large part of the U.S. population will retire soon and will need the services of occupational therapists. Medical science has also improved the chances of survival for those with traumatic brain injuries. These people will need ongoing assistance to learn new ways of life.

In mid-2008, occupational therapists were earning an annual median income of $66,780. Most occupational therapists work for home health care services, nursing homes, health care practitioners, hospitals, and schools.

Robert Hensel was born with spina bifida, a birth defect that affects the spine. He said, *"Placing one foot in front of the other, I've climbed to higher lengths. Reaching beyond my own limitations, to show my inner strength. No obstacle too hard, for this warrior to overcome. I'm just a man on a mission, to prove my disability hasn't won."* One of the many things he accomplished was to become the Guinness world-record holder for the longest non-stop wheelie in a wheelchair.

An occupational therapist probably helped him.

LOOKING FORWARD

14. Using personal experience and information from the article, discuss whether occupational therapy would be a good career choice for you. How would you be able to help others overcome difficulties they face on a daily basis? Would you prefer to work in a hospital, homebound, or school setting? Why?

Looking Forward

_____
_____
_____
_____
_____
_____
_____
_____
_____
_____

ETHICAL DILEMMA

15. You are an occupational therapist who believes that your elderly client should no longer be allowed to drive. He refuses to allow you to test him because he has no other source of transportation available if he fails the test. Do you report him to the driver's license bureau in your state as an unsafe driver? Do you have any other options?

Ethical Dilemma

_____
_____
_____
_____
_____
_____
_____
_____
_____
_____

UNIT VOCABULARY ASSESSMENT

Matching

Match each word in Column I to its definition in Column II.

Column I
_____ 1. diagnose
_____ 2. amnesia
_____ 3. degenerative
_____ 4. sensitivity

Column II
A. partial or total loss of memory
B. to identify a disease or condition
C. tending to lose functional activity
D. state of being easily affected

Multiple Choice

Choose the word that MOST NEARLY replaces the underlined word in each sentence.

5. If we don't use them, our muscles can begin to underlined{deteriorate}.
   A. grow
   B. dilate
   C. weaken
   D. protect

6. The underline{severity} of the injury is unknown at this point.
   A. scene
   B. regularity
   C. seriousness
   D. selectiveness

7. As she read the detective novel, she tried to underline{ascertain} who committed the crime.
   A. aspire
   B. protect
   C. conceal
   D. determine

Fill in the Blank

Choose a word from the word bank to fill in the blank in the sentence below.

8. My grandmother suffers from _____, sometimes not even recognizing me.

9. After negative reviews in the newspaper, the restaurant decided to _____ its menu.

10. When you say that you won the competition because of luck, you _____ the fact that you spent many hours in practice.

11. The _____ of her injuries causes us great concern.

12. After serving his prison sentence, the man still faced years of _____.

Word Bank

dementia

discount

gravity

probation

revamp

AUTHENTIC ASSESSMENT

Students will participate in a constructed response based on the unit "Invisible Injury."

Instructions for Constructed Response

1. **Brainstorming.** Students will spend time brainstorming and/or researching well-known professional sports players who have sustained multiple or career-ending head injuries. Some sports in which this is common include football, hockey, and baseball. Students may use the website SportsConcussions.org (www. sportsconcussions.org). Players discussed in the high-interest and technical articles may be included as a starting point. Students should make a list of these athletes.

2. **Research.** Each student should select one person from the list to study. The student should research that athlete and his or her sports-related head injury. Depending on the person chosen, students may use Internet sources, encyclopedias, books, or other periodicals for research. To guide research, students will turn in notes that answer the following questions:

   a. Who is the person, and what sport did he/she play?

   b. What was his/her sports background?

   c. What type of head injury was sustained?

   d. How did a head injury affect his/her career?

   e. Did his/her head injury cause any controversy?

   f. Was he/she able to overcome the injury to play again?

3. **Response.** After completing the research, students will write an extended constructed response to the following question: After sustaining head injuries, players often continue to play, going so far as to hide the severity of their injuries from their coaches and teammates. How do you think the person you chose to research would respond to a player who ignored medical advice and continued to play with a concussion? What would this person say about the benefits, dangers, or criticism other players may receive? Offer <u>specific</u> examples from the articles and your research to support your answer.

4. **Assessment.** Work will be assessed using the rubric that follows.

RUBRIC

Points	Requirements
31–40	The response correctly answers the question in the context of the person the student chose. The student's answer is correct, complete, and addresses all aspects of the prompt. The response uses information from well-documented research for support. Any additional information provided by the student is related to the assigned task and acts as a support for his/her response.
21–30	The response correctly answers the question in the context of the person the student chose. The student's answer is correct and addresses most aspects of the assigned task. The student provides detail and support, but it is not complete or from well-documented research.
11–20	The response correctly answers the question in the context of the person the student chose. The student's answer is correct; however, it is generalized and not specific enough. The student is missing specific details and support research that would prove his/her full understanding of the assigned task.
1–10	The response shows very little understanding of what is being asked in the assigned task and does not answer the question in the context of the person the student chose. The answer is incomplete, has many things wrong with it, or addresses very little of the question.
0	The answer is completely incorrect, has nothing to do with the assigned task, or no answer is provided.

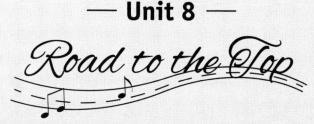

READING INSTRUCTIONAL GUIDE FOR HIGH-INTEREST ARTICLE

BEFORE READING

Looking at the Words

Determining How the Word Sounds (Phonics)

Using the Syllable Guide and the Reading Instructional Guide Template found in the beginning of the book, read the steps to learn how to break a word into manageable parts.

Determining What the Word Means (Vocabulary)

Words to Study	Breaking into Syllables	Short Definition
confounded	con-found-ed	(adj.) completely confused
covet	cov-et	(v.) to wish for
diligent	dil-i-gent	(adj.) hardworking
minority	mi-nor-i-ty	(n.) a group outside the majority
overshadow	o-ver-shad-ow	(v.) to be more important than something else
prolific	pro-lif-ic	(adj.) productive
reportedly	re-port-ed-ly	(adv.) according to rumor

Activating Background Knowledge

Anticipation Guide

Mark each of the following statements True or False:

1. _____ Taylor Swift plays only country music.

2. _____ Taylor Swift writes many of her country songs.

3. _____ *Fearless* was the name of Swift's first hit single.

4. _____ Taylor Swift won the 2009 CMA Award for Entertainer of the Year.

5. _____ Darius Rucker won the 2009 Dove Award for New Artist of the Year.

Starter Questions

After completing the Anticipation Guide, participate in a group or class discussion using the following questions:

1. What uncomfortable moment did Taylor Swift experience on live television in 2009?

2. What is the inspiration behind Taylor Swift's music?

3. What awards has Taylor Swift received?

4. What musical instrument is Swift most comfortable with?

5. Who is Darius Rucker?

Make a prediction about what you think the article will be about.

DURING READING

- Skim the article for 45–60 seconds. Circle any words you don't know.

- When you are finished, decode and determine the meaning of unknown words.

- Skim the questions for 30–45 seconds.

- Predict what the article is about.

- Read the article.

- Reread to clarify as needed.

- Answer the questions.

AFTER READING

Discussion Starter Questions

1. If Taylor Swift were to write a song about meeting you, what would the song be about?

2. How are Darius Rucker and Taylor Swift similar?

3. How do you think country music stars differ from pop music stars?

4. Do you think Taylor Swift is a role model? Why or why not?

5. What advice would you give Taylor Swift about avoiding the pitfalls that some other young stars have experienced?

It was the interruption heard around the entertainment world. At the 2009 Video Music Awards, Taylor Swift was poised to accept her first VMA trophy for Best Female Video. As she began her acceptance speech, Kanye West stormed the stage. West took the microphone from Swift and said, "Yo Taylor, I'm really happy for you, I'll let you finish, but Beyoncé has one of the best videos of all time. One of the best videos of all time!" And as quickly as he came on stage, West was gone. He left a silent audience, an embarrassed Beyoncé, and a confounded Swift.

Although Taylor was reportedly seen crying backstage afterwards, how she behaved later revealed her character. She was able to recover and perform almost immediately following West's outburst. Character seems to be something that Swift takes pretty seriously. She appears to be a diligent young woman who sticks to what she believes in. She's become a superstar who sells out concerts in two minutes flat, produces hit after hit, and has seen more success at 19 years old than most do in a lifetime.

Taylor had early ambitions for a career in the music industry. At just 11 years old she took a trip from her hometown in Pennsylvania to Nashville, known as the capital of country music. She hoped to get a record deal by making a demo tape of karaoke songs. She took it to every record label in town. She was rejected by them all, but that didn't stop her.

Road To The Top

Taylor learned three guitar chords from a computer repairman. From that she wrote her first song, "Lucky You." By the time she was 12, she could play a twelve-string guitar and was a prolific songwriter. Writing songs gave her a way to deal with all of the things she was going through, like not fitting in at school. As she has grown older, her songs have reflected those experiences. She recounts how kids used to tease her as she set up her karaoke equipment at town festivals. This made her take her music career even more seriously. "The only thing I can do is look back and thank [them]. If I hadn't been so driven to music because I didn't have anyone to hang out with, if I hadn't written songs because I didn't have anyone to talk to, I wouldn't be sitting here right now." Writing also set her apart from the crowd. Not only was she a girl with a great voice, but she also told her unique story. It was the beginning of her career in country music.

Taylor Swift admits that she couldn't have made it as far as she has today without the support of her family. Proving their belief in her abilities, Taylor's family moved with her to a suburb of

Nashville when she was 14 years old. Their gamble paid off. She was recruited by multiple record companies, ultimately signing with Big Machine Records, and became the youngest staff songwriter ever employed by Sony.

By the time she released her first album in October 2006, she was already well known among country music listeners because of her debut single, "Tim McGraw." She has matched and broken countless album and digital music milestones, including the best online debut for any country album ever with her newest album, *Fearless*.

Although such overwhelming success has led many teen stars down a dark path, Taylor insists that she's different. She values her fans, especially the young ones. She doesn't want to do anything to let them down. As she puts it, "When you lose someone's trust, it's lost, and there are a lot of people out there who are counting on me right now." Swift doesn't need controversy to make her a star. She was the top-selling recording artist of 2008 and is number 69 on the *Forbes* list of most powerful celebrities. She was nominated for more American Music Awards than any other artist and was the youngest-ever nominee and winner of the coveted Entertainer of the Year award at the 2009 CMAs. She won four Grammy Awards in 2010. Even with her squeaky clean reputation, and maybe even because of it, Taylor Swift is about as big of a star as there can be.

And as for her embarrassment at the VMAs? She's handling it with grace and a bit of humor. In accepting one of her four 2009 CMA awards, she joked, "I want to thank every single person in this room tonight for not running up on this stage." Based on her long list of awards and the incredible support she has received since the incident with Kanye, it is unlikely that anyone will overshadow Taylor Swift in the near future.

Darius Rucker: Pursuing a Dream

Darius Rucker was part of the 1990s pop sensation band Hootie & the Blowfish, but he dreamed of being a solo artist as well. He made the unlikely transition to country music. His first single, "Don't Think I Don't Think About It," was the first country chart-topping song by an African-American artist since Charley Pride in 1983. In 2009 Rucker became the first African American to ever win the Best New Artist CMA. Rucker believes that despite being a minority in the world of country music, his success has come from the fact that people identify with his songs. He shows a deep appreciation for the acceptance from fans and country radio. Rucker is well on his way to breaking racial barriers and being an example of pursuing one's dream, no matter the obstacles.

READING COMPREHENSION

After reading "Taylor Swift: Road to the Top," choose the options that best answer questions 1–14.

1. Read this sentence.

   At the 2009 Video Music Awards, Taylor Swift was poised to accept her first VMA trophy for Best Female Video.

   What is the meaning of the word *poised* as it is used in this sentence?
   A. set
   B. fearful
   C. nervous
   D. hesitant

2. Read this sentence.

   Taylor had early ambitions for a career in the music industry

   What is the meaning of the word *ambitions* as it is used in this sentence?
   F. ideas
   G. doubts
   H. laziness
   I. desired goals

3. From this article, the reader can tell that
   A. Songwriting serves as a stress reliever for Swift.
   B. Beyoncé must have been jealous of Swift's success.
   C. Taylor Swift does not like to perform in front of others.
   D. Life on the road has limited Swift's ability to write chart-topping songs.

4. Which of the following is an example of an obstacle that Taylor Swift turned into an opportunity?
   F. After meeting Kanye West, Swift decided to perform a duet with him.
   G. Hiding behind her shyness, writing songs encouraged Swift to make new friends.
   H. After having social difficulties, Swift wrote songs as a way to deal with the issues.
   I. Swift is now motivated to write country songs for many of the recording studios that rejected her.

5. In the author's opinion,
   A. Swift has shown more character than other celebrities.
   B. Taylor Swift has the best-selling country album of all time.
   C. Country music is more suitable for Swift's songs than pop music.
   D. Swift should not have pursued her dream of music at such a young age.

6. The author organizes the article by
   F. portraying the major events in Swift's music life.
   G. comparing the country music artists over the years.
   H. describing the process Taylor Swift undergoes when writing a song.
   I. listing the reasons why Taylor Swift deserved to win Artist of the Year.

7. Why does the author mention Darius Rucker?
    A. to encourage the reader to purchase his album
    B. to prove that male artists have a difficult time with country music
    C. to introduce the reader to another country music artist who is following a dream
    D. to compare and contrast the various awards that Taylor Swift and Darius Rucker have received

8. Which title BEST fits the article?
    F. Charting Music
    G. Soaring into Stardom
    H. A Little Bit of Country
    I. Overcoming the Burdens of Stardom

9. Taylor Swift credits her success to
    A. her agent.
    B. her formal education.
    C. her popularity at school.
    D. the devotion and support of her family.

10. Making friends used to be difficult for Taylor Swift because
    F. she didn't fit in with the crowd.
    G. many of her friends were jealous of her talents.
    H. her busy schedule never allowed her to spend time with friends.
    I. her career forced her to move frequently and made it impossible to meet new people.

11. Rucker is compared to Swift because
    A. both pursued their dreams.
    B. they are from the same hometown.
    C. Swift was a former backup singer for Hootie and the Blowfish.
    D. Rucker helped Swift write the majority of her chart-topping hits.

12. Which fact from the article provides the BEST evidence that Taylor Swift's success is extraordinary?
    F. She could play a 12-string guitar at age 12.
    G. Her debut single, "Tim McGraw," was a huge success.
    H. Her family moved with her to Nashville when she was 14.
    I. She was the youngest-ever winner of the CMA Entertainer of the Year award.

13. People who read this article will learn
    A. about Swift's rise to success.
    B. a detailed history of country music.
    C. why Nashville is such a popular city to live in.
    D. the pros and cons of being a best-selling artist like Swift.

14. Based on the information provided about Swift throughout the article, which of these conclusions is accurate?
    F. Swift will soon take a break from country music.
    G. Writing songs will likely continue to be a passion for Swift.
    H. Swift's family will return to Pennsylvania and begin a new life.
    I. Swift will dedicate her next album to all of those who did not believe in her.

READING STRATEGY

Directions: Taylor Swift's rise to the top of country music depended on a series of events. Determine the major events that contributed to her successful music career and then write the events between the guitar frets, arranging them in chronological order. (One event is completed for you.) Finally, write a summary of the main idea of the article as it relates to her rise to successful recording artist.

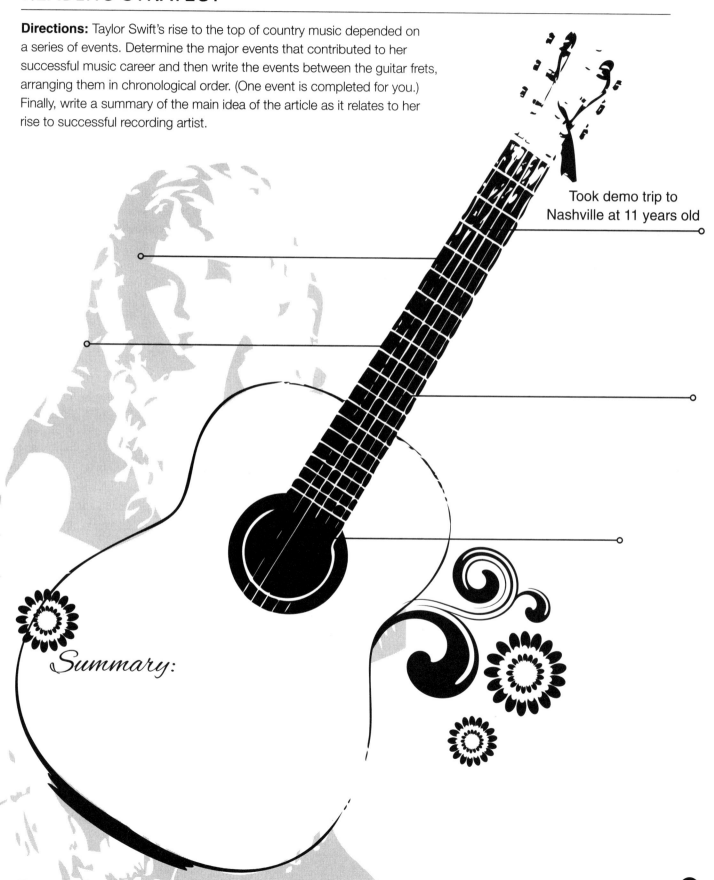

Took demo trip to Nashville at 11 years old

Summary:

INTERPRETING THE DATA

PART I

Taylor Swift's Billboard Success

Virtually unknown in 2005, Taylor Swift had a quick and successful rise on the Billboard charts between 2006 and 2009.

Table 1. Taylor Swift's top singles

Year	Single	Peak single spot by chart	
		Hot Country Songs	Billboard Hot 100
2006	Tim McGraw	6	40
2007	Teardrops on My Guitar	2	13
2007	Our Song	1	16
2007	Last Christmas	28	—
2007	Christmases When You Were Mine	48	—
2007	Santa Baby	43	—
2007	Silent Night	54	—
2007	White Christmas	59	—
2008	Picture to Burn	3	28
2008	Should've Said No	1	33
2008	Love Story	1	4
2008	White Horse	2	13
2008	Change	57	10
2008	You're Not Sorry	—	11
2008	Forever & Always	—	34
2008	The Way I Loved You	—	72
2008	Hey Stephen	—	94
2008	The Best Day	56	103
2009	You Belong With Me	1	2
2009	Fifteen	7	23
2009	Crazier	—	17
2009	Jump Then Fall	59	10
2009	Untouchable	—	19
2009	Come In With the Rain	—	30
2009	Superstar	—	26
2009	The Other Side of the Door	—	22
2010	Today Was a Fairytale	52	2

15. In what year did Taylor Swift earn her first #1 single, and for what song?

_____

16. What are the highest-ranking singles she has ever had on the Billboard Hot 100? (Hint: there are two.)

_____

17. Based on the previous information, which year do you think has been Taylor Swift's most successful so far? Use specific examples from Table 1 to support your answer.

ANALYZE EVALUATE EXPLAIN

_____

_____

_____

_____

_____

_____

_____

18. What is the difference in the way Taylor Swift's singles have charted on the two different charts? Make a prediction about how her songs might chart in the future. Be specific and support your answer with details from Table 1.

ANALYZE EVALUATE EXPLAIN

_____

_____

_____

_____

_____

_____

_____

PART II

Charting Singles in a Digital Age

For decades, the Billboard charts have been a reflection of the music that the American public is listening to. With the relatively recent emergence of digital media as a major source of the music being purchased, Billboard has had to come up with creative ways to keep up with the ever-changing music world in order to accurately rank the most popular music.

Table 2. Taylor Swift's singles in the Billboard Hot 100 the week of November 5, 2009

Song	Place on the Billboard Hot 100
Jump Then Fall*	#10
You Belong With Me	#14
Untouchable*	#19
The Other Side of the Door*	#23
Superstar*	#26
Come In With the Rain*	#30
Forever & Always	#34
Fifteen	#46
Two Is Better Than One (by Boys Like Girls, featuring Swift)	#79

*digital singles that were new songs on the re-release of her 2008 album, *Fearless*, and were simultaneously released the week of November 5, 2009

19. What percentage of the singles in the Billboard Hot 100, as listed in Table 2, were in the top 20?

_____

20. What percentage of the singles in Table 2 were released the week of November 5, 2009?

_____

21. Taylor Swift's 9 listings on the Hot 100 give her the record for the most charted singles in one week by any female artist in history. All-male rock group The Beatles hold the current record (set in 1964) for the most charted singles in the same week, with 14 radio singles, none of which were released at the same time as another. What are some of the similarities and differences between the two records?

ANALYZE EVALUATE EXPLAIN

22. Some critics believe that the ability to release digital singles simultaneously is an unfair way for artists to "stack the charts" in their favor and break records. Using the previous Taylor Swift/Beatles example, state whether you agree or disagree with this viewpoint.

ANALYZE EVALUATE EXPLAIN

REFLECT AND RESPOND

23. Do you believe that digital media has overall been a positive or negative force when it comes to today's rising music stars and the music industry as a whole? Use specific examples from the high-interest article and the data in this section to support your opinion.

READING INSTRUCTIONAL GUIDE FOR TECHNICAL EXTENSION

BEFORE READING

Looking at the Words

Determining What the Word Means (Vocabulary)

Words to Study	Breaking into Syllables	Short Definition
abstract	ab-stract	(adj.) related to theory; complex
aspire	as-pire	(v.) to aim or seek
attentive	at-ten-tive	(adj.) alert
concentration	con-cen-tra-tion	(n.) the act of focusing attention on one thing or idea
induce	in-duce	(v.) to bring about or cause
trigger	trig-ger	(v.) to start something

Activating Background Knowledge

Graphic Organizer

Either individually or in groups, brainstorm about multiple intelligences, recalling anything previously learned and any prior experience with the subject. Next, complete the idea wheel by listing examples in each section of the wheel to demonstrate what you already know about the different ways people can learn.

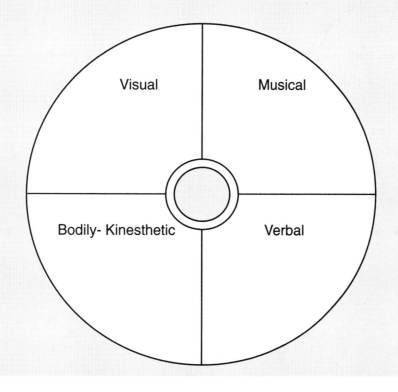

Starter Questions

After completing the Graphic Organizer, participate in a group or class discussion to come up with questions about the subject, a prediction about the article, and at least one learning goal. The first question has been provided for you.

Question: How is music currently incorporated into your learning environment?

Question: _____

Prediction: _____

Goal: _____

DURING READING

- Skim the article for 45–60 seconds. Circle any words you don't know.

- When you are finished, decode and determine the meaning of unknown words.

- Skim the questions for 30–45 seconds.

- Predict what the article is about.

- Read the article.

- Reread to clarify as needed.

- Answer the questions.

AFTER READING

After reading, you may do the following:

- Review, paraphrase, and summarize

- Participate in main-idea discussions by describing the information in their own words

- Reflect on concept maps and generate additional discussion starter questions based on the mappings

- Participate in small-group discussions using discussion starter questions

Discussion Starter Questions

The first question has been provided for you.

1. After looking at the list of multiple intelligences, which one best describes your area of strength? Why?

2. _____

3. _____

TECHNICAL EXTENSION

Can My Music Make Me Smarter?

"Music can change the world because it can change people." –Bono, U2

Taylor Swift has said that her music reflects her experiences growing up as an outsider. Lady Gaga recently told an interviewer, "Every bit of me is devoted to love and art, and I aspire to be a teacher to my young fans who feel like I did at their age: like a freak." These two very different performers seem to agree on one thing: music "opens the heart, soul and mind of individuals, and is the most powerful way to express yourself."

And science seems to agree, too. American psychologist Howard Gardner presented his theory of multiple intelligences in a 1983 book called *Frames of Mind.* His theory outlines the different ways people learn new things. For example, people like Swift and Lady Gaga most likely have sensitivity to rhythm, melody, and sound. They also may notice sounds in the world that others don't notice. They probably learn new information easily if is sung or tapped out in rhythm. People with musical intelligence also have the ability to memorize songs quickly, and they can tell when a note if off-key. They often have a song in their heads, and they have a passion for many kinds of music.

Gardner says that the different categories of learning fit together in unique ways for each of us. By understanding how we learn, we can improve in the other categories when necessary. We can also focus as much as possible on our areas of strength. Teachers can use this information by teaching in ways that each of their students understands best.

Aside from Howard Gardner, many other people believe that music has effects on the human brain that cannot be ignored. Some studies have shown that listening to certain musical notes produces serotonin, a chemical neurotransmitter. This chemical lessens the effects of depression. There are even studies indicating that flat musical notes induce sleep, while natural notes make us more alert.

Another study shows actual changes in the brain from exposure to music and the arts. Brain cell connections are created along active cell transmitters, which helps us learn and apply information. All of this is good news for learning in all subjects, not just music.

Have you ever told someone that you have to listen to music when you study or do homework? You might be right! Music can improve concentration as well as memory. A study showed that the silence between two musical notes actually triggers the brain cells that improve memory. It also showed that the music from some types of musical instruments and strong beats make us more attentive as we learn.

This type of information has led to the support of the arts in schools. A study done with 3-year-olds in the 1990s showed that music lessons improved their ability to put puzzles together. This is the same abstract reasoning ability that engineers, chess players, and mathematicians use in their tasks. Other programs have been developed that teach basic fractions and multiplications using rhythm.

Students also showed an increase in self-confidence and a better attitude toward math in general, a subject many find difficult. This then flows over into other tasks that students must perform during the school day. Mary Jane Collett, Director of the Office of Arts and Cultural Education in the New York public schools, speaks out for arts in the curriculum. She states that "learning through all the senses expands the learning process to accommodate different learning styles." Supporters of the arts in schools argue that subjects like band, chorus, and art are essential parts of any young person's education.

The way we learn new information is the way we learn to express ourselves, too. This takes us back to Taylor Swift and Lady Gaga. Both felt like they were outsiders

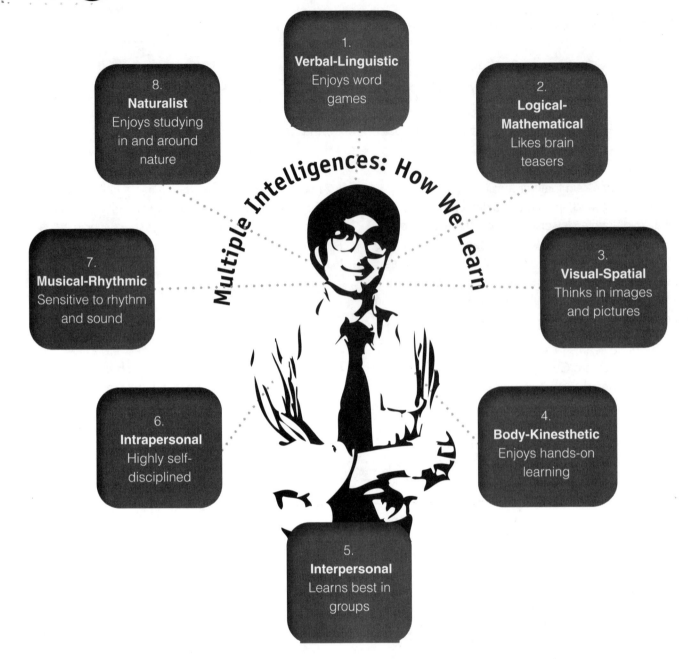

Multiple Intelligences: How We Learn

1.
Verbal-Linguistic
Enjoys word games

2.
Logical-Mathematical
Likes brain teasers

3.
Visual-Spatial
Thinks in images and pictures

4.
Body-Kinesthetic
Enjoys hands-on learning

5.
Interpersonal
Learns best in groups

6.
Intrapersonal
Highly self-disciplined

7.
Musical-Rhythmic
Sensitive to rhythm and sound

8.
Naturalist
Enjoys studying in and around nature

as they grew up. They turned to music to communicate with others. However, there are many young people who struggle to be understood, and many never find a way that allows them to express themselves. The results are things like low academic achievement and boredom with school, lack of positive conflict resolution skills, poor peer and adult relationships, and a lack of self-esteem and self-respect.

Music can improve our ability to learn by changing our brains. It is also an important learning tool and can provide a path toward communication and understanding. As Swift put it in her song entitled "A Place in This World,"

I don't know what I want, so don't ask me
Cause I'm still trying to figure it out
Don't know what's down this road, I'm just walking
Trying to see through the rain coming down
Even though I'm not the only one
Who feels the way I do.

READING COMPREHENSION

After reading "Can My Music Make Me Smarter?" answer questions 1–12.

1. Which of these words best describes Lady Gaga's attitude about her role with her fans?
   A. annoying
   B. disturbing
   C. distressing
   D. comforting

2. As stated in the article, Mary Jane Collett *advocates* for arts in schools in New York. This means that
   F. she thinks the arts should be taught outside of school.
   G. she supports keeping the arts in schools' coursework.
   H. the arts are not included in the budget for schools in New York.
   I. she believes that, although important, the arts should be cut when budgets are tight.

3. From the article, we can tell that
   A. brain function is not affected by musical training.
   B. musical intelligence comes only from music lessons.
   C. various academic subjects can use music as a learning tool.
   D. brain studies show musical training is important primarily at early ages.

4. How could teachers use knowledge of multiple intelligences *most effectively* in their classrooms?
   F. They could require every student to learn in each intelligence.
   G. They could present each lesson in a variety of ways to reach more students.
   H. They could grade all assignments using information about one intelligence category at a time.
   I. They could require their students to learn about multiple intelligences at the beginning of each year.

5. What writing strategy does the author use to create interest in the topic of multiple intelligences?
   A. by starting and ending with facts about current recording artists
   B. discussing the personal backgrounds of two current recording artists
   C. using a great deal of research data on the topic of multiple intelligences
   D. comparing and contrasting the musical backgrounds of Taylor Swift and Lady Gaga

6. If this article were a newspaper column, what would be the BEST headline to get people to read about the effects of music on learning?
   F. Lady Gaga and Taylor Swift
   G. Examining Multiple Intelligences
   H. Which Intelligence Do YOU Use?
   I. Keeping Music in Our Schools Can Help Students Achieve

7. According to the information in the article, learning through the arts is important because
   A. students' senses are used to connect with their learning strengths.
   B. all students are especially sensitive to some degree to rhythm, melody, and sound.
   C. all students need to be exposed to great artists as part of their education.
   D. college and university admission requirements include a certain number of arts courses.

8. The song quote at the end of the article supports Lady Gaga's quote in the first paragraph because
    F.   the song shows a search for the meaning of life.
    G.   Lady Gaga shocks many of her fans on purpose.
    H.   both refer to young people who need connections with others like them.
    I.   Swift also wants to be a teacher to her fans who need help with communication.

9. Bono's quote is included at the beginning of the article because
    A.   it shows us how we can use music to change how we study.
    B.   Bono has done a lot of charity work that has changed the world.
    C.   knowledge about multiple intelligences allows people to see how they learn.
    D.   the research presented in the article shows many ways that music changes people.

10. The information in the text box supports the idea in the article that
    F.   group activities must be used in all classrooms.
    G.   brain changes occur through the use of music in education.
    H.   teachers can help more students succeed by using a variety of methods.
    I.   people like Taylor Swift and Lady Gaga were not able to learn through traditional methods.

11. Which of the following statements BEST matches how Taylor Swift and Lady Gaga might react to these lines from Christelle Duvenage's poem "Nothing Girl"?

    Maybe you look at me and think: Gee, what a nothing girl.

    A.   They would understand the poet's feelings of being disconnected.
    B.   They would think that Duvenage might not be able to understand their music.
    C.   Both Swift and Lady Gaga would reject the poet's belief that she was "nothing."
    D.   Neither artist would be able to identify with Duvenage's work as presented in this poem.

12. How does music affect our learning? Use information from both the article and your personal experience.

    _____
    _____
    _____
    _____
    _____
    _____
    _____
    _____
    _____

TECHNICAL WRITING PROMPT

13. Refer to the illustration in the technical extension. Using the chart titled "Multiple Intelligences: How We Learn," make a list of eight jobs that might be performed well based on each of the eight intelligences. For example, a person with verbal-linguistic intelligence might be a good speech writer. After each example in the list, clearly and concisely explain your reasoning.

Technical Writing

VOCATIONAL EXTENSION

Teachers have the responsibility and satisfaction of preparing young people for their future, and music teachers know they are passing on their love of their craft as well. As Jean Paul Richter puts it, "Music is the poetry of the air." Music teachers translate that poetry for hundreds of students every year.

HELP WANTED:

Music teacher wanted for local high school. Responsibilities include basic instruction in music theory and history, as well as serving as chorus director. Bachelor's degree and state certification required. Applicants must also play at least one instrument and should enjoy working with young people.

There are many opportunities available for teaching music. Public and private schools offer the most teaching positions. Teachers in an elementary school or day care center offer instruction in singing, listening, and movement, as well as in learning music patterns. Children can learn things like keeping a beat and identifying a melody. They might be introduced to simple instruments, like bongos, maracas, tambourines, recorders, flutes, and xylophones.

In middle and high school, music educators might also teach and lead band or chorus. Large schools often have small ensemble groups and musical theater classes. Music instruction at this level adds music theory and music history to the basic lessons taught in elementary school. Elementary and secondary teachers must have a bachelor's degree along with state certification. Usually music teachers need to play at least one instrument. The national average salary for teachers at these levels is approximately $46,000 per year.

College music professors must have at least a master's degree, although most have a doctorate. A professor might teach music theory, music history and literature, performance, electronic music, composition, conducting, or music therapy. The national average for college music teachers is between $25,000 and $70,000 per year.

If you are interested in a career in music but the classroom doesn't appeal to you, there are other ways to pass on your love of music. You may offer private lessons in your home or travel to your students' homes. Those who teach privately have the freedom to set their own schedules.

Music therapy is also an exciting field. Music therapists reach their clients, both children and adults, through a combination of therapy and music. They first evaluate the emotional and physical needs of the client and then design music sessions to meet those needs. They use improvisation, listening, songwriting, discussing lyrics, and performing. People with Alzheimer's disease, substance abuse problems, brain injuries, physical disabilities, or pain can benefit from music therapy.

Music therapists work in a wide range of places, such as hospitals, rehab centers, clinics, mental health centers, senior centers, nursing homes, and prisons. Those who want to practice this type of therapy must complete a college-approved music therapy program and an internship. The average salary for an experienced music therapist is $70,000 per year. Music gives us a unique way to express ourselves and can add rich background to our lives. Like all educators, music teachers must be patient, understanding, and knowledgeable in their subject. They must be able to communicate their lessons well and relate to a diverse population of students at different ability levels. They must be masters at organization and management. Most of all, they must genuinely like young people and want them to succeed!

Are you ready to make music?

LOOKING FORWARD

14. Music is normally offered through public schools as either a resource class at the elementary level or an elective at the secondary level. Unfortunately, due to budget cuts, some school districts are considering removing music from the school system. Imagine that you are employed as a music teacher in one of these districts. Using your personal experience and information from the article, write a letter to persuade your local school board to keep music alive in the classroom.

Looking Forward

ETHICAL DILEMMA

15. Your music teacher has finally been able to arrange a private audition with a well-known musician during your next lesson. At your last session, your teacher discussed the level of practice that would be necessary to prepare for this audition; however, you went on a vacation and were not able to practice. You still feel confident that you will perform adequately, but probably not to the level your teacher expects. Do you proceed with the audition date or ask your teacher to try to reschedule? Are there any other options?

Ethical Dilemma

UNIT VOCABULARY ASSESSMENT

Matching

Match each word in Column I to its definition in Column II.

Column I

_____ 1. overshadow
_____ 2. diligent
_____ 3. trigger
_____ 4. covet
_____ 5. concentration

Column II

A.   to start something
B.   to be more important than something else
C.   focusing attention on one thing or idea
D.   to wish for
E.   hardworking

Multiple Choice

Choose the word that MOST NEARLY replaces the underlined word in each sentence.

6. Many young people <u>aspire</u> for the lifestyle they see celebrities living on television.
    A.   aim
    B.   plan
    C.   fear
    D.   work

7. Thanks to a <u>prolific</u> writing session in the mountains, the author was finally able to complete her book.
    A.   difficult
    B.   profound
    C.   productive
    D.   disappointing

8. Fearing that the decision might <u>induce</u> anger in the community, the mayor decided to delay the ruling.
    A.   cause
    B.   prevent
    C.   increase
    D.   encourage

9. One way to be successful is to be very <u>attentive</u> to detail.
    A.   alert
    B.   remiss
    C.   certain
    D.   confused

Word Bank

abstract

confounded

minority

reportedly

Fill in the Blank

Choose a word from the word bank to fill in the blank in the sentence below.

10. My preference for more homework puts me in the _____.

11. The _____ student was baffled by many of the challenging math problems.

12. Solving word puzzles is an excellent way to improve _____ thinking.

13. The celebrity was _____ in trouble with the law for drug use.

AUTHENTIC ASSESSMENT

Students will create song lyrics based on the unit "Road to the Top."

Instructions for Song Lyrics

1. **Planning.** Students may work in self-chosen or teacher-designed groups of two to four. Writing song lyrics is one way to express an emotion or make a point. Groups should first discuss a topic for the song, recording their brainstorming session on paper. Guidelines set by the teacher may include the following:

   a. a topic that is relevant to the students' everyday lives

   b. a topic that is appropriate to the classroom

   c. a topic that makes a social commentary

2. **Progress monitoring.** In order to track the progress of group participation and cooperation, each group will turn in a planning record that monitors group progress. The following questions should be answered:

   a. What is the basis of your song? What are you trying to explain, teach, etc.?

   b. From whose point of view is the song written?

   c. Will the song be upbeat or somber?

   d. How many verses does the song have?

   e. Who came up with the title of the song?

   f. What was the extent of participation of each group member in writing the song?

3. **Product.** Each group should complete song lyrics based on the specifications given by the teacher. Once the song is written, it should be approved by the teacher. A tune may be assigned and the song performed according to the teacher's instructions.

4. **Assessment.** Planning and cooperative behaviors are major factors in the success of this project. Work will be assessed using the rubric that follows.

COOPERATIVE LEARNING RUBRIC

Instructions: Assess yourself in each of the areas below by circling the number that best reflects your participation in the cooperative learning assignment. On the lines below, list the specific ways you participated in each area.

1. You were active in determining the topic/subject of your song.

   3- a lot   2- some   1- very little   0- not at all

   Specific contributions: _____

   _____

2. You participated in the brainstorming for your lyrics.

   3- a lot   2- some   1- very little   0- not at all

   Specific contributions: _____

   _____

3. Your song holds relevance and meaning for your life.

   3- a lot   2- some   1- very little   0- not at all

   Specific contributions: _____

   _____

4. You contributed specific content for the lyrics.

   3- a lot   2- some   1- very little   0- not at all

   Specific contributions: _____

   _____

5. You worked collaboratively and successfully with your group.

   3- a lot   2- some   1- very little   0- not at all

   Specific contributions: _____

   _____

— Unit 9 —
2ndChances

READING INSTRUCTIONAL GUIDE FOR HIGH-INTEREST ARTICLE

BEFORE READING

Looking at the Words

Determining How the Word Sounds (Phonics)

Using the Syllable Guide and the Reading Instructional Guide Template found in the beginning of the book, read the steps to learn how to break a word into manageable parts.

Determining What the Word Means (Vocabulary)

Words to Study	Breaking into Syllables	Short Definition
bankruptcy	bank-rupt-cy	(n.) the state of being unable to pay debts
endorsement	en-dorse-ment	(n.) the act of supporting a product
redeem	re-deem	(v.) to make up for (a fault)
reinstatement	re-in-state-ment	(n.) the act of putting back in a previous position
remorse	re-morse	(n.) deep and painful regret
skeptical	skep-ti-cal	(adj.) having doubt; questioning
testament	tes-ta-ment	(n.) something that serves as proof
unattainable	un-at-tain-a-ble	(adj.) impossible to reach

Activating Background Knowledge

Anticipation Guide

Mark each of the following statements True or False:

1. ____ Michael Vick is a famous NFL quarterback.

2. ____ Tony Dungy is Vick's former head coach.

3. ____ Michael Vick is currently playing for the Atlanta Falcons.

4. ____ Robert Downey Jr. starred in *Iron Man*.

5. ____ Michael Vick served time in prison.

Starter Questions

After completing the Anticipation Guide, participate in a group or class discussion using the following questions:

1. What crime did Michael Vick commit in 2007?

2. Who is Robert Downey Jr.?

3. How are Michael Vick and Robert Downey Jr. similar?

4. What is a halfway house?

5. How has Tony Dungy helped Michael Vick?

Make a prediction about what you think the article will be about.

DURING READING

- Skim the article for 45–60 seconds. Circle any words you don't know.
- When you are finished, decode and determine the meaning of unknown words.
- Skim the questions for 30–45 seconds.
- Predict what the article is about.
- Read the article.
- Reread to clarify as needed.
- Answer the questions.

AFTER READING

Discussion Starter Questions

1. Do you agree with Tony Dungy that Michael Vick deserves a second chance? Why or why not?

2. Do you think the Falcons were right to release Vick from his contract? Why or why not?

3. Should celebrities be held to a higher standard when it comes to committing crimes? Why or why not?

4. Should the public welcome back celebrities who have committed crimes?

5. How has Harold Jonas used his addiction to help other people?

2nd Chances

Quarterback Michael Vick was once the highest-paid player in football. When he was sent to prison for his connection to an illegal dogfighting ring, many critics stated that his NFL career was over. His life truly did seem to take a lasting turn for the worse. He lost his lucrative NFL salary as well as millions of dollars of endorsement money. To top it off, his financial advisors badly managed his money. He was left with almost nothing and filed for bankruptcy.

"I have said several times in recent weeks that I want Michael to be one of the NFL's success stories as an individual and as a football player… I know the Eagles will provide strong support but, ultimately, Michael's success is up to him and the decisions he makes." – Roger Goodell, NFL commissioner

Vick served almost two years. When he was released, he promised to be a new man, ready to work and be the role model he should have been before. He hoped to play professional football again, but the path would be long. Vick had to show true remorse in order for the NFL commissioner to consider his reinstatement. He would also have to find a team willing to take a chance on him. And then there was the question of proving himself to the fans, perhaps the hardest job of all.

When Vick was released, the NFL commissioner lifted his suspension. However, Atlanta Falcons owner Arthur Blank stated that he was not welcome to play for the Falcons again. The NFL assigned former Indianapolis Colts coach Tony Dungy to be Vick's mentor as part of his reinstatement. Dungy and Vick worked together in finding a good team fit for Vick, reportedly getting interest from several teams. They settled on Philadelphia. The City of Brotherly Love would be the place that gave Vick his second chance at football and the opportunity to redeem himself to NFL fans.

Vick signed a one-year, $1.6 million contract with the Philadelphia Eagles for the 2009 season, with an option for a second year. It brought the Eagles much expected negative press, including picketing and even some threats. There was also a surprising amount of support. The team asked fans to trust that they did their research and Vick had truly changed. Vick promised not only to prove himself as a good player and role model again, but also to do as much as he could to advance animal rights.

"I'm a believer that as long as people go through the right process, they deserve a second chance. He's got great people on his side; there isn't a finer person than Tony Dungy. He's proven he's on the right track." – Andy Reid, Eagles Coach

After both positive and negative reactions, Vick was able to settle into a supporting role on the Eagles' offense. He had been out of the game for a long time and had lost some of his conditioning. The fact that he's playing at all is a long way from where many expected him to be after 2007. His career isn't what it once was and probably isn't what he wishes it were. In fact,

"Our country is a country of second chances. I paid my debt to society. I spent two years in prison ... That was a humbling experience. I can't explain how deeply hurt and how sorry I was … I'm glad that Coach Reid and the rest of the organization stepped forward," Vick said. "I'm glad I got the opportunity and the second chance. I won't disappoint." –Michael Vick

he stated shortly after his prison release that he hoped to be an NFL starter. That has yet to happen. However, Vick's second chance has just begun and can be as great as he makes it. Just his playing in the NFL stands as a powerful testament to how a second chance can change a life.

While Vick's controversial story is popular, he's certainly not the first celebrity to benefit from a second (or third, or fourth) chance. Many famous celebrities have endured personal, social, and legal struggles. And many have overcome them to once again be accepted in the public eye.

Robert Downey Jr. gained success as a young actor in the 1980s, even winning a nomination for an Oscar in 1992. However, between 1996 and 2001 he was arrested many times on drug charges. Despite multiple tries at rehab, he couldn't stay sober and out of trouble. He even landed a role on the popular series *Ally McBeal* but was fired after two seasons when he was arrested twice. Downey was ordered again into a treatment program, but few had hopes that he could change. But he finally did and was accepted back into Hollywood with a few minor films. In 2007 he was cast in the leading role of *Iron Man*. The next year he earned a second Academy Award nomination for *Tropic Thunder*, showing that his comeback was for keeps.

Michael Vick and Robert Downey Jr. sank to their lowest, only to come out stronger and ready to make something better of their lives. Their comebacks may seem unattainable to those of us who aren't celebrities, but the world is full of everyday people who have overcome odds and made the most of their second chances.

Harold Jonas is an average person who is using his second chance to make a difference. He was addicted to drugs for most of his life. He tried for years to stop using but was never sober for long. His father asked him to try one more time, and this time he made it work. Jonas now runs a drug recovery assistance website called Sober.com and owns three halfway houses in Florida. He is using his knowledge to give back to his community.

Like Vick and Downey Jr., Jonas has been through the trenches, but he has turned his shortcomings into a way to help others. Only time will tell whether Vick and Downey Jr. will stay on the right side of the law and in public favor. But these stories, and the countless others like them, remind us all to take advantage of every opportunity that comes our way. We can benefit our own lives and the lives of those around us.

Michael Vick is hardly the first NFL player to find legal trouble. The largeness of his offense and his controversial reinstatement makes his case different. His situation will probably be referenced in cases of other professional athletes who find themselves in trouble and later want to return to their sport. How Vick conducts himself will likely have an impact on how players such as Plaxico Burress, currently in prison on weapons charges, work out their returns to the NFL. Likewise, Robert Downey Jr.'s sobriety and return to fame may impact how the public and the entertainment industry accept stars who have had trouble with the law, such as Britney Spears and Amy Winehouse.

READING COMPREHENSION

After reading "Second Chances," choose the options that best answer questions 1–14.

1. Read this sentence.
    Like Vick and Downey Jr., Jonas has been through the trenches, but he has turned his shortcomings into a way to help others.

    What is the meaning of the phrase "through the trenches" as it is used in this sentence?
    A. through ditches
    B. through openings
    C. through rainstorms
    D. through difficult times

2. Read this sentence.
    He lost his lucrative NFL salary as well as millions of dollars of endorsement money.

    What is the meaning of the word *lucrative* as it is used in this sentence?
    F. small
    G. profitable
    H. commercial
    I. unfortunate

3. From this article, the reader can infer that in the near future Vick will
    A. start dogfighting again.
    B. be closely watched by NFL fans.
    C. become the starting quarterback for the Eagles.
    D. go on to retire from the National Football League.

4. Which of the following is an example of how Harold Jonas turned an obstacle into a contribution?
    F. He learned from his drug addiction and now helps others overcome it.
    G. Due to the media attention he received, he is starring in a new movie about addiction.
    H. Jonas is mentoring Robert Downey Jr. to help him battle the lingering effects of addiction.
    I. Jonas gives some of his charitable proceeds to the local humane society in support of Vick.

5. In the author's opinion,
    A. we will always get second chances.
    B. the Falcons were right to release Vick from his contract.
    C. Vick should not have been given another shot in the NFL.
    D. we need to welcome any opportunities we receive in life.

6. The author organizes the article by
    F. listing Michael Vick's statistics in football.
    G. describing and then presenting key events in the life of Harold Jonas.
    H. comparing Robert Downey Jr.'s acting career with careers of other well-known actors.
    I. providing examples of people who have overcome obstacles to get a second chance in life.

7. Why does the author include quotes from people who have a connection to Michael Vick?
    A. to demonstrate how others are giving Vick a second chance
    B. to provide more information about the National Football League
    C. to introduce the reader to important people who coach in the NFL
    D. to prove that dogfighting is a serious offense that should not be taken lightly

8. Which title BEST fits the article?
    F. Football Fans
    G. Attacking Addiction
    H. Conquering Challenges
    I. The Lives of Today's Celebrities

9. Why was Michael Vick paired up with Tony Dungy?
    A. Vick needed a new coach.
    B. Dungy and Vick have similar backgrounds.
    C. Dungy was appointed to serve as Vick's mentor.
    D. Like Vick, Dungy was looking for a second chance in life.

10. What seemed to make Downey Jr. decide to change his life?
    F. a new contract
    G. the uproar of fans
    H. the influence of other celebrities
    I. numerous arrests and court-ordered treatment programs

11. What is true of both Downey Jr. and Vick?
    A. They are both professional athletes.
    B. Both had to overcome obstacles in the public eye.
    C. Tony Dungy mentored both of them and helped them overcome their challenges.
    D. Both Downey Jr. and Vick were offered starring roles in the blockbuster movie *Iron Man*.

12. Which person's quotation BEST supports the claim that Vick is trying to change his life?
    F. Andy Reid
    G. Tony Dungy
    H. Harold Jonas
    I. Roger Goodell

13. According to the text box,
    A. Vick was the first NFL player to be arrested.
    B. Britney Spears and Robert Downey Jr. are friends.
    C. Vick visits and mentors Plaxico Burress on a regular basis.
    D. Vick's and Downey Jr.'s actions can affect how the public views other celebrities.

14. In the fall of 2009, Michael Vick told students at his former middle school that they should avoid making bad decisions like he did.

    After reading the article about second chances, what does this new information suggest?
    F. Vick will most likely fail at his second chance.
    G. Vick hopes to get a better NFL deal for improved behavior.
    H. Vick appears to be using his second chance as a way to help others.
    I. Vick may be using his second chance to convince the school to offer a scholarship in his name.

READING STRATEGY

Directions: One of the major factors in Michael Vick's ability to make a comeback was the support team that surrounded him. Referring to the article, summarize Vick's quotation and the quotations of the three members of Vick's support team listed in the graphic organizer below. Then explain the role that each person played in his comeback. At the bottom of the page, write a summary of how others aided Vick in reestablishing himself.

Circle of Support

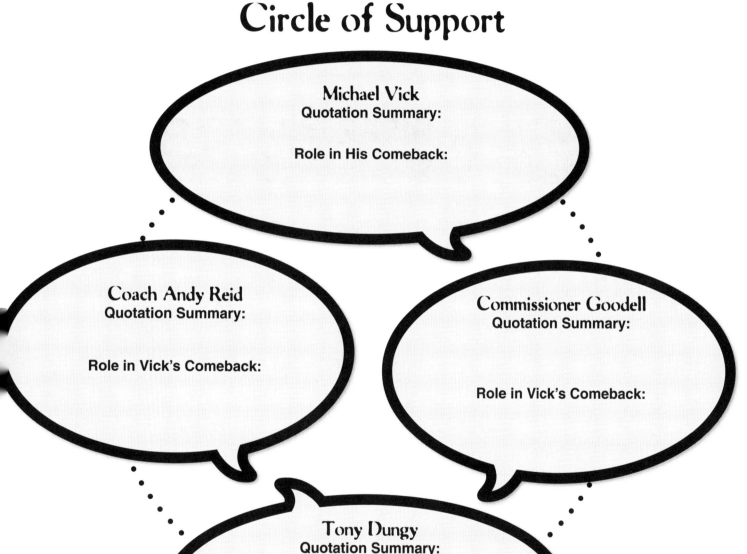

Michael Vick
Quotation Summary:

Role in His Comeback:

Coach Andy Reid
Quotation Summary:

Role in Vick's Comeback:

Commissioner Goodell
Quotation Summary:

Role in Vick's Comeback:

Tony Dungy
Quotation Summary:

Role in Vick's Comeback:

Summary:

INTERPRETING THE DATA

PART I

What is the state of Michael Vick's career?

Michael Vick returned to the NFL in 2009 as a backup quarterback on a team with a well-established starting quarterback. How did his 2009–2010 statistics compare to his statistics in the first part of his career?

Use the data given in Table 1 to determine the answers to questions 15–18 (yards per game). The first shaded box has been completed for you.

Table 1. Michael Vick's career statistics

Season	Games played	Pass attempts	Passing yards completed	Pass comple-tions	Yards per game	Passing TDs	Intercep-tions	Rusing yards completed	Rushing TDs	Fumbles
2001-2002	8	113	785	50	785 ÷ 8= 98.1	2	3	289	1	6
2002-2003	15	421	2,936	231	**15.**	16	8	777	8	9
2003-2004	5	100	585	50	**16.**	4	3	255	1	4
2004-2005	15	321	2,313	181	154.2	14	12	902	3	16
2005-2006	15	387	2,412	214	160.8	1	13	597	6	11
2006-2007	16	388	2,474	204	**17.**	20	13	1,039	2	9
2009-2010	12	13	86	6	**18.**	1	0	95	2	0

19. In which season did Vick pass:

    a) the most yards per game? _____

    b) the least yards per game? _____

20. What is Vick's career total for rushing yards?

    _____

21. Determine Vick's percentage of passing yards completed
    (pass completions/pass attempts) in the following seasons:

    a) 2001–2002: _____

    b) 2006–2007: _____

    c) 2009–2010: _____

22. With the exception of the 2003–2004 season when he
    was injured, during which season did Vick play the fewest
    games? How did that season compare to his first season
    back in the NFL (2009–2010) after his time in prison?

ANALYZE EVALUATE EXPLAIN

_____

_____

_____

_____

_____

_____

_____

_____

PART II

What do you predict for Vick's future quarterback rating?

Quarterback rating is a measure of the efficiency of the passing skills of a quarterback. It is based on percentage of completions per attempt, average yards gained per attempt, percentage of touchdown passes per attempt, and percentage of interceptions per attempt.

Table 2. Michael Vick's quarterback ratings

Season	Quarterback rating
2001–2002	62.7
2002–2003	81.6
2003–2004	69.0
2004–2005	78.1
2005–2006	73.1
2006–2007	75.7
2009–2010	93.8

23. In what season did Vick show the:

    a) lowest quarterback rating? _____

    b) highest quarterback rating? _____

24. With the exception of the 2003–2004 season (when Vick was injured) what do you notice about the trend of his quarterback ratings? What would you expect it to do in 2010-2011?

ANALYZE EVALUATE EXPLAIN

_____
_____
_____
_____
_____
_____
_____
_____

25. A quarterback rating tends to be higher when a player throws less. If Vick were to be a starter next year, would you expect his quarterback rating to be lower or higher? Base your answer on the information in this question as well as Vick's history of quarterback ratings.

ANALYZE
EVALUATE
EXPLAIN

26. On January 9, 2010, in a playoff game, Vick threw the longest completed touchdown pass of his career. It was a 76-yard pass. Vick says that he is ready to be a starter in the NFL. Based on this statement, and looking at his overall career statistics from Part I, would you give him a starting position if you were a coach?

ANALYZE
EVALUATE
EXPLAIN

REFLECT AND RESPOND

27. At the end of the 2009–2010 season, Vick received the Ed Block Courage Award. Players receiving this award are selected by teammates, and the award is given to players who "exemplify commitment to the principles of sportsmanship and courage." Based on what you know from the article and the statistics, would you have awarded Vick this honor?

Reflect
&
Respond

READING INSTRUCTIONAL GUIDE FOR TECHNICAL EXTENSION

BEFORE READING

Looking at the Words

Determining What the Word Means (Vocabulary)

Words to Study	Breaking into Syllables	Short Definition
chronological	chron-o-log-i-cal	(adj.) arranged in the order of time
dilemma	di-lem-ma	(n.) a difficult problem
mechanism	mech-an-ism	(n.) the process by which an effect is produced
mollusk	mol-lusk	(n.) an animal with no backbone that has a soft body often enclosed in a shell (e.g., clam, oyster)
neuroscientist	neu-ro-sci-en-tist	(n.) a scientist who studies the nervous system
precept	pre-cept	(n.) something regarded as true; principle
transitional	tran-si-tion-al	(adj.) moving from one stage to another

Activating Background Knowledge

Graphic Organizer

Either individually or in groups, brainstorm about teens' decision making, recalling anything previously learned and any prior experience with the subject. Next, complete the three-column chart to demonstrate what you already know about the dangerous or risky behavior of teens.

Types of peer pressure	Resulting behavior or decisions	Possible consequences

Starter Questions

After completing the Graphic Organizer, participate in a group or class discussion to come up with questions about the subject, a prediction about the article, and at least one learning goal. The first question has been provided for you.

Question: Why do you think teens often act in ways that involve risky or dangerous behavior?

Question: _____

Prediction: _____

Goal: _____

DURING READING

- Skim the article for 45–60 seconds. Circle any words you don't know.

- When you are finished, decode and determine the meaning of unknown words.

- Skim the questions for 30–45 seconds.

- Predict what the article is about.

- Read the article.

- Reread to clarify as needed.

- Answer the questions.

AFTER READING

After reading, you may do the following:

- Review, paraphrase, and summarize

- Participate in main-idea discussions by describing the information in their own words

- Reflect on concept maps and generate additional discussion starter questions based on the mappings

- Participate in small-group discussions using discussion starter questions

Discussion Starter Questions

The first question has been provided for you.

1. How have your personal experiences affected your development?

2. _____

3. _____

TECHNICAL EXTENSION

The Success Mechanism

"Everyone has a success mechanism and a failure mechanism. The failure mechanism goes off by itself. The success mechanism only goes off with a goal. Every time we write down and talk about a goal, we push the button to start the success mechanism."
- Charles Jones

Michael Vick, Robert Downey Jr., and Harold Jonas appear to have worked through their failures. They each activated the "success mechanism." However, where exactly is that mechanism, and can we turn ours on, too?

The answer may lie in the science of human development. This is the study of the physical, emotional, and psychological stages of our growth. Are the mistakes we make simply a result of poor judgment? Or are there physical changes at work, also? This question has interested scientists for hundreds of years.

There are several leaders in this field of study. Probably the most well known is Jean Piaget (1896-1980). Piaget was a biologist who went from studying mollusks to learning how human thought develops. He spent most of his career observing the changes in the thought processes of people at different ages. He then recorded what he saw. From his study, he then came up with four major stages of how people learn to reason and think.

Based on his studies, Piaget believed that humans entered the final phase of this type of development at about age 12. He thought that this is when we begin "adult type thinking." He did not seem to believe there was much growth after reaching that period.

However, some scientists who came after Piaget disagreed with some of his findings. Erik Erikson (1902-1994) was a German psychologist who observed eight stages of development during a human's life.

An important precept in Erikson's work is that our development is greatly affected by what he called natural "crises." He believed these crises happen to all of us at certain times in our lives. How we resolve these crises can change the rest of our lives in good and bad ways. It depends on how we deal with them. However, he also said that we learn important skills from dealing with these dilemmas. These skills can then help us become more successful from that point on in our lives.

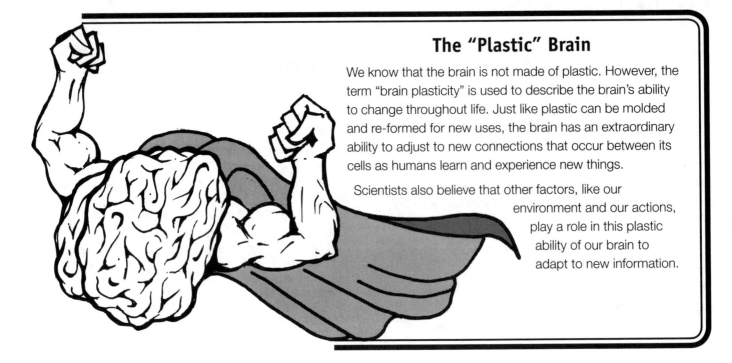

The "Plastic" Brain

We know that the brain is not made of plastic. However, the term "brain plasticity" is used to describe the brain's ability to change throughout life. Just like plastic can be molded and re-formed for new uses, the brain has an extraordinary ability to adjust to new connections that occur between its cells as humans learn and experience new things.

Scientists also believe that other factors, like our environment and our actions, play a role in this plastic ability of our brain to adapt to new information.

Another important scientist in this field is Daniel J. Levinson (1920-1994). Levinson was a psychologist who believed that our thinking is divided into five stages, or eras. These eras match up with a human's chronological age, beginning with birth and lasting until age 80 or older.

Levinson then grouped the five eras into two major periods. He called these periods *stable* and *transitional*, and felt that they occur over and over in our lives. Levinson believed that the *stable* periods are when we deal with important choices in life. The *transitional* periods fall between the end of one stable period and the beginning of the next.

So, what does this mean for us as we struggle with our own tough decisions? If Michael Vick can turn his life around, maybe the "success mechanism" exists for the rest of us, too.

Recent studies on the human brain seem to think it does. Scientists today think that we grow and mature far longer than Piaget believed. According to Fulton Crews, a neuroscientist at the University of North Carolina at

Chapel Hill, at around age 11 the brain experiences a major overhaul. Our social behavior changes in important ways. This begins a period in our lives when our brains are greatly affected by things like abuse, drug use, and other unhealthy influences.

New technologies like MRIs and PET scans have allowed better pictures of the human brain. These have shown that our brains continue to grow and develop into our mid-twenties. This is much longer than has been believed by earlier scientists. Experts believe this might explain why teens do not handle pressure from their peers very well. It also might explain why teens often act in ways that involve dangerous or risky behavior. Their brains simply are not able to engage in more mature thinking yet.

We can use this information to make very careful decisions as we grow and develop. It also proves that making poor choices and failing does not have to be the final judgment for our lives. Humans all experience the "failure mechanism," but we can also tap into the "success mechanism" to correct those mistakes.

READING COMPREHENSION

After reading "The Success Mechanism," answer questions 1–12.

1. Read this sentence.
   They each activated the "success mechanism."

   What does the word *activated* mean as used in this sentence?
   A. quit
   B. turned on
   C. completed
   D. discouraged

2. Read this sentence.
   How we resolve these crises affects the rest of our lives, both in positive and negative ways.

   What does the word *resolve* mean as it is used in this sentence?
   F. fix
   G. resist
   H. combine
   I. continue

3. What does the author suggest is the most important reason for teens to learn how humans think and learn?
   A. to understand that failure is not forever
   B. to interest young people in scientific theory
   C. to learn that scientific study is an ongoing process
   D. to introduce the newer technology that is now used in scientific study

4. Important new information on brain development has been possible because
   F. scientists are better trained today.
   G. there are more people studying this topic.
   H. there is better technology today to study the brain.
   I. more people are interested in this topic and follow the progress of the research.

5. The author organizes the article by
   A. discussing Michael Vick's background.
   B. comparing three scientists and their theories.
   C. describing flashbacks from the lives of three scientists.
   D. discussing opinions from those who have allowed people to have second chances.

6. What is the main idea of the article's final paragraph?
   F. Poor choices are always a result of our development.
   G. The "failure mechanism" triggers our stages of development.
   H. People like Michael Vick who get a second chance are just lucky and will likely fail again.
   I. Because we know that teens' brains are not fully developed, teens can use this information to make better choices and learn from past mistakes.

7. According to the article, why are young people more likely than older people to be affected by things like drug use and abuse?
   A. They haven't had as many experiences yet.
   B. The brain experiences many changes beginning in the pre-teen years.
   C. Human reasoning ability is finished by the time a person has reached adulthood.
   D. Young people cannot learn from the new information about brain research because they are not yet fully developed.

8. According to the article, what is the major difference between Piaget's theories and those of Erikson and Levinson?
   F. Piaget was a biologist.
   G. Erikson and Levinson were psychologists.
   H. Erikson and Levinson believed that human reasoning ability develops throughout life.
   I. Levinson's theory of human development is divided into five stages, while Erikson thought there were eight.

9. Which one of the following facts from the article makes us believe that newer brain research is probably better than the older research?
   A. Piaget was a biologist, not a psychologist.
   B. Erikson and Levinson were both scientists of the 20th century.
   C. Theories of human reasoning ability have gone through many changes.
   D. New technologies that provide images of the brain are now used in research studies on brain development.

10. Using the quotation at the beginning of the article and the information in the article, the reader can tell that
    F. important brain research is done only by psychologists.
    G. permanent human failure is programmed into all human experience.
    H. teenagers must work harder to learn from their mistakes and set new goals.
    I. it is possible for humans at any age to actively set new goals and change their behavior.

11. What additional information does the text box bring to the article?
    A. The brain develops throughout life.
    B. Brain development is easier when we are younger.
    C. There are factors other than physical brain development that cause changes in the brain.
    D. Teens sometimes do not handle difficult situations effectively because their brains are not yet fully developed.

12. What is the major difference between Jean Piaget's ideas about human intellectual development and the most current research on this subject? Support your answer with facts from the article.

TECHNICAL WRITING PROMPT

13. You are a college professor of a beginning psychology class. You want to show your students a clear and concise presentation of the differing viewpoints on human development and growth stages. Design four PowerPoint slides giving a brief overview of the four views of development discussed in the article:

    1. Jean Piaget   2. Erik Erikson   3. Daniel J. Levinson   4. Modern Scientists

Technical Writing

VOCATIONAL EXTENSION

Athletes like Michael Vick rely on many people to guide their careers. This group might include friends, relatives, and coaches. But probably one of the most important to any athlete is the sports agent.

HELP WANTED:

Intern for small sports management firm. Clerical duties to include tracking stats on client athletes and arranging travel for agents. Small stipend available to those with at least two years of college. E-mail current resume to diane@sportsmasters.com.

A basic task for sports agents is advising their clients in all aspects of their lives that affect their sport. This includes promoting their clients for future or current contracts and helping their clients improve their performance by hiring trainers or coaches to work with the athletes.

Some agents offer a full range of other services that will help their clients be successful on and off the field. These services might include arranging speaking opportunities and endorsement deals, as well as providing legal services, financial planning, and tax consulting.

As we can see, the job of a sports agent requires a lot of flexibility. There is not a one-size-fits-all job description for this career. An agent might be negotiating an athlete's multi-million dollar contract one day and waiting for a client to come out of surgery the next. Agents must be ready to give plenty of time and attention to the athletes they represent.

Agents must also be able to recognize new talent and help those athletes grow into the best they can be. For this reason, some agents specialize in a particular sport, like football, baseball, soccer, or hockey. They can then identify young athletes who might have the necessary skills and work habits to someday be professionals.

According to agent Scott Casanover, the single most important characteristic for a good agent is honesty. Clients must be able to trust their agents to do the best thing for them at all times. He says being an agent also "takes a tremendous work ethic and self sacrifice," including "a willingness to work all hours, while spending a great deal of time away from your family."

So, what can an agent expect to make for all those hours at the office? An agent's pay can be set up in several ways. Some agents charge a flat fee for their services, while others are paid a percentage of their clients' deals. Some attorneys act as their clients' agents, so these attorneys charge their normal hourly rate, which can be up to $400 per hour. Depending on experience, the median salary range for this profession is between $40,000 and $120,000.

Representing professional athletes can be an exciting way to make a living, but it takes time, experience, and hard work to reach the top levels of this profession. Are you ready to get started?

LOOKING FORWARD

14. Sports and entertainment agents represent the interests of their clients. Imagine that you have accepted a position as an agent for a famous celebrity either in entertainment or sports. First decide which celebrity you would like to represent. Then, using personal knowledge and information from the article, explain how you could develop and improve the career of your client. Be sure to include specific advice for this celebrity.

ETHICAL DILEMMA

15. You are a summer intern at an agency that represents high-profile professional athletes. At the end of your first month, the agent you work for asks you to fill out his phone log even though you don't know how long he talked to each one of his clients. You are uncomfortable "making up" this important document that is used to bill the clients. How do you handle this? What are your choices?

UNIT VOCABULARY ASSESSMENT

Matching
Match each word in Column I to its definition in Column II.

Column I

_____ 1. redeem
_____ 2. mollusk
_____ 3. neuroscientist
_____ 4. mechanism
_____ 5. unattainable

Column II

A.   process by which an effect is produced
B.   scientist who studies the nervous system
C.   an animal with a soft body and no backbone
D.   to make up for (a fault)
E.   impossible to reach

Multiple Choice
Choose the word that MOST NEARLY replaces the underlined word in each sentence.

6. After his guilty plea, the criminal showed <u>remorse</u> and apologized to the victim's family.
   A.   regret
   B.   happiness
   C.   uneasiness
   D.   friendliness

7. Ethical questions often pose confusing <u>dilemmas</u>.
   A.   needs
   B.   problems
   C.   discussions
   D.   expectations

8. Companies that have green practices get my <u>endorsement</u>.
   A.   money
   B.   support
   C.   skepticism
   D.   disapproval

9. The constitution lays out the <u>precepts</u> of America.
   A.   history
   B.   proceeds
   C.   principles
   D.   mannerisms

Word Bank

bankruptcy
chronological
reinstatement
skeptical
testament
transitional

Fill in the Blank
Choose a word from the word bank to fill in the blank in the sentence below.

10. The couple was forced to file for _____ after losing their main source of income.

11. The _____ of the college president came after he was cleared of all wrongdoing.

12. Timelines allow us to see events in _____ order.

13. The student's improvement in grades is a _____ to the value of hard work.

14. Middle school is often seen as a _____ time of growing from child to teenager.

15. Because she has lied to me before, I am _____ of her honesty and sincerity.

AUTHENTIC ASSESSMENT

Students will create a mock draft based on the unit "Second Chances."

Instructions for Mock Classroom Draft

1. **Group assignment.** Six to eight teams of students will set up athletic teams based on those in a professional sports association such as the NFL (football), NBA (basketball), or MLB (baseball). Students should name the teams.

2. **Research.** Using research, prior knowledge, or information from the teacher, students will learn about how a draft works. If possible, students should look at information from a previous draft for the sport chosen.

3. **Planning.** After gaining a solid understanding of how a draft works, students should use real-life data to look at players who either will be included in an upcoming draft or have been in a recent draft for the sport chosen. Students will look to see how many players of a certain position are generally drafted, as well as what important statistics mean. Fantasy draft sites (yahoo.com, ESPN.com) as well as the official sites for professional sports (NFL.com, NBA.com, MLB.com) are excellent places to gather information.

4. **Draft.** Groups will draw numbers to determine who goes first. Each team should have access to the list of players, their rankings, and their positions. Each team should also have a draft sheet marked with the number of positions to fill. Teams take turns in order to draft players and complete the teams.

5. **Assessment.** Work will be assessed using the rubric that follows.

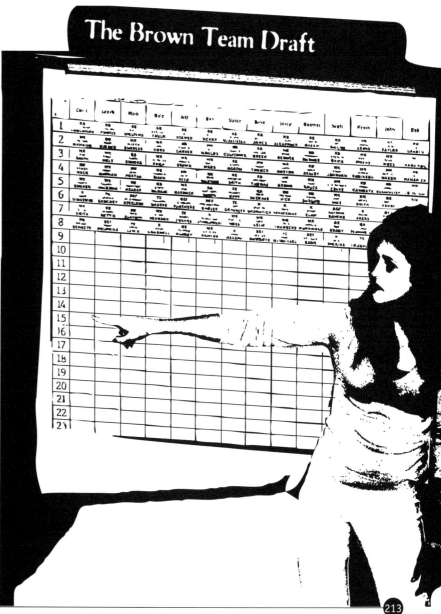

COOPERATIVE LEARNING RUBRIC

Instructions: Assess yourself in each of the areas below by circling the number that best reflects your participation in the cooperative learning assignment. On the lines below, list the specific ways you participated in each area.

1. You were active in learning about how a draft works.

   3- a lot   2- some   1- very little   0- not at all

   Specific contributions: _____

   _____

2. You fully understood how a draft works.

   3- a lot   2- some   1- very little   0- not at all

   Specific contributions: _____

   _____

3. You researched real-life drafts.

   3- a lot   2- some   1- very little   0- not at all

   Specific contributions: _____

   _____

4. You participated in picking your team.

   3- a lot   2- some   1- very little   0- not at all

   Specific contributions: _____

   _____

5. You worked collaboratively and successfully with your group.

   3- a lot   2- some   1- very little   0- not at all

   Specific contributions: _____

   _____

—Unit 10—

incredible goals

READING INSTRUCTIONAL GUIDE FOR HIGH-INTEREST ARTICLE

BEFORE READING

Looking at the Words

Determining How the Word Sounds (Phonics)

Using the Syllable Guide and the Reading Instructional Guide Template found in the beginning of the book, read the steps to learn how to break a word into manageable parts.

Determining What the Word Means (Vocabulary)

Words to Study	Breaking into Syllables	Short Definition
coincidentally	co-in-ci-dent-al-ly	(adv.) happening or occurring by chance
conquistador	con-quis-ta-dor	(n.) a conqueror (Spanish)
contender	con-ten-der	(n.) one who competes
derive	de-rive	(v.) to form from a source
embark	em-bark	(v.) to set out or begin
noteworthy	note-wor-thy	(adj.) deserving attention
rudimentary	ru-di-men-ta-ry	(adj.) basic or unrefined; primitive

Activating Background Knowledge

Anticipation Guide

Mark each of the following statements True or False:

1. _____ Cuauhtémoc Blanco Bravo is a famous city in Mexico.

2. _____ Soccer is referred to as football in Mexico.

3. _____ David Beckham plays for the Chicago Fire.

4. _____ The use of hands is not permitted in soccer.

5. _____ Soccer is the world's most popular sport.

Starter Questions

After completing the Anticipation Guide, participate in a group or class discussion using the following questions:

1. Are there any similarities between Blanco and David Beckham?

2. What team does Blanco currently play for?

3. What is the World Cup?

4. What is Club America?

5. How are American soccer and American football different?

Make a prediction about what you think the article will be about.

DURING READING

- Skim the article for 45–60 seconds. Circle any words you don't know.
- When you are finished, decode and determine the meaning of unknown words.
- Skim the questions for 30–45 seconds.
- Predict what the article is about.
- Read the article.
- Reread to clarify as needed.
- Answer the questions.

AFTER READING

Discussion Starter Questions

1. What was the significance of Blanco's first game-winning goal for the Chicago Fire?

2. What is the "Blanco Bounce"?

3. Do you think professional sports should be able to recruit athletes from other countries? Why or why not?

4. How do you think Blanco could use his childhood difficulties to inspire others?

5. Why do you think David Beckham received more attention than Blanco at the beginning of the 2007 season?

Blanco: Mexican Soccer Legend

In 2007 British football player David Beckham joined Major League Soccer as a member of the Los Angeles Galaxy. He embarked on a season known for heavy publicity and controversy. That same year, although with much less media hype, Mexican soccer legend Cuauhtémoc Blanco Bravo entered the league as part of the Chicago Fire.

In a poor section of Mexico City, Blanco grew up playing football in abandoned fields and streets. For most children, football was just a way to pass time. But Blanco, often called Cuau or Temo, showed early promise. He developed a creative, if aggressive, manner of playing. This style could be a reflection of the crime that surrounded him in the Tepito neighborhood. His unique style was enough to gain him notice. He made his debut in the Mexican First Division for Club America while still a teenager. Except for a few brief stints elsewhere, Blanco stayed with Mexico's Club America until he joined Major League Soccer in the United States.

Blanco played for Mexico in two World Cups, in 1998 and 2002, and is expected to be a contender in the 2010 World Cup in South Africa. He was also a member of the winning Mexican team in the 1999 Confederations Cup. He is one of the highest scorers ever for Club America. He has more than 100 goals made while playing for the club and 35 goals scored as part of the Mexican national football team. His game-winning first goal for the Chicago Fire, a 25-yard volley, was named the 2007 Goal of the Year.

But Blanco may be best known for his signature move, the "Blanco Bounce." He first performed it in the 1998 World Cup. In this move, also referred to as the "Bunny Hop," he holds the ball between his ankles and leaps over opponents while still holding the ball between his legs. It was later named the "Cuauhtémiña" and became an official move in Major League Soccer.

Blanco by the Numbers

1- Number of Olympics he has competed in

2- Number of World Cups he has competed in

5- Number of times he has been named MVP

9- Most goals he has scored in a single game

16- Number of goals he has scored for the Chicago Fire

19- Age at which he made his debut for Club America

34- Goals he has made for the Mexican national team

97- Number of international appearances he has made for the Mexican national team

100- Caps he has earned

Soccer, called football in most of the world, has likely been around for a very long time. Evidence suggests that over 2,000 years ago, people in China played a game in which they kicked a rudimentary ball. The modern sport was born in 1863 in Great Britain, when rules to a popular ball game were established. The rules included that players could not trip their opponents and could not touch the ball with their hands.

The FIFA World Cup is an international soccer competition between men's national teams from all over the world. The competition is held every four years in the summer. Teams must qualify over the three-year period preceding each World Cup. The first World Cup was played in Uruguay in 1930. Since then, the tournament has become the most prestigious soccer competition in the world. Brazil has won a record five World Cup titles, followed by Italy with four wins.

Blanco's career hasn't been without controversy. His aggressive style, including lashing out, has made headlines. He was not named to the 2006 Mexican national team, and many think that this was because of his disagreements with former national coach Ricardo Lavolpe. In the summer of 2008, the U.S. Soccer Federation suspended him from the U.S. Open Cup for illegal moves like head butting and eye gouging.

Despite the controversies, Blanco's career has been noteworthy for the impact he has made on soccer outside his homeland—where it's already a well-established sport. He's also helped the rise of Major League Soccer in the United States. Over 6,000 American Fire fans came out to a welcome ceremony when he joined MLS. And when fans were initially worried about his chemistry with the team, Blanco answered their concerns by scoring that first game-winning goal. His presence in MLS increased ticket sales for his team. His ability to make plays gave the Fire an advantage in the league. At the end of his 3-year contract, Blanco returned to Mexico at the end of 2009 to play for team Veracruz.

Most recently, Blanco has been given the chance to star in his own television program, "La Hora de Cuauhtémoc (Cuauhtémoc's Hour)," on Fox Sports in the United States and Latin America. The show is a one-hour Spanish-language talk show featuring celebrities and sports figures discussing important issues in the world of soccer.

In all of his success, Blanco has never forgotten his Mexican roots. His first name, Cuauhtémoc, is derived from the Aztec word *Cuahtli*, which means "eagle." The eagle is coincidentally also the mascot of Club America. When Blanco makes a goal, he strikes the famous pose of ancient ruler Tlatoani Cuauhtémoc, who tried to save the Aztecs from the Spanish Conquistadors. True to his name, Blanco has risen above the poverty and violence that surrounded his childhood to become a legend of his generation.

READING COMPREHENSION

After reading "Blanco: Mexican Soccer Legend," choose the options that best answer questions 1–14.

1. Read this sentence.
   When Blanco makes a goal, he strikes the famous pose of ancient ruler Tlatoani Cuauhtémoc, who tried to save the Aztecs from the Spanish Conquistadors.

   What is the meaning of the word *strikes* as it is used in this sentence?
   A. models
   B. assaults
   C. protests
   D. researches

2. Read this sentence.
   Except for a few brief stints elsewhere, Blanco stayed with Mexico's Club America until he joined Major League Soccer in the United States.

   What is the meaning of the word *stints* as it is used in this sentence?
   F. actions
   G. interests
   H. limitations
   I. periods of time

3. From this article, the reader can tell that Blanco
   A. and Beckham both brought excitement to Major League Soccer.
   B. was frustrated that Americans don't understand the rules of soccer.
   C. is more interested in being a television star than he is in playing soccer.
   D. is a quiet player who likes to remain to himself without a lot of attention from fans.

4. According to the article, which of the following is true?
   F. Blanco and Beckham played for the same Major League Soccer team.
   G. Blanco is starring in a Spanish-language television program featuring soccer issues.
   H. After finishing a career as a soccer player, Blanco will go on to become a soccer coach.
   I. Blanco will soon retire from playing soccer and will go on to make a career in television.

5. From the author's point of view,
   A. soccer is a better sport than football.
   B. Blanco has always shown poor sportsmanship.
   C. Blanco should play for the American World Cup team.
   D. Blanco rose above difficult childhood surroundings to become a star.

6. The author organizes the article by
   F. comparing Beckham and Blanco.
   G. describing the rules and procedures of soccer.
   H. contrasting the World Cup and Major League Soccer.
   I. providing background information on Blanco's childhood and career.

7. Why does the author list the facts in the "Blanco by the Numbers" text box?
   A. to emphasize Blanco's accomplishments
   B. to introduce the reader to soccer terminology
   C. to emphasize the effort it takes to play professional soccer
   D. to show how professional soccer's international following has increased

8. Which title BEST fits the article?
    - F.   The Yellow Card
    - G.   Blanco's Savvy Skills
    - H.   Playing in the World Cup
    - I.   Professional Soccer in the United States

9. Why was Blanco suspended from the Open Cup in 2008?
    - A   drug use
    - B.   scheduling conflict
    - C.   illegal and aggressive play
    - D.   inappropriate actions off the field

10. According to the article, one of the ways Blanco affected the Chicago Fire the most was
     - F.   modeling leadership.
     - G.   influencing more fans to buy tickets.
     - H.   persuading team owners to keep the team in Chicago.
     - I.   assisting coaches with selecting and drafting the right players.

11. The major difference between soccer in the United States and soccer in Mexico is that
     - A.   Mexico uses a rudimentary ball.
     - B.   the sport is called football in Mexico.
     - C.   the United States has different rules than Mexico.
     - D.   the matches are longer in the United States than in Mexico.

12. Which of the following is the BEST evidence that Blanco is a talented soccer player?
     - F.   He started playing in the United States at the age of 19.
     - G.   He overcame adversity to become a professional athlete.
     - H.   He was signed by the United States after playing in Mexico.
     - I.   He scored 16 goals in just 3 years while playing for the Chicago Fire.

13. People who read this article will learn
     - A.   that soccer is popular around the world.
     - B.   that Mexico has more soccer fans than any other country.
     - C.   that soccer is becoming more popular than football in the United States.
     - D.   how to become a professional soccer player for the U.S. Soccer Federation.

14. When Blanco decided to return to Mexico, a Fire representative stated, **"We respect his desire to continue playing in Mexico during the MLS offseason and continue preparing for the 2010 World Cup, which is a top priority for him."**

     Based on this quotation and the information in the article, which of the following conclusions is valid?
     - F.   The Chicago Fire team was happy to see Blanco go.
     - G.   Mexican soccer players make more money in the World Cup than U.S. players.
     - H.   Training for the World Cup was one of Blanco's reasons for returning to Mexico.
     - I.   Blanco's top priority was to play in Mexico, where the coaches are more qualified.

READING STRATEGY

Directions: Identify the main idea of the article and write it in the center pentagon. Write supporting facts from the article in the surrounding spots on the soccer ball. Finally, write a summary statement explaining how the supporting facts taken together have made a difference in Blanco's career.

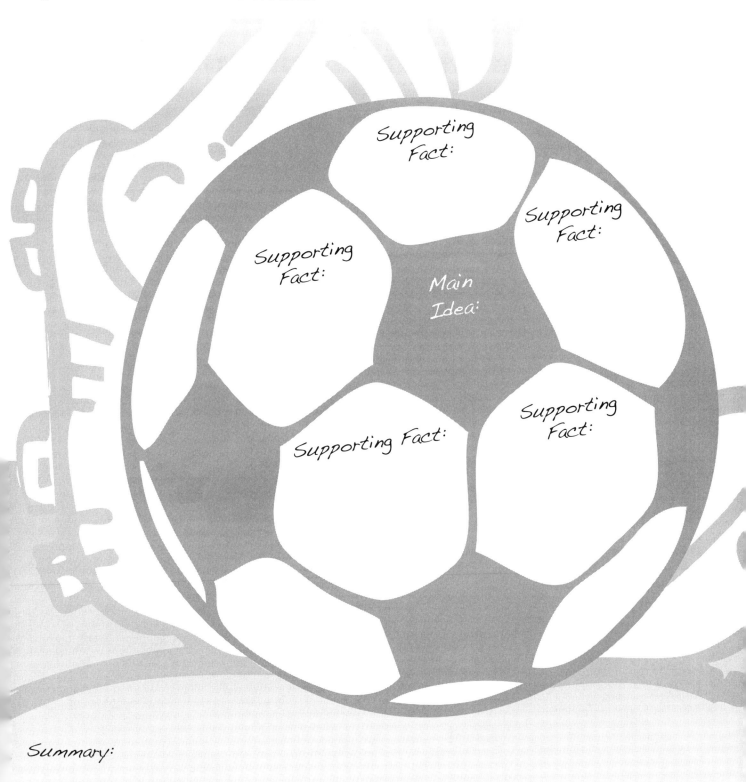

Supporting Fact:

Supporting Fact:

Supporting Fact:

Main Idea:

Supporting Fact:

Supporting Fact:

Summary:

INTERPRETING THE DATA

World Cup Winners

Like many sporting events, the World Cup awards a first-, second-, and third-place winner.

Table 1. Top-3 team finishes in the World Cup since 1982

Year	Host country	1st place	2nd place	3rd place
1982	Spain	Italy	Germany	Poland
1986	Mexico	Argentina	Germany	France
1990	Italy	Germany	Argentina	Italy
1994	United States	Brazil	Italy	Sweden
1998	France	France	Brazil	Croatia
2002	Korea & Japan	Brazil	Germany	Turkey
2006	Germany	Italy	France	Germany

15. According to Table 1, what team won first place in the year in which they were the host country?

_____

16. Which team won first place the most times? _____

17. Fill in Table 2 to tally the number of first-, second-, and third-place finishes by each country as listed in Table 1.

Table 2. Totals for top-3 team finishes in the World Cup since 1982

Country	1st-place finishes	2nd-place finishes	3rd-place finishes	Number of top 3 finishes
Argentina				
Brazil				
France				
Germany				
Italy				

18. Rank the top five countries according to total number of top-3 finishes in the World Cup since 1982. Use Table 2 to support your answer.

ANALYZE EVALUATE EXPLAIN

_____
_____
_____
_____
_____
_____
_____
_____

19. Which team would you consider the most successful since 1982—Germany or Brazil? Support your answer with facts and statistics from the tables.

ANALYZE EVALUATE EXPLAIN

_____
_____
_____
_____
_____
_____
_____
_____

Since the very first World Cup in 1930, Brazil has overwhelmingly had the most success. Consider the following graph showing its top finishes.

Figure 1. Brazil's top-4 team finishes in the World Cup

20. There were 18 World Cup contests from 1930 to 2006. According to Figure 1, in how many of these did Brazil NOT place in the top 4?

Examine this similar chart of Italy's and Germany's top places since 1930.

Figure 2. Italy's and Germany's top-4 team finishes in the World Cup

Legend:
- 1st place
- 2nd place
- 3rd place
- 4th place

Y-axis: Number of finishes (0 to 4)

Germany, Italy

21. After considering Figure 1 and Figure 2, which team would you now consider the most successful overall—Germany, Italy, or Brazil? Support your answer with facts and statistics from the charts.

ANALYZE EVALUATE EXPLAIN

REFLECT AND RESPOND

22. Why do you think national pride is such an important part of major worldwide sporting events? Do you think this pride helps or hinders the sense of sportsmanship that surrounds sporting events such as the World Cup?

Reflect & Respond

READING INSTRUCTIONAL GUIDE FOR TECHNICAL EXTENSION

BEFORE READING

Looking at the Words

Determining What the Word Means (Vocabulary)

Words to Study	Breaking into Syllables	Short Definition
acclaim	ac-claim	(n.) enthusiastic approval
coveted	cov-et-ed	(adj.) desired or wished for
infinite	in-fi-nite	(adj.) unlimited
spectacle	spec-ta-cle	(n.) something impressive that can be seen; wonder
unfold	un-fold	(v.) to become clear
wondrous	won-drous	(adj.) wonderful

Activating Background Knowledge

Graphic Organizer
Either individually or in groups, brainstorm about soccer, recalling anything previously learned and any prior experience with the subject. Next, complete the T-Chart to demonstrate what you already know about the similarities and differences between soccer and American football.

Soccer	American Football

Starter Questions

After completing the Graphic Organizer, participate in a group or class discussion to come up with questions about the subject, a prediction about the article, and at least one learning goal. The first question has been provided for you.

Question: What is the World Cup?

Question: _____

Prediction: _____

Goal: _____

DURING READING

- Skim the article for 45–60 seconds. Circle any words you don't know.

- When you are finished, decode and determine the meaning of unknown words.

- Skim the questions for 30–45 seconds.

- Predict what the article is about.

- Read the article.

- Reread to clarify as needed.

- Answer the questions.

AFTER READING

After reading, you may do the following:

- Review, paraphrase, and summarize

- Participate in main-idea discussions by describing the information in their own words

- Reflect on concept maps and generate additional discussion starter questions based on the mappings

- Participate in small-group discussions using discussion starter questions

Discussion Starter Questions

The first question has been provided for you.

1. Why is soccer such a popular sport?

2. _____

3. _____

TECHNICAL EXTENSION

Soccer: Ballet of the Masses

"I love soccer. Call it football, futbol, calico, voetbol, soccer, whatever . . . I love this game. The game unfolds slowly, as we learn what we are up against. But the action can take place in a breathless rush where art, science, physics and magic all collide in a wondrous spectacle. . . . But like the best music or the richest art, the simplicity combines into infinite complexity. No two games are ever exactly alike." –Sachin, BigSoccer Moderator, BigSoccer.com

Mention football in the United States, and images of players like Tom Brady, Maurice Jones-Drew, and Randy Moss come to mind. But in nearly every other country in the world, "football" refers to what we call soccer. It is the major team sport of nearly every country in Asia, Africa, Europe, and South America. Players like Cristian Ronaldo or Zlatan Ibrahimovic, unknown to most Americans, command the attention and acclaim of the soccer world. However, more and more people in our country are playing soccer all the time.

According to a global count of soccer players in 2006, 265 million men and women participate in the game. Add another 5 million referees and officials, and you have nearly 4% of the world's population chasing that ball around soccer fields!

What makes this game so wildly popular? Many think that it is because players of different ability levels can play together and still be competitive. Those interested in fitness believe that it provides one of the best workouts of any sport. Others say that it isn't a complicated game to play, and it is easy for spectators to understand. The BigSoccer Moderator, Sachin, explains this by saying, "Every player has a role, but the players are all equal in responsibility."

Unlike baseball or American football, soccer can be played alone. All you need is a soccer ball and a few spare minutes in order to practice. This means that it is not an expensive sport, which might explain why it is popular in many countries that don't have the advantages of wealthier nations.

Soccer has also become a huge source of national pride. Countries of all sizes put together "futbol" teams that carry their flags and generate intense feelings of support. The International Federation of Association Football (FIFA) lists 207 member associations with teams from countries as small as Fiji and Togo, along with large countries like the United States and Australia.

Once every four years, the World Cup tournament is held in a member nation. Its founder, former FIFA president Jules Rimet, hoped that "soccer could reinforce the ideals of a permanent and real peace" by bringing players together from all over the world. The first World Cup competition was held in 1930 in Uruguay. Five European countries plus the United States, Mexico, and six other South American teams also competed for the coveted title. The host country took home that first World Cup trophy. In 2010, the World Cup tournament will be held in South Africa, home of FIFA.

Soccer players in other countries become sports idols just like American football players do in the United States. One way to determine the most popular players around the world is to take a look at their salaries. Cristiano Ronaldo, who plays for a team from Spain called the Real Madrid, signed the most expensive contract in soccer in 2009 when the team paid him $126 million to move from the Manchester United (England).

Before Ronaldo's deal, the top player in the world had been David Beckham, a former British star who now plays for The Galaxy, a Los Angeles team. His salary is listed as over $42 million. The other top players on the list are Lionel Messi ($38 million–Barcelona, Spain), Ronaldinho ($26 million–Milan, Italy), and Thierry Henry ($23 million–Barcelona, Spain). Like athletes in other major sports, these stars earn millions more in endorsement deals with companies like Nike, Fuji, Adidas, and Pepsi.

American football is seldom played outside the borders of our country. However, as one soccer blogger states, "Soccer is not just a game. . . . It is all about passion and the deep love for the sport. Wherever you go, people will talk about soccer. It isn't surprising that it is the number one sport in the world."

The World's Highest-Paid Athletes, 2009

Tiger Woods	Golf	$100	Million
Kiki Raikkonen	Auto Racing	$45	Million
Michael Jordan	Basketball	$45	Million
Kobe Bryant	Basketball	$45	Million
David Beckham	Soccer	$42	Million
Manny Pacquiao	Boxing	$40	Million

READING COMPREHENSION

After reading "Soccer: Ballet of the Masses," answer questions 1–12.

1. Read the following sentence.
    Countries of all sizes put together "futbol" teams that carry their flags and generate intense feelings of support.

    What is the meaning if the word *generate* as it is used in the sentence?
    A. stop
    B. break
    C. create
    D. discourage

2. Read the following sentence.
    Its founder, former FIFA president Jules Rimet, hoped that "soccer could reinforce the ideals of a permanent and real peace" by bringing players together from all over the world.

    What is the meaning of the word *reinforce* as it is used in the sentence?
    F. destroy
    G. to make inferior
    H. to become outdated
    I. to strengthen or make more effective

3. From reading the article, the reader can infer that the winner of the first World Cup competition was
    A. Uruguay.
    B. South Africa.
    C   the United States.
    D. a European country.

4. Which of the following BEST supports the statement that soccer is the number one sport in the world?
    F. Soccer can be played alone.
    G. David Beckman plays for an American team.
    H. Soccer has become a huge source of national pride.
    I. Two hundred sixty-five million people play soccer.

5. What writing strategy does the author use to illustrate the passion that people have for soccer?
    A. using quotations
    B. comparing data from various countries
    C. discussing the reasons for starting the World Cup
    D. outlining the organization of the 207 member nations into the FIFA

6. If this article were published in a newspaper, which would be the most informative headline?
    F. Ronaldo: A Star!
    G. The Rise of Beckham
    H. Soccer: The World's Game
    I. The World Cup and the FIFA

7. According to the article, what is one reason that soccer is popular in small countries?
    A. FIFA's home is South Africa.
    B. 4% of the world's population plays.
    C. Soccer doesn't cost much to play.
    D. All soccer players on a team play all positions.

8. Based on the given 2009 figures, how do the salaries of top soccer players compare to those of high-profile athletes in other sports?
    F. Soccer players' salaries are all higher.
    G. David Beckham is the highest paid soccer player ever.
    H. American football players make less than soccer players.
    I. The highest-paid soccer player earns less than half of the income of the highest-paid athlete.

9. Which fact from the article BEST supports the fact that the United States is becoming as interested in soccer as the rest of the world?
    A. American football is not played in many countries.
    B. One of the world's highest paid soccer players is on an American team.
    C. The United States is a member of the International Federation of Association Football.
    D. The game's popularity comes from its simplicity and the fact that it is inexpensive to play.

10. What is the most likely reason that Cristiano Ronaldo is NOT included in the text box list of the World's Highest-Paid Athletes in 2009?
    F. The information presented is incorrect.
    G. His $126 million contract was not signed until late in 2009.
    H. The text box includes figures from both salaries and endorsements.
    I. David Beckham did not start playing for the LA Galaxy until after 2009.

11. Pierre de Courbetin of France is credited with bringing the Olympic Games back into modern times. He said, **"Let us export our oarsmen, our runners, our fencers into other lands... the day it [the Olympics] is introduced into Europe the cause of Peace will have received a new and strong ally."**

    Pierre de Courbetin and Jules Rimet have similar ideas in believing that
    A. sports promote good will.
    B. soccer is more important than other sports.
    C. European nations can lead the way in trade.
    D. American football will soon become more popular than soccer.

12. What evidence is presented in the article that supports a soccer fan's statement that "soccer is the number one sport in the world"?

TECHNICAL WRITING PROMPT

13. You have just been hired as a writer for a soccer fan website. Your first assignment is to write the text for the home page on the website. Write a paragraph about the popularity of soccer in the world, a bit of history, and why it is such a well-loved sport. Because it is the opening text of the website, it should be short, powerful, and to the point. Use information from the text and any personal experience you might have to capture the attention of your audience.

Technical
Writing

VOCATIONAL EXTENSION

There are a handful of soccer players who are millionaires. But most people who enjoy "futbol" play only for the love of the game. Kids show up on fields every weekend all over the world to compete in games coached and officiated by volunteers who don't expect to be paid.

Since the earliest days of our country, volunteerism has been a way neighbors have supported one another. French writer Alexis de Tocqueville wrote *Democracy in America* in 1831. He noted that the United States was a "nation of joiners" that worked together to achieve common goals. Barn raisings, quilting bees, pot luck dinners, and coaching youth sports are examples of volunteers providing service to one another.

HELP WANTED

Individual to work 6 hours per week as a volunteer soccer coach for Community Youth Soccer League. Training and certification by the National Alliance for Youth Sports is required. Apply at nearest city recreation center.

People who volunteer are also helped in many ways. They learn new skills that can help them reach career goals. There is a great sense of satisfaction found through helping others with no thought of pay. In fact, many states require students to complete a set number of volunteer hours in order to graduate. Families enjoy the social aspect of meeting others with similar interests, too.

People of all ages and backgrounds offer assistance through volunteering. Statistics show, though, that the average volunteer has a college education, is in good health, has an interest in recreation, and simply believes in helping others. Churches, social service organizations, civic and cultural groups, schools, political groups, hospitals, and senior centers are the most common places where volunteers lend a hand.

Many projects in U.S. history have been the result of volunteering on a large scale. The Civilian Conservation Corps planted trees and also built roads and bridges beginning in the 1930s. The Peace Corps was organized in the 1960s to help some of the poorest countries in the world. Today, AmeriCorps and Learn and Serve America use volunteers of all ages to help throughout the United States.

There are some interesting cultural and ethnic characteristics about volunteers, too. African Americans have a long history of serving their communities. This is done through their neighborhoods, social groups, and churches. Latinos provide high expectations and support for the families within their community. Native Americans share their communal lifestyle with their neighbors. Agencies sponsored by Jewish organizations are known for their efforts to help immigrants around the world.

Teens are valuable sources of volunteer help, with about 59% of youth in America volunteering in some way. This is a higher percentage than adult participation. Volunteers of all ages feel more connected to their communities and schools, too. However, some barriers to teens volunteering are a lack of time, having too many other responsibilities, no transportation, or simply that no one has ever asked them to help.

Famous American boxer Muhammad Ali said, "Service to others is the rent you pay for your room here on Earth." As we can see, volunteers are all about paying the rent!

LOOKING FORWARD

14. Volunteering is a great way to strengthen leadership skills. Using personal experience and information from the article, share your most rewarding volunteer experience. What did you do? Whom did you meet? How did the experience change you? If you have not yet volunteered, write about an organization you would like to help in the future. What strengths would you bring to this organization?

Looking
Forward

ETHICAL DILEMMA

15. Your father coaches your soccer team, and the assistant coach is your dad's boss. Your team is sponsored by their company. The assistant coach belittles a teammate who is autistic. This is the only player the assistant coach mistreats, and he always does it when your dad isn't around. You want to tell your dad, but you know it might cause problems for him at work and might also jeopardize the team. What are your options? Do you tell your father?

Ethical
Dilemma

UNIT VOCABULARY ASSESSMENT

Matching

Match each word in Column I to its definition in Column II.

Column I
_____ 1. derive
_____ 2. unfold
_____ 3. coincidentally
_____ 4. embark
_____ 5. coveted

Column II
A. happening by chance
B. desired or wished for
C. to form from a source
D. to become clear
E. to set out

Multiple Choice

Choose the word that MOST NEARLY replaces the underlined word in each sentence.

6. Although she didn't win the scholarship, her accomplishments were certainly <u>noteworthy</u>.
   A. many   C. remarkable
   B. finished   D. understandable

7. There are so many ways to design a room that the possibilities seem <u>infinite</u>.
   A. limited   C. unlimited
   B. imperfect   D. incomplete

8. Mastering <u>rudimentary</u> math is necessary to understand more complicated math.
   A. basic   C. complex
   B. obscure   D. complementary

Fill in the Blank

Choose a word from the word bank to fill in the blank in the sentence below.

9. The Spanish _____ defeated many opponents.

10. The fifth wonder of the world is a _____ to be seen.

11. The German figure skater will be a strong _____ in the Olympics.

12. The band has received _____ for their popular debut album.

13. Our family always looks forward to watching the _____ fireworks display on the 4th of July.

Word Bank

acclaim

conquistador

contender

spectacle

wondrous

AUTHENTIC ASSESSMENT

Students will write and give a speech based on the unit "Incredible Goals."

Instructions for Speech

1. **Topic.** Each student will choose a speech topic approved by the teacher. Suggestions include individual soccer players (current or past) or the history/influence of soccer on an individual country.

2. **Research.** Students will research their chosen topics using periodicals, Internet resources, and any other sources approved by the teacher. Research should be organized in an effective way and available for teacher review.

3. **Speech preparation.** Students will learn about elements of an effective speech. The following guidelines may be helpful.
   a. **Organization**
      • Speech has an opening, middle, and conclusion.
      • All thoughts are linked to the main idea.
   b. **Originality**
      • Thoughts are given in student's own words.
      • Although based on fact, the student adds personal touches that make the speech original.
   c. **Delivery**
      • Student uses eye contact with audience.
      • Student speaks in a clear, projected voice.
      • Body language is appropriate and not distracting.

4. **Speech.** Student will use research and knowledge about the elements of speech to deliver a 2-minute speech on his or her given subject.

5. **Assessment.** Work will be assessed using the rubric that follows.

RUBRIC

Requirement	8–10 Points	4–7 Points	0–3 Points	Points Earned
Topic and Research	The student's topic is appropriate, and research is complete and appropriate.	The student's topic is appropriate, and research is appropriate but incomplete.	The student's topic is inappropriate, and/or the research is not complete.	
Organization	The speech is well organized, focused on the main idea with supporting points.	The speech is somewhat organized, sometimes straying from the main idea.	The speech is disorganized and may not have a main idea.	
Originality	The speech is written from the student's perspective and uses the student's own language.	The speech is somewhat personal but is missing some of the student's own language.	The speech uses language from the research sources or is plagiarized (automatic zero for assignment).	
Delivery	The speech is easy to understand, with appropriate eye contact and body language.	The speech can be understood, with some lapses in eye contact and body language.	The speech is difficult to understand. The speaker may read directly from a card or have distracting body language.	

Rubrics

Reading Short-Response Rubric	
2 points	The student fully understands what is being asked for. The student's answer is correct, complete, and addresses all aspects of the assigned task. The student provides detail and support from the text in order to support his/her answer. Any additional information provided by the student is related to the assigned task and acts as support for his/her response.
1 point	The student partially understands what is being asked for. The student's answer is correct; however, it is generalized and not specific enough. The student is missing any specific details and support from the text that would prove his/her full understanding of the text and the assigned task.
0 points	The answer is completely incorrect, has nothing to do with the assigned task, or no answer is provided.

Reading Extended-Response Rubric	
4 points	The student fully understands what is being asked for. The student's answer is correct, complete, and addresses all aspects of the assigned task. The student provides detail and support from the text in order to support his/her answer. Any additional information provided by the student is related to the assigned task and acts as support for his/her response.
3 points	The student understands what is being asked for. The student's answer is correct and addresses all aspects of the assigned task. The student provides detail and support, but it is not fully complete or directly from the text.
2 points	The student partially understands what is being asked for. The student's answer is correct; however, it is generalized and not specific enough. The student is missing any specific details and support from the text that would prove his/her full understanding of the text and the assigned task.
1 point	The student has very little understanding of what is being asked for in the task. The answer is not complete, has many things wrong with it, or addresses very little of what has been asked for.
0 points	The answer is completely incorrect, has nothing to do with the assigned task, or no answer is provided.

Interpreting the Data Short-Response Rubric	
2 points	The student fully understands what is being asked for. The work is completed correctly and efficiently. There is a full demonstration of the know-how necessary to accurately answer the problem provided. If applicable, the explanations and interpretations are clear, complete, and concise. Any small mistakes do not take away from the overall display of understanding.
1 point	The student seems to understand what is being asked for, but the answer is only partially correct. The answer may be correct, but it is apparent that there is a lack of full awareness in the know-how necessary to complete the problem. Or there is a full awareness of the know-how necessary to complete the problem, but the answer is incorrect.
0 points	No answer is provided, the answer is completely incorrect, or there is absolutely no demonstration of the know-how necessary to complete the problem (even if the answer provided is correct).

Interpreting the Data Extended-Response Rubric

4 points	The student fully understands what is being asked for. The work is completed correctly and efficiently. There is a full demonstration of the know-how necessary to accurately answer the problem provided or others like it. If applicable, the explanations and interpretations are clear, complete, and concise. Any small mistakes do not take away from the overall display of understanding.
3 points	The student understands what is being asked for. The answer is essentially correct, but the demonstration of the know-how necessary to explain how the student came to the answer is slightly flawed. The answer contains some minor errors that could be due to lack of attention to detail in the demonstration of the know-how necessary to answer the problem or others like it.
2 points	The student seems to understand what is being asked for, but the answer is only partially correct. The answer may be correct, but it is apparent that there is a lack of full awareness in the know-how necessary to complete the problem or others like it. Or there is a full awareness of the know-how necessary to complete the problem, but the answer provided is incorrect.
1 point	There is a very limited understanding of what is being asked for. The answer is incomplete and has errors. There is some demonstration of the know-how necessary to answer the problem or others like it, but the answer is incomplete, totally incorrect, or inadequate.
0 points	No answer is provided, the answer is completely incorrect, or there is absolutely no demonstration of the know-how necessary to complete the problem (even if the answer provided is correct).

Character Education Rubric

4 points	The student uses information from the reading selection and his/her life and formulates a strong answer that demonstrates what conclusions about character he/she has drawn from the article.
3 points	The student gives examples from either only his/her life or only the reading selection and formulates a strong answer that demonstrates what conclusions about character he/she has drawn from the article.
2 points	The student gives few examples from his/her life or the reading selection, but formulates an answer that demonstrates what conclusions about character he/she has drawn from the article.
1 point	The student does not use examples from his/her life or from the reading selection. It is difficult to determine whether the student has drawn any conclusions about character from the article.
0 points	The student has provided no response or a completely incorrect response. The student does not demonstrate that he/she has drawn any conclusions about character from the article.

Technical Writing Rubric

4 points	The student clearly and concisely conveys specialized information in a way that shows a keen understanding of the specific audience/purpose and supports general statements with an abundance of relevant facts.
3 points	The student communicates specialized information in a way that shows a general understanding of the specific audience/purpose and supports statements with a sufficient number of relevant facts.
2 points	The student communicates information in a way that is unclear, shows limited understanding of the audience/purpose, and/or uses few relevant facts.
1 point	The student communicates information in a way that is unclear, shows minimal understanding of the audience/purpose, and/or uses very few facts.
0 points	The student either does not answer the question at all or shows no understanding of the assigned writing task.

Notes

Unit 1: Animation Domination
High-Interest Article

Character biographical information from: "SpongeBob Characters," SpongeBob.com, http://spongebob.nick.com/backstage/characters/spongebob/ and "Character Bios," TheSimpsons.com, http://www.thesimpsons.com/bios/bios_family_index.htm.

Intepreting the Data

The creator of…: Hamilton, Don, "Matt Groening's Portland," *The Portland Tribune*, July 19, 2002, http://www.portlandtribune.com/news/story.php?story_id=12392.

SpongeBob's creator has…: "Encyclopedia: SpongeBob SquarePants," NationMaster.com, http://www.statemaster.com/encyclopedia/SpongeBob-SquarePants.

Table 1: Data from City-Data.com, http://www.city-data.com/city/Portland-Oregon.html; http://www.city-data.com/city/Seattle-Washington.html.

Figure 1: Data and Statistics compiled from information provided on http://www.the-numbers.com.

Technical Extension

But what about…: Mackenzie, Chris, "Top 25 Anime Characters of All Time," IGN, http://movies.ign.com/articles/103/1036651p5.html.

Fans are known…: Newitz, Annalee, "Anime Otaku: Japanese Animation Fans Outside Japan," Bad Subjects, April 1994, http://bad.eserver.org/issues/1994/13/newitz.html.

When it was…: Bhartiya, Pratush, "History of Animation: Before Disney," EzineSeeker.com, January 10, 2010, http://technology.ezineseeker.com/history-of-animation-before-disney-144476d467.html.

Prior to this…: Swygert, Nancy Maria, "History of Multimedia Animation," Animation Tutorial, University of South Carolina Master's Educational Technology Program, April 2004, http://www.usca.edu/swygert/Animation/history.htm.

Then in 1937…: Swygert.

Next, these artists…: O'Connell, Michael, "A Brief History of Anime," Otakon 1999 program book, http://www.corneredangel.com/amwess/papers/history.html.

Before this, stories…: O'Connell.

Tezuku was inspired…: O'Connell.

Anime also includes…: Aeschliman, Lesley, "What Is Anime?" BellaOnline, 2009, http://www.bellaonline.com?ArticlesP/art4260.asp.

The plot lines…: Aeschliman.

One characteristic of…: Ho Lin, "Lack of Narrative Closure in Anime," Cyberspace, Hypertext, & Critical Theory, http:ww.cyberartswebweb.org/cpace/anime/closure.html.

Each format might…: Newitz, Annalee, "Anime Otaku: Japanese Animation Fans Outside Japan," Bad Subjects, April 1994.

The racial composition…: Newitz.

There have been…: Newitz.

Today, it is…: Newitz.

Technical Multiple-Choice Questions

One article about (Question 11)…: Newitz, Annalee, "Anime Otaku: Japanese Animation Fans Outside Japan," Bad Subjects, April 1994, http://bad.eserver.org/issues/1994/13/newitz.html.

Unit 2: Pitching Anxiety
High-Interest Article

His first year…: Posnanski, Joe, "Zack Greinke Is in Total Control," SI.com, April 28, 2009, http://sportsillustrated.cnn.com/2009/writers/joe_posnanski/04/28/zack.greinke/index.html.

Greinke was expected…: Donovan, John, "A Long Way to Go: Greinke Battles Depression in Bid for K.C. Rotation," SI.com, March 15, 2007, http://sportsillustrated.cnn.com/2007/writers/john_donovan/03/15/royals.greinke/index.html.

Social anxiety disorder…: "Social Phobia," athealth.com, August 23, 2007, http://www.athealth.com/Consumer/disorders/SocialPhobia.html.

Even during his…: Donovan.

But for already…: Cuncic, Arlin, "Famous People with Social Anxiety Disorder: Zack Greinke," About.com, April 30, 2009, http://socialanxietydisorder.about.com/od/celebritieswithsad/p/zackgreinke.htm.

He dreaded even…: Posnanski.

They told him…: Posnanski.

He left the…: Donovan.

Feeling better, he…: Posnanski.

He spent the…: Donovan.

The first season…: Cuncic.

"Really, all that…: Dutton, Bob, "Sports Illustrated Putting Greinke on Cover," The Kansas City Star, April 27, 2009, http://www.kansascity.com/sports/royals/story/1166062.html.

But for now…: Posnanski.

He was a (text box)…: Cuncic, Arlin, "Famous People with Social Anxiety Disorder: Ricky Williams," About.com, May 10, 2009, http://socialanxietydisorder.about.com/od/celebritieswithsad/p/zackgreinke.htm.

He explained, "I (text box)…: Moore, Donnica, "Social Anxiety Disorder with Ricky Williams (interview)," Dr.Donnica.com, December 20, 2003, http://www.drdonnica.com/celebrities/00007874.htm.

"If my story (text box)…: Cuncic, "Famous People with Social Anxiety Disorder: Ricky Williams."

Intepreting the Data

Table 1: Schoenstadt, Arthur, MD, "Anxiety Disorder Statistics," eMedTV.com, http://anxiety.emedtv.com/anxiety-disorder/anxiety-disorder-statistics.html.

"In any social…: Schoenstadt, Arthur, MD, "Social Phobia," eMedTV.com, http://anxiety.emedtv.com/social-phobia/social-phobia.html.

Another study indicates…: Kessler RC, et al., "Lifetime Prevalence and Age-of-Onset Distributions of DSM-IV Disorders in the National Comorbidity Survey Replication," *Archives of General Psychiatry*, 2005. (The statistics in this study have been simplified for ease of comprehension and instruction.)

Table 2: "Social Anxiety Disorder (SAD) Statistics," Social Anxiety Center.org, http://www.socialanxietycenter.org/about-social-anxiety-disorder/social-anxiety-disorder-statistics.php.

Technical Extension

He was overwhelmed…: King, Peter, "The New Zack Greinke," Sports Illustrated, May 3, 2009, p. 42.

The average episode…: "Teenage Depression Statistics," 2005, http://www.teendepression.org/articles5.html.

However, this might…: "Teenage Depression Statistics."

The change in…: "Types of Depression," Teen Depression—Help for Troubled Teens, 2005, http://www.teendepression.org/articles49.html.

These events could…: "Causes of Teen Depression," National Institutes of Health, http://www.teendepression.org/articles2.html.

Hopefully, then they…: "Teenage Depression Statistics."

However, it wasn't…: King.

These sessions often…: "Teen Depression: A Guide for Parents and Teachers," HelpGuide.org, http://www.helpguide.org/mental/depression_teen.htm.

Other therapies in…: "Depression Health Center: Questions and Answers About Depression," WebMD.com, http://www.webmd.com/depression/questions-and-answers-about-depression.

Experts do not…: Teen Depression: A Guide for Parents and Teachers."

Symptoms of teen (text box)…: "Types of Depression."

Vocational Extension

However, at that…: "Definition," Holistic Medicine, Answers.com, http://www.answers.com/topic/holistic-health.

The body is…: "Definition," Holistic Medicine.

They also encourage…: "Holistic Healing and Holistic Physicians," http://www.holisticpractitioner.net/.

Holistic medicine emphasizes…: "Definition," Holistic Medicine.

Those seeking the…: "Holistic Medicine: Training and Certification,"Answers.com, http://www.answers.com/topic/holistic-medicine-training-and-certification.

Their income matches…: "Holistic Medicine," Medical Career Training, http://www.medical-career-training.com/holistic_physician.htm.

Benefits like paid…: Harrison, Hayley, "How Much Money Do Naturopathic Doctors Make?" ehow.com, http://www.ehow.com/facts_5232607_much-do-naturopathic-doctors-make.html.

Unit 3: Online Communities
High-Interest Article

He is a…: Maag, Christopher, "A Hoax Turned Fatal Draws Anger but No Charges," New York Times, November 28, 2007, http://www.nytimes.com/2007/11/28/us/28hoax.html.

According to prosecutors…: Associated Press, "Judge to Reverse Conviction in MySpace Hoax," July 2, 2009, MSNBC.com, http://today.msnbc.msn.com/id/31708526.

However, a jury…: Associated Press.

While police were…: Poltilove, Josh, "Police Looking into Teen Girls Fight Video in Tampa," The Tampa Tribune, April 2, 2009, http://www2.tbo.com/content/2009/apr/02/021353/police-looking-teen-girls-fight-video-tampa/.

Companies are looking…: Skinner, Carrie-Ann, "Employers Admit Checking Facebook before Hiring," PC World, September 14, 2008, http://www.pcworld.com/businesscenter/article/151044/employers_admit_checking_facebook_before_hiring.html.

America Online recently…: Malachowski, Dan, "Wasted Time at Work Costing Companies Billions," Salary.com, July 11, 2005, http://www.salary.com/.../crel_display_nocat_Ser374_Par555.html.

Employees of all…: Braid, Mary, "Learn to Love Social Network Sites," Times Online, January 27, 2008, http://business.timesonline.co.uk/tol/business/career_and_jobs/recruiter_forum/article3255962.ece.

Many sites allow…: Khadaroo, Stacy Teicher, "Efforts to Reign in Online Fight Videos," July 27, 2008, ABC News, http://abcnews.go.com/Technology/Story?id=5452699&page=1.

Keeping Facebook Private (text box)…: Facebook, http://www.facebook.com/policy.php.

Tweeting Too Loudly (text box)…: Selix, Casey, "Trouble in Twitter Land: Tweeting without Thinking," MinnPost.com, June 8, 2009, http://www.minnpost.com/stories/2009/06/08/9340/trouble_in_twitter-land_tweeting_without_thinking.

Tucker, Doug, "Chiefs Cut Enigmatic Larry Johnson," San Diego News Network, November 9, 2009, http://www.sdnn.com/sandiego/2009-11-09/sports/football/chiefs-cut-enigmatic-rb-larry-johnson.

Intepreting the Data

Table 1: Adapted from iStrategyLabs, http://www.istrategylabs.com/wpcontent/uploads/2009/01/facebook_demographics_statistics_2009.png.

Consider the following…: "25 Interesting Facebook Statistics and Facts," Penn Olson, http://www.penn-olson.com/.../25-interesting-facebook-statistics-and-facts/?...PennOlson+(Penn+Olson).

Table 2: Adapted from "Internet," Nielsen NetView, http://enus.nielsen.com/rankings/insights/rankings/internet.

Technical Extension

So, what provides…: Swartz, Jon, "Social-Networking Sites Work to Turn Users into Profits," USA Today, May 12, 2008, http://www.usatoday.com/tech/techinvestor/industry/2008-05-11-social-networking_N.htm.

Facebook, the biggest…: Stelter, Brian, "Facebook's Users Ask Who Owns Information," New York Times Feb. 16, 2009, http://www.nytimes.com/2009/02/17/technology/internet/17facebook.html?_r=1.

Recent figures show…: Swartz.

According to the…: Facebook Advertising, Facebook, 2009, http://www.facebook.com/advertising/?src=pf.

Facebook says that…: Facebook Advertising.

"[Our company] generated…: Facebook Advertising

It also tells…: Swartz.

Facebook hoped to…: Swartz.

MySpace, for one…: Swartz.

Top 10 Social (text box)…: McCarthy, Caroline, "Whee! New Numbers on Social Network Usage!" CNET News, Feb. 10, 2009, http://news.cnet.com/8301-17939_109-10160850-2.html.

Vocational Extension

Besides copywriting, below…: Jain, Geetika, "A Career in Advertising," Articlesbase, February 27, 2009, http://www.articlesbase.com/careers-articles/a-career-in-advertising-792540.html.

The copywriter cannot…: Jain.

One expert says…: O'Barr, William M., "What Is Advertising?" Advertising and Society Review, The Advertising Educational Foundation, 2005, https://muse.jhu.edu/journals/advertising_and.../6.3unit01.html.

A degree in…: Rensch, Randall, "Frequently Asked Questions about Advertising, Copywriting, Freelancing, and Life in General," Absolute Write, http://www.absolutewrite.com/specialty_writing/faq_advertising.htm.

The copywriters are…: Sivak, Cathy, "Advertising Everything from Soup to Nuts…Literally!" Art School.com, October 8, 2004, http://www.artschools.com/articles/advertising/careers.html.

However, those who…: Sivak.

Lance Kinney, an…: Sivak.

Unit 4: Beating the Odds
High-Interest Article

He and his…: Bell, Jarrett, "From Homeless to the NFL: Oher's Journey to Draft Unique," *USA Today*, April 23, 2009, http://www.usatoday.com/sports/football/nfl/2009-04-23-michael-oher-cover_N.htm.

Fortunately for Michael…: Bell.

Sean Tuohy recalls…: Bell.

He went from…: Lewis, Michael, "The Ballad of Big Mike," *New York Times Magazine*, September 24, 2006, http://www.nytimes.com/2006/09/24/magazine/24football.html?scp=1&sq=Michael%20Oher,%20Homeless&st=cse.

Oher earned such…: "Micheal Oher," NFL Draft, CBS Sports, http://www.cbssports.com/nfl/draft/players/559237.

However, it isn't…: Ridenour, Marla, "Mississippi Prospect Michael Oher Lives Real-Life Rags-to-Riches Story," *Akron Beacon Journal / Fox Sports*, 2009, http://msn.foxsports.com/cbk/story/9495420/Mississippi-prospect-Michael-Oher-lives-real-life-rags-to-riches-story-.

Regardless of his…: Collette, Tim, "Michael Oher-From Foster Child to Top NFL Draft Prospect," Seahawk Nation Blog, April 24, 2009, seahawknationblog.com/.../michael-oher-from-foster-child-to-top-nfl-draft-prospect/.

Being Homeless (text box)…: "Why Are People Homeless?" National Coalition for the Homeless, July 2009, http://www.nationalhomeless.org/factsheets/why.html.

Overcoming the Odds (text box)…: The Donald Driver Foundation, http://www.donalddriverfoundation.com/flash/index.html.

Intepreting the Data

Figure 1: Data from National Coalition for the Homeless, http://www.nationalhomeless.org/.

Figure 2: National Alliance to End Homelessness, http://www.endhomelessness.org.

Technical Extension

It is virtually…: "Executive Summary," State Report Card on Child Homelessness, Campaign to End Child Homelessness, 2009, http://www.homelesschildrenamerica.org.

As he says…: "Michael Oher Quotes from NFL Presser," Chris Pika's Blog," 2009, http://wnst.net/wordpress/chrispika/2009/04/26/michael-oher-quotes-from-nfl-presser.

1.3 million of…: "Overview: Homelessness & Poverty in America," National Law Center on Homelessness & Poverty, 2008, http://www.nlchp.org/hapia.cfm.

And 42% of…: "Report: 1 in 50 U.S. Children Face Homelessness," CNN.com, 2008, http://www.cnn.com/2009/US/03/10/homeless.children/index.html.

One study found…: "Report: 1 in 50 U.S. Children Face Homelessness."

According to the…: "Executive Summary," State Report Card on Child Homelessness.

These programs provide …: "Homelessness & Poverty in America: Real Solutions," National Law Center of Homelessness & Poverty, 2008, http://www.nlchp.org/hapia_solutions.cfm.

Incomes for those…: "Overview: Homelessness & Poverty in America."

Both shelters and…: "Youth Homelessness in America: The Changing Face of the Homeless," Suite 101.com, July 7, 2009, http://homelessness.suite101.com/article.cfm/youth_homelessness_in_america.

Cash donations would…: "Youth Homelessness in America: The Changing Face of the Homeless."

Housing and Income (text box)…: "Risk Factors for Child Homelessness: Housing Market Factors," Campaign to End Child Homelessness, 2009, http://www.homelesschildrenamerica.org/findings_risk-factors_housing.php.

Vocational Extension

A non-profit, or…: Fritz, Joanne, "What Is a Nonprofit?" About.com, http://nonprofit.about.com/od/qathebasics/f/whatisnonprofit.htm.

Although less well…: "10 Super Sized Agencies," Charity Navigator, http://www.charitynavigator.org/index.cfm?bay=topten.detail&listid=24.

The most effective…: Fritz, Joanne, "So You Want a Nonprofit Job?" About.com, http://nonprofit.about.com/od/nonprofitwork/tp/gettingjob.htm.

Therefore, jobs within…: Fritz, Joanne, "Three Things You Must Include on Your Resume When Applying for a Nonprofit Job," About.com, http://nonprofit.about.com/od/nonprofitwork/qt/resumetips.htm.

An accounting clerk…: "Accounting Clerk—US National—All Nonprofits," Abbott, Langer Association Surveys, http://www.abbott-langer.com/content/All_Nonprofits_Salary_Survey/Accounting_Clerk_4002/US_National.htm.

Positions that carry…: "Employee Training Specialist - US National - All Nonprofits," Abbott, Langer Association Surveys, http://www.abbott-langer.com/content/All_Nonprofits_Salary_Survey/Employee_Training_Specialist_1822/US_National_Average.htm.

The highest salaries…: VanHuss, Katrina, "NPR Study Finds Non-profit CEO Salaries Are Up," Turnkey Promotions, September 29, 2009, http://turnkeywow.wordpress.com/2009/09/29/npr-ceo-study/.

Mahatma Gandhi, a…: "Quote DB," http://www.quotedb.com/quotes/2050.

Unit 5: The Sound of Success

Intepreting the Data

"Top Ten Greatest Speeches," *Time* magazine website, http://www.time.com/time/specials/packages/article/0,28804,1841228_1841749_1841743,00.html.

Technical Extension

"Managers are people…: Clark, Donald, "Team Building," May 11, 1997, http://www.depts.ttu.edu/aged/leadership/leadtem.htm.

"Management is based…: Owen, Hilary, "What Makes a Leader?" *USA Today*, December 9, 2002, http://www.usatoday.com/money/jobcenter/workplace/successstrategies/2002-11-14-leader_x.htm.

They seek to…: Larson, Sandra, "What Makes for an Effective Leader?" Free Management Library, http://www.managementhelp.org/mgmnt/leader.htm.

These qualities are…: Goleman, Daniel, "What Makes a Leader?" *Harvard Business Review*: On Point, January 2004, http://hbr.org/hb-main/resources/pdfs/comm/microsoft/makes-leader.pdf.

It is also…: Goleman.

The 21st century…: Dick, Gary, "What Makes a Leader in a Flat World?" Heidrick and Struggles, http://www.heidrick.com/NR/rdonlyres/DA5CADA6-6D8D-4F30-BD50-E545655FB242/0/HS_LeaderInFlatWorld.pdf.

Based on his…: Dick.

British General Bernard…: "Quotes on Leadership," Leading Thoughts: Building a Community of Leaders, http://www.leadershipnow.com/leadershipquotes.html.

Traits of an (text box)…: Dick.

Vocational Extension

If your actions…: *The Free Dictionary*, http://forum.thefreedictionary.com/postst1572_If-your-actions-inspire-others-to-dream-more--learn-more--do-more-and-become-more--you-are-a-leader-.aspx.

According to one…: Clark, D.R., "Concepts of Leadership," Instructional System Design Concept Map, 2004, http://nwlink.com/~donclark/hrd/ahold/isd.html.

Professor Boyd at…: Boyd, Barry, "Bringing Leadership Experiences to Inner-City Youth," *Journal of Extension*, August 2001, http://www.joe.org/joe/2001august/a6.php.

Unit 6: Home Front
High-Interest Article

Many have credited…: Saletan, William, "Girls in the Hood: If women can defend Fort Hood, they can defend America," Slate.com, November 6, 2009, http://www.slate.com/id/2234862.

As one sergeant…: Hefling, Kimberly, "Back from Combat, Women Struggle for Acceptance," *Associated Press*, December 14, 2009, http://news.yahoo.com/s/ap/20091214/ap_on_go_ca_st_pe/us_female_veterans_finding_a_place.

Elder comments, "I'm…: Schmidt, Carol, "Studentlivin'@msu: Elder Designs Life after Iraq," Montana State University, March 7, 2006, http://www.montana.edu/cpa/news/nwview.php?article=3472.

Her PTSD is…: Hefling.

"You're sitting on…: Patterson, Thom, "U.S. Seeing More Female Homeless Veterans," *CNN*, September 25, 2009, http://www.cnn.com/2009/LIVING/09/25/homeless.veterans/.

Female veterans have…: Hefling.

Resolved, That the…: "Services and Achievements of Military Women Recognized," American Women Veterans, http://americanwomenveterans.org/home/2009/11/services-and-achievements-of-military-women-recognized/.

"Invisible Soldier" (text box)…: Lintecum, Sarge, 1995, posted on PTSD Support Services website, http://www.ptsdsupport.net/thefemale_soldier.html.

Women in the (text box)…: "Frequently Asked Questions: Women in Combat," Center for Military Readiness, November 22, 2004, http://www.cmrlink.org/WomenInCombat.asp?DocID=237.

Intepreting the Data

Table 1: Data from Epstein, Jack, and Johnny Miller, "U.S. Wars and Post-Traumatic Stress Disorder," *San Francisco Chronicle*, June 22, 2005, http://www.sfgate.com/cgi-bin/article.cgi?f=/c/a/2005/06/22/MNGJ7DCKR71.DTL&type=health.

National Center for PTSD, United States Department of Veterans Affairs, http://www.ptsd.va.gov/public/pages/how-common-is-ptsd.asp

Table 2: Data from Epstein and Miller.

Technical Extension

In the early…: "Clinton-Era Policy Changes Affect Women in War Today," Center for Military Readiness/Women in Combat, April 2, 2003, http://www.cmrlink.org/WomenInCombat.asp?docID=187.

By 2003, she…: Brennan, Carol, "Black Biography: Shoshana Johnson," Answers.com, http://www.answers.com/topic/shoshana-johnson.

She later received…: "Women in the Military," *New World Encyclopedia*, http://www.newworldencyclopedia.org/entry/Women_in_the_military.

It was 3…: "Women in the Military."

During the 1950s…: "Women in the Military."

They also realized…: "Women in the Military."

And it might…: "Women in Land Combat," Center for Military Readiness Policy Analysis, April 2003, http://www.cmrlink.org/CMRNotes/M38V8CCMRRPT16.pdf.

And those areas…: "Clinton-Era Policy Changes Affect Women in War Today."

As a traditionally…: Francis, Samuel, "Clinton Seeks to 'Ungender' the Military," April 8, 1997, http://www.militarywoman.org/academic.htm.

They say that…: Francis.

She refused to…: McManus, Kathy, "Single Mothers in the Military: Kids or Country?" January 14, 2010, http://www.responsibilityproject.com/blog/post/single-mothers-in-the-military-kids-or-country/.

Hutchinson was briefly…: McManus.

Some Military Women (text box)…: "Military Women 'Firsts,'" Military Women "Firsts" and Their History, http://userpages.aug.com/captbarb/firsts.html.

Vocational Extension

Uncle Sam Wants…: "The Most Famous Poster," American Treasure of the Library of Congress, March 15, 2007, http://www.loc.gov/exhibits/treasures/trm015.html.

Only a limited…: "Military Plain Facts: Get the Plain Facts About the US Military," http://military.plainfacts.net/category/enlistment/.

You must also…: "Entrance Requirements FAQ," Today's Military, http://www.todaysmilitary.com/faq/entrance-requirements.

Those married with…: "Military Plain Facts: Get the Plain Facts About the US Military."

The results determine…: "Military Plain Facts: Get the Plain Facts About the US Military."

You must pass…: "Army Weight Charts," U.S. Army Weight Charts for Males, About.com US Military, http://usmilitary.about.com/od/army/l/blmaleweight.htm.

"Height and Weight Standards for the United States Navy," Navy Height and Weight Standards for the United States Navy, http://www.navycs.com/navyheightweightchart.html.

Those with convictions…: "Military Plain Facts: Get the Plain Facts About the US Military."

If you have…: "Military Plain Facts: Get the Plain Facts About the US Military."

The Army, Navy …: "Military Plain Facts: Get the Plain Facts About the US Military."

Days begin at…: "Military Plain Facts: Get the Plain Facts About the US Military."

Training covers the…: "Military Plain Facts: Get the Plain Facts About the US Military,"

Some of the…: "Military Plain Facts: Get the Plain Facts About the US Military."

The Army will…: "Active Duty Enlistment Bonus," Army Enlistment Incentives, About.com US Military, http://usmilitary.about.com/od/armyjoin/a/incbonus.htm?p=1.

Recruits with college…: "Active Duty Quick Ship (Seasonal) Bonus," Army Enlistment Incentives, About.com US Military, http://usmilitary.about.com/od/armyjoin/a/incbonus.htm?p=1.

Bonuses of less…: "Active Duty Education Bonus," Army Enlistment Incentives, About.com US Military, http://usmilitary.about.com/od/armyjoin/a/inced.htm?p=1.

Higher bonuses are…: "Active Duty Enlistment Bonus."

Officers, of course…: "Assessing Pay and Benefits for Military Personnel," Economic and Budget Issue brief, August 15, 2007, http://www.cbo.gov/ftpdocs/85xx/doc8550/08-15-MilitaryCompensation_Brief.pdf.

Unit 7: Invisible Injury
High-Interest Article

The teammate's comment…: Bishop, Greg, "As Signs of Concern Spread, N.F.L. Revisits Concussions," *New York Times*, November 29, 2009, http://www.nytimes.com/2009/11/30/sports/football/30steelers.html.

There have even…: Mihoces, Gary, "Concussions Force Hard Look Inward Around NFL," *USA Today*, June 18, 2007, http://www.usatoday.com/sports/football/nfl/2007-06-18-concussions-cover_N.htm.

Scientists at the…: Smith, Stephanie, "Dead Athletes' Brains Show Damage from Concussions," *CNN*, January 27, 2009, http://www.cnn.com/2009/HEALTH/01/26/athlete.brains/index.html#cnnSTCVideo.

According to the…: "Heads Up: Concussions in Youth Sports," Centers for Disease Control and Prevention," December 8, 2009, http://www.cdc.gov/concussion/HeadsUp/youth.html.

The symptoms of…: "Heads Up: Concussions in Youth Sports."

They warn that…: "Heads Up: Concussions in Youth Sports."

Intepreting the Data

Tables 1–4; Figure 2: Data from "Injuries," NFL.com, http://www.nfl.com/injuries.

Table 5: Information from "Schedule," NFL.com, http://www.nfl.com.

Figures 3–5: Data from "Nonfatal Traumatic Brain Injuries from Sports and Recreation Activities—United States, 2001—2005," Table 2, *Morbidity and Mortality Weekly Report*, July 27, 2007, http://www.cdc.gov/mmwr/preview/mmwrhtml/mm5629a2.htm#tab1.

Technical Extension

"I dropped down…: "Athletes Beware of Concussion-Caused Dementia," *CBS Broadcasting, Inc.*, January 29, 2009, http://cbs2chicago.com/health/willie.baun.Chronic.2.921183.html.

Webster even went…: "Former Steeler Webster Dies at Age 50," *ESPN Classic*, October 3, 2002, http://espn.go.com/classic/obit/s/2002/0924/1435977.html.

The SLI uses…: "Our Story," Sports Legacy Institute, 2009, http://www.sportslegacy.org/index.php?option=com_content&view=article&id=47&Itemid=60.

The scientific name…: "Our Story."

He sustained one…: "Concussion Expected to Sideline Roethlisberger," WJZ.com, November 29, 2009, http://wjz.com/sports/ben.roethlisberger.2.1338305.html.

He experienced the: "Doctor: Symptoms from Concussions Can Linger," KDKA.com, December 29, 2009, http://kdka.com/sports/Ben.Roethlisberger.Concussion.2.896731.html

Receiver Hines Ward…: Cohn, Bob, "Players and NFL Accelerate Strategy for Concussions and Head Injuries," AARP Bulletin Today, February 5, 2010, http://bulletin.aarp.org/yourhealth/healthyliving/articles/players_and_nfl_accelerate_strategy_for_concussions_and_head_injuries.html.

NFL team doctors…: "Doctor: Symptoms from Concussions Can Linger."

A head injury…: "Dementia: Warning Signs," FamilyDoctor.org, December 2009, http://familydoctor.org/online/famdocen/home/seniors/mental-health/662.printerview.html.

As the condition…: "Dementia: Warning Signs.

He explains that…: "Athletes Beware of Concussion-Caused Dementia."

Some NFL Players (text box): Cohn.

Vocational Extension

They help people…: Burke, Harold, Ph.D., "Brain Injury: Traumatic Brain Injury Post Concussion Syndrome Rehabilitation and Treatment," Brain Therapy Center, http://www.brain-injury-therapy.com/articles/brain_injury.htm.

Many brain injuries…: "Occupational Therapists," Occupational Outlook Handbook, 2010-11 Edition, Bureau of Labor Statistics, http://www.bls.gov/oco/ocos078.htm.

The therapist sometimes…: "Occupational Therapists."

The therapist might…: "Occupational Therapists."

They evaluate clients'…: "Occupational Therapists."

Home health therapists …: "Occupational Therapists."

Finally, you must …: "Occupational Therapists."

These people will …: "Occupational Therapists."

Most occupational therapists …: "Occupational Therapists."

"I'm just a…: "Disability Quotes," Finest Quotes, http://www.finestquotes.com/select_quote-category-Disability-page-0.htm.

One of the…: O'Toole, Catie, "A Ride Into the Record Book; When It Comes to Wheelchair Wheelies, the Ultimate Can Be Found in the City of Oswego," *The Post-Standard*, October 3, 2003, http://www.highbeam.com/doc/1G1-108454472.html.

Unit 8: Road to the Top
High-Interest Article

West took the…: Kreps, Daniel, "Kanye West Storms the VMAs Stage During Taylor Swift's Speech," *Rolling Stone*, September 19, 2009, http://www.rollingstone.com/rockdaily/index.php/2009/09/13/kanye-west-storms-the-vmas-stage-during-taylor-swifts-speech/?rand=84857.

She was able…: Rodriguez, Jayson, "Kanye West Crashes VMA Stage During Taylor Swift's Award Speech," MTV.com, September 13, 2009, http://www.mtv.com/news/articles/1621389/20090913/west_kanye.jhtml.

"The only thing…: "Taylor Swift: My Bullies Helped Me Succeed," Radar Online.com, February 18, 2009, http://www.radaronline.com/exclusives/2009/02/taylor-swift-my-bullies-helped-me-succeed.php.

As she puts…: "Taylor Swift: Don't Picture Me Naked!" *US Magazine*, February 18, 2009, http://omg.yahoo.com/news/taylor-swift-don-t-picture-me-naked/19038.

Even with her…: Hockenberry, John, Celeste Headlee, and Kristen Meinzer, "Taylor Swift on Role Models, Advice," The Takeaway, November 6, 2009, http://www.thetakeaway.org/stories/2009/nov/06/taylor-swift-role-models-advice/.

Based on her…: Guerra, Joey, "Taylor Swift Dominates the CMAs," Peep: Blogging Entertainment with the Chronicle Staff, *The Houston Chronicle*, November 11, 2009, http://blogs.chron.com/peep/2009/11/taylor_swift_dominates_the_cma.html.

Darius Rucker, Pursuing (text box)…: Darden, Beville, "Darius Rucker Wins 2009 CMA Best New Artist," The Boot.com, AOL, Music, Inc., November 11, 2009, http://www.theboot.com/2009/11/11/2009-cma-award-best-new-artist/.

Intepreting the Data

Table 2: Pietroluongo, Silvio, "DeRulo Tops Hot 100, But Swift Swoops in with Record-Breaking Debut Sum," Billboard.com, November 5, 2009, http://www.billboard.com/#/news/derulo-tops-hot-100-but-swift-swoops-in-1004033394.story.

Technical Extension

Lady Gaga recently…: "Lady Gaga on Barbara Walters 'Most Fascinating People," YouTube, http://www.youtube.com/watch?v=-3u5x__EIFM.

These two very…: "Quotes About Music," GAIA Community, http://www.gaia.com/quotes/topics/music.

They probably learn…: Mills, Susan, "Introduction: What Is Intelligence? (Gardner, Howard. *Frames of Mind*, 1983)," September 2001, http://www.soundpiper.com/mln/mi.htm.

They often have…: "Musical Intelligence," MyPersonality.info, http://www.mypersonality.info/multiple-intelligences/musical/.

We can also…: Mills, Susan.

There are even…: Oak, Manali, "Effects of Music on the Mind and Brain," Buzzle.com, November 3, 2008, http://www.buzzle.com/articles/effects-of-music-on-the-mind-and-brain.html.

Brain cell connections…: Inglish, Patty, "Listen to Music—It Can Save the Brain," Hubpages, http://hubpages.com/hub/Music-Can-Save-the-Brain.

It also showed…: Oak.

She states that…: Olson, Kristian David, "The Effects of Music on the Mind: Beyond Soothing the Savage Beast," February 22, 1996, http://www.reversespins.com/effectsofmusic.html.

The results are…: Olson.

I don't know…: "Taylor Swift — A Place in This World," Lyricsty, http://www.lyricsty.com/lyrics/t/taylor_swift/a_place_in_this_world.html.

Multiple Intelligences: How (text box)…: Mills.

Vocational Extension

As Jean Paul Richter…: "Quotations About Music," The Quote Garden, http://www.quotegarden.com/music.html.

Public and private…: "Music Careers," Careers in Music, National Association for Music Education, 2001, http://www.kenfoster.com/Articles/Careers.htm.

Teachers in an…: "Music Teacher Jobs and Careers," Music Teacher Salary, Job Description and Career Information, http://www.moneyinmusic.com/music-teacher.html.

They might be…: "Job Description of a General Music Teacher," eHow.com: How to Do Just About Everything, http://www.ehow.com/about_4741247_job-description-general-music-teacher.html.

Music instruction at…: "Music Careers."

The national average…: "Music Teacher Salaries in Jacksonville, FL," indeed.com, January 4, 2010, http://www.indeed.com/salary?q1=music+teacher&l1=Jacksonville%2C+FL+32220.

A professor might…: "Music Careers."

The national average…: "Salary Survey for Job: Art, Drama, or Music Teacher, Post-Secondary," PayScale—Art, Drama, or Music Teacher, Postsecondary Salary, Average Salaries, January 2, 2010, http://www.payscale.com/research/US/Job=Art,_Drama,_or_Music_Teacher,_Postsecondary/Salary.

Income as a…: "Music Teacher Jobs and Careers."

Music therapists reach…: "Frequently Asked Questions About Music Therapy," American Music Therapy Association, http://www.musictherapy.org/faqs.html.

People with Alzheimer's…: "Frequently Asked Questions About Music Therapy."

Those who want…: "Frequently Asked Questions About Music Therapy."

The average salary…: "Music Therapist Salaries," indeed.com, January 8, 2010, http://www.indeed.com/salary/Music-Therapist.html.

Unit 9: Second Chances
High-Interest Article

"I think Michael…: Associated Press, "Dungy Believes Vick Focused," *ESPN.com*, July 28, 2009, http://sports.espn.go.com/nfl/news/story?id=4361284.

"I have said… Associated Press, "Vick Looking for Second Chance with Eagles," August 14, 2009, *CBS*, http://cbs3.com/local/Philadelphia.Eagles.NFL.2.1127901.html.

"I'm a believer… Mortensen, Chris, and others, "Vick, Eagles Agree to Two-Year Deal," *ESPN.com*, August 14, 2009, http://sports.espn.go.com/nfl/news/story?id=4397938.

"Our country is… Associated Press, "Vick Looking for Second Chance with Eagles."

The next year… Carter, Sharon, "Three Best Celebrity Comebacks," EduBook.com, August 23, 2009, http://www.edubook.com/3-best-celebrity-comebacks/11873/.

He is using… "Been There, Done That: Former Drug Addict Turns His Life Around," Sober.com, April 23, 2002, http://www.sober.com/blogs/press/pages/been-there-done-that.aspx.

Intepreting the Data

Data in Table 1 and Table 2: "NFL Career Stats: Michael Vick." *Yahoo! Sports*, 2010, http://sports.yahoo.com/nfl/players/5448/career.

Technical Extension

From his study…: Boeree, Dr. C. George, "Jean Piaget," 2006, http://webspace.ship.edu/cgboer/piaget.html.

He did not…: Boeree.

Erik Erikson (1902…: "Erik Erikson," NNDB Tracking the Entire World, Soylent Communications, 2009, http://www.nndb.com/people/151/000097857/.

These skills then…: "Erik Erikson."

These eras match…: "Developmental Stages, Levinson," SIL International, 1999, http://www.sil.org/lingualinks/literacy/ImplementALiteracyProgram/DevelopmentalStagesLevinson.htm.

The transitional periods…: "Daniel Levinson," Theories of Life Stages and Human Development, http://humangrowth.tripod.com/id3.html.

This begins a…: Crenson, Matt, "Brain Changes, Not Hormones, Explain Many Adolescent Behaviors," SouthCoast Today, http://archive.southcoasttoday.com/daily/12-00/12-31-00/e05li127.htm.

Their brains simply…: Crenson.

The "Plastic" Brain (text box)…: Michelon, Dr. Pascale, "Brain Plasticity: How Your Brain Learns," Sharp Brains: Brain Fitness for All, February 26, 2008, http://www.sharpbrains.com/blog/2008/02/26/brain-plasticity-how-learning-changes-your-brain/.

Vocational Extension

This includes promoting…: "Sports Agent: Occupation Overview," Illinois workNet, http://www.illinoisworknet.com/vos_portal/residents/en/Jobs/Prepare/Careers/career_listings.htm?occId=100228&occText=Sports+Agent&occType=overview&jobId=3.

These services might…: "Sports Agent: Occupation Overview."

They can then…: Eppel, Max, "Identifying the Strengths and Weaknesses of an Agent," Oct. 2, 2009, http://www.sportsagentblog.com/2009/10/12/identifying-the-strengths-and-weaknesses-of-an-agent/.

He says being…: Casanover, Scott, "Sports Agent Blog," Sports Agent News, http://www.sportsagentblog.com/interview-with-the-agent/scott-casanover.

Some attorneys act…: "Sports Agent Salary," Become-A-Sports-Agent, http://www.become-a-sports-agent.com/salary.asp.

Depending on experience…: "Salary Survey for Job: Sports Agent," PayScale, http://www.payscale.com/research/US/Industry=Sports_Agency/Salary.

Unit 10: Incredible Goals
High-Interest Article

His game-winning…: Amoia, Steve, "Cuauhtémoc Blanco of the Chicago Fire," Soccerlens, May 4, 2008, http://soccerlens.com/profile-of-cuauhtemoc-blanco-bravo-of-the-chicago-fire/6590/.

It was later…: "Cuauhtémoc Blanco," Roster: Player Bio, Chicago Fire, http://chicago.fire.mlsnet.com/players/bio.jsp?player=blanco_c&playerId=bla435579&statType=current&team=t100.

He was not…: "Cuauhtémoc Blanco Biography and Wallpapers," Sportsvideo24.com, Zimbio, Inc., September 6, 2009, http://www.zimbio.com/Cuauhtemoc+Blanco/articles/gpEoMWo8W0b/Cuauhtemoc+Blanco+Biography+Wallpapers.

In the summer…: "Blanco No Go for U.S. Open Cup," Gruffgoat.blogspot.com, Zimbio, Inc., July 30, 2008, http://www.zimbio.com/Cuauhtemoc+Blanco/articles/4/Blanco+No+Go+for+US+Open+Cup.

His presence in…: Amoia.

The show is…: "Cuauhtémoc Blanco Starts TV Program," SI.Com, January 21, 2010, http://sportsillustrated.cnn.com/2010/soccer/wires/01/21/2080.ap.soc.blanco.tv.1st.ld.writethru.0143/index.html.

When Blanco makes…: "Cuauhtémoc Blanco," Roster: Player Bio.

Blanco by the (text box)…: Amoia.

Evidence suggests that (text box)…: Fédération Internationale de Football Association (FIFA) website, http://fifa.com.

Technical Extension

I love soccer…: Sachin, "Why I Love Soccer," BigSoccer.com, April 15, 2004, http://www.bigsoccer.com/forum/showthread.php?t=106450.

Players like Cristian…: "The Top 50 Highest Paid Players in World Football Revealed in Full," Mirror Football, June 2, 2010, http://www.mirrorfootball.co.uk/opinion/blogs/mirror-football-blog/The-Top-50-highest-paid-players-in-world-football-revealed-in-full-featuring-Cristiano-Ronaldo-Lionel-Messi-Kaka-Wayne-Rooney-David-Beckham-John-Terry-Ashley-Cole-Wayne-Bridge-and-Ronaldinho-article324875.html.

Add another 5…: "Big Count," FIFA.com, http://www.fifa.com/worldfootball/bigcount/index.html.

Others say that…: "Basics," Soccer, http://library.thinkquest.org/3570/.

The BigSoccer Moderator…: Sachin.

This means that…: "10 Reasons Why I Love Soccer," The Footie, January 7, 2008, http://www.everyjoe.com/thefootie/ten-reasons-why-i-love-soccer/.

The International Federation…: "World Football," Fifa.com, http://www.fifa.com/worldfootball/index.html.

The host country….: "How It All Began," World Cup History, http://www.world-cup-info.com/history.htm.

Cristiano Ronaldo, who…: "Ronaldo Completes £80m Real Move," Football, July 1, 2009, http://news.bbc.co.uk/sport2/hi/football/teams/m/man_utd/8121951.stm.

The other top…: Mondal, Subhankar, "Top 10 Highest Paid Footballers," Soccer Info, http://www.sportspundit.com/article/3460/.

Like athletes in…: Settimi, Christina, "The World's Best Paid Soccer Players," Forbes.com, April 30, 2008, http://www.forbes.com/2008/04/30/best-paid-soccer-biz-soccer08-cx-cs_0430players_intro_print.html.

"Soccer is not…: "10 Reasons Why I Love Soccer."

The World's Highest (text box)…: Badenhausen, Kurt, "The World's Highest Paid Athletes," Forbes.com, June 17, 2009, http://www.forbes.com/2009/06/17/top-earning-athletes-business-sports-top-earning-athletes_print.html.

Technical Multiple-Choice Questions

Question 11 quotation…: Rosenberg, Jennifer, "History of the Olympics: Creating the Modern Olympic Games," About.com: 20th Century History, http://history1900s.about.com/od/fadsfashion/a/olympicshistory.htm.

Vocational Extension

Training and certification…: "Officials," National Alliance for Youth Sports, http://www.nays.org/officials.

He noted that…: Young, Richard D., "Volunteerism: Benefits, Incidence, Organizational Models, and Participation in the Public Sector," http://ipspr.sc.edu/publication/Volunteerism%20FINAL.pdf.

Families enjoy the…: Young.

Churches, social service…: Young.

Today, AmeriCorps and…: Young.

Agencies sponsored by….: Young.

Volunteers of all…: de Guzman, Maria R. T., "Youth Volunteerism," NebGuide, University of Nebraska, Lincoln, http://www.ianrpubs.unl.edu/epublic/pages/publicationD.jsp?publicationId=833.

However, some barriers…: de Guzman.

Famous American boxer…: "Quotes on Volunteerism," Energize, http://www.energizeinc.com/reflect/quote1.html.